D1276871

Casenote™ Legal Briefs

CONTRACTS

Keyed to
Dawson, Harvey, and Henderson's
Contracts: Cases and Comment, Eighth Edition

ΛSPEN

P U B L I S H E R S

1185 Avenue of the Americas, New York, NY 10036
www.aspenpublishers.com

© 2003 Aspen Publishers, Inc.
A WoltersKluwer Company
www.aspenpublishers.com

Permissions
Aspen Publishers
1185 Avenue of the Americas
New York, NY 10036

Printed in the United States of America.

ISBN 0-7355-4518-9

1 2 3 4 5 6 7 8 9 0

About Aspen Publishers

Aspen Publishers, headquartered in New York City, is a leading information provider for attorneys, business professionals, and law students. Written by preeminent authorities, our products consist of analytical and practical information covering both U.S. and international topics. We publish in the full range of formats, including updated manuals, books, periodicals, CDs, and online products.

Our proprietary content is complemented by 2,500 legal databases, containing over 11 million documents, available through our Loislaw division. Aspen Publishers also offers a wide range of topical legal and business databases linked to Loislaw's primary material. Our mission is to provide accurate, timely, and authoritative content in easily accessible formats, supported by unmatched customer care.

To order any Aspen Publishers title, go to *www.aspenpublishers.com* or call 1-800-638-8437.

For more information on Loislaw products, go to *www.loislaw.com* or call 1-800-364-2512.

For Customer Care issues, e-mail CustomerCare@aspenpublishers.com; call 1-800-234-1660; or fax 1-800-901-9075.

Aspen Publishers
A Wolters Kluwer Company

FORMAT FOR THE CASENOTE LEGAL BRIEF

PARTY ID: Quick identification of the relationship between the parties.

NATURE OF CASE: This section identifies the form of action (e.g., breach of contract, negligence, battery), the type of proceeding (e.g., demurrer, appeal from trial court's jury instructions) or the relief sought (e.g., damages, injunction, criminal sanctions).

FACT SUMMARY: This is included to refresh the student's memory and can be used as a quick reminder of the facts.

CONCISE RULE OF LAW: Summarizes the general principle of law that the case illustrates. It may be used for instant recall of the court's holding and for classroom discussion or home review.

FACTS: This section contains all relevant facts of the case, including the contentions of the parties and the lower court holdings. It is written in a logical order to give the student a clear understanding of the case. The plaintiff and defendant are identified by their proper names throughout and are always labeled with a (P) or (D).

ISSUE: The issue is a concise question that brings out the essence of the opinion as it relates to the section of the casebook in which the case appears. Both substantive and procedural issues are included if relevant to the decision.

HOLDING AND DECISION: This section offers a clear and in-depth discussion of the rule of the case and the court's rationale. It is written in easy-to-understand language and answers the issue(s) presented by applying the law to the facts of the case. When relevant, it includes a thorough discussion of the exceptions to the case as listed by the court, any major cites to other cases on point, and the names of the judges who wrote the decisions.

CONCURRENCE / DISSENT: All concurrences and dissents are briefed whenever they are included by the casebook editor.

EDITOR'S ANALYSIS: This last paragraph gives the student a broad understanding of where the case "fits in" with other cases in the section of the book and with the entire course. It is a hornbook-style discussion indicating whether the case is a majority or minority opinion and comparing the principal case with other cases in the casebook. It may also provide analysis from restatements, uniform codes, and law review articles. The editor's analysis will prove to be invaluable to classroom discussion.

QUICKNOTES: Conveniently defines legal terms found in the case and summarizes the nature of any statutes, codes, or rules referred to in the text.

PALSGRAF v. LONG ISLAND R.R. CO.
Injured bystander (P) v. Railroad company (D)
N.Y. Ct. App., 248 N.Y. 339, 162 N.E. 99 (1928).

NATURE OF CASE: Appeal from judgment affirming verdict for plaintiff seeking damages for personal injury.

FACT SUMMARY: Helen Palsgraf (P) was injured on R.R.'s (D) train platform when R.R.'s (D) guard helped a passenger aboard a moving train, causing his package to fall on the tracks. The package contained fireworks which exploded, creating a shock that tipped a scale onto Palsgraf (P).

CONCISE RULE OF LAW: The risk reasonably to be perceived defines the duty to be obeyed.

FACTS: Helen Palsgraf (P) purchased a ticket to Rockaway Beach from R.R. (D) and was waiting on the train platform. As she waited, two men ran to catch a train that was pulling out from the platform. The first man jumped aboard, but the second man, who appeared as if he might fall, was helped aboard by the guard on the train who had kept the door open so they could jump aboard. A guard on the platform also helped by pushing him onto the train. The man was carrying a package wrapped in newspaper. In the process, the man dropped his package, which fell on the tracks. The package contained fireworks and exploded. The shock of the explosion was apparently of great enough strength to tip over some scales at the other end of the platform, which fell on Palsgraf (P) and injured her. A jury awarded her damages, and R.R. (D) appealed.

ISSUE: Does the risk reasonably to be perceived define the duty to be obeyed?

HOLDING AND DECISION: (Cardozo, C.J.) Yes. The risk reasonably to be perceived defines the duty to be obeyed. If there is no foreseeable hazard to the injured party as the result of a seemingly innocent act, the act does not become a tort because it happened to be a wrong as to another. If the wrong was not willful, the plaintiff must show that the act as to her had such great and apparent possibilities of danger as to entitle her to protection. Negligence in the abstract is not enough upon which to base liability. Negligence is a relative concept, evolving out of the common law doctrine of trespass on the case. To establish liability, the defendant must owe a legal duty of reasonable care to the injured party. A cause of action in tort will lie where harm, though unintended, could have been averted or avoided by observance of such a duty. The scope of the duty is limited by the range of danger that a reasonable person could foresee. In this case, there was nothing to suggest from the appearance of the parcel or otherwise that the parcel contained fireworks. The guard could not reasonably have had any warning of a threat to Palsgraf (P), and R.R. (D) therefore cannot be held liable. Judgment is reversed in favor of R.R. (D).

DISSENT: (Andrews, J.) The concept that there is no negligence unless R.R. (D) owes a legal duty to take care as to Palsgraf (P) herself is too narrow. Everyone owes to the world at large the duty of refraining from those acts that may unreasonably threaten the safety of others. If the guard's action was negligent as to those nearby, it was also negligent as to those outside what might be termed the "danger zone." For Palsgraf (P) to recover, R.R.'s (D) negligence must have been the proximate cause of her injury, a question of fact for the jury.

EDITOR'S ANALYSIS: The majority defined the limit of the defendant's liability in terms of the danger that a reasonable person in defendant's situation would have perceived. The dissent argued that the limitation should not be placed on liability, but rather on damages. Judge Andrews suggested that only injuries that would not have happened but for R.R.'s (D) negligence should be compensable. Both the majority and dissent recognized the policy-driven need to limit liability for negligent acts, seeking, in the words of Judge Andrews, to define a framework "that will be practical and in keeping with the general understanding of mankind." The Restatement (Second) of Torts has accepted Judge Cardozo's view.

QUICKNOTES
FORESEEABILITY – The reasonable anticipation that damage is a likely result from certain acts or omissions.

NEGLIGENCE - Failure to exercise that degree of care which a person of ordinary prudence would exercise under similar circumstances.

PROXIMATE CAUSE – Something which in natural and continuous sequence, unbroken by any new intervening cause, produces an event, and without which the injury would not have occurred.

NOTE TO STUDENTS

Aspen Publishers is proud to offer *Casenote Legal Briefs*–continuing thirty years of publishing America's best-selling legal briefs.

Casenote Legal Briefs are designed to help you save time when briefing assigned cases. Organized under convenient headings, they show you how to abstract the basic facts and holdings from the text of the actual opinions handed down by the courts. Used as part of a rigorous study regime, they can help you spend more time analyzing and critiquing points of law than on copying out bits and pieces of judicial opinions into your notebook or outline.

Casenote Legal Briefs should never be used as a substitute for assigned casebook readings. They work best when read as a follow-up to reviewing the underlying opinions themselves. Students who try to avoid reading and digesting the judicial opinions in their casebooks or on-line sources will end up shortchanging themselves in the long run. The ability to absorb, critique, and restate the dynamic and complex elements of case law decisions is crucial to your success in law school and beyond. It cannot be developed vicariously.

Casenote Legal Briefs represent but one of the many offerings in Aspen's Study Aid Timeline, which includes:

- Casenotes *Legal Briefs*
- Emanuel *Outlines*
- *Examples & Explanations* Series
- *Introduction to Law* Series
- Emanuel *Law in a Flash* Flashcards
- Emanuel *CrunchTime* Series

Each of these series is designed to provide you with easy-to-understand explanations of complex points of law. Each volume offers guidance on the principles of legal analysis and, consulted regularly, will hone your ability to spot relevant issues. We have titles that will help you prepare for class, prepare for your exams, and enhance your general comprehension of the law along the way.

To find out more about Aspen Study Aid publications, visit us on-line at www.aspenpublishers.com or e-mail us at legaledu@aspenpubl.com. We'll be happy to assist you.

Free access to Briefs and Updates on-line!

Download the cases you want in your notes or outlines using the full cut-and-paste feature accompanying our on-line briefs. On-line briefs will also contain the latest updates. Please fill out this form for full access to these useful features. No photocopies of this form will be accepted.

① **Name:** _____ **Phone:** (____) _____

     Address: _____ **Apt.:** _____

     City: _____ **State:** _____ **ZIP Code:** _____

     Law School: _____ **Year (circle one):** **1st 2nd 3rd**

② **Cut out the UPC found on the lower left-hand corner of the back cover of this book. Staple the UPC inside this box. Only the original UPC from the book cover will be accepted. (No photocopies or store stickers are allowed.)**

> ### Attach UPC inside this box.

③ **E-mail:** _____ **(Print LEGIBLY or you may not get access!**

④ **Title (course subject) of this book** _____

⑤ **Used with which casebook (provide author's name):** _____

⑥ **Mail the completed form to:**   Aspen Publishers, Inc.
                                       Legal Education Division
                                       Casenote On-line Access
                                       1185 Avenue of the Americas
                                       New York, NY 10036

I understand that on-line access is granted solely to the purchaser of this book for the academic year in which it was purchased. Any other usage is not authorized and will result in immediate termination of access. Sharing of codes is strictly prohibited.

_____

Signature

Upon receipt of this completed form, you will be e-mailed codes so that you may access the Briefs and Updates for this Casenote Legal Brief. On-line Briefs and Updates may not be available for all titles. For a full list of available titles please check www.aspenpublishers.com/casenotes.

HOW TO BRIEF A CASE

A. DECIDE ON A FORMAT AND STICK TO IT

Structure is essential to a good brief. It enables you to arrange systematically the related parts that are scattered throughout most cases, thus making manageable and understandable what might otherwise seem to be an endless and unfathomable sea of information. There are, of course, an unlimited number of formats that can be utilized. However, it is best to find one that suits your needs and stick to it. Consistency breeds both efficiency and the security that when called upon you will know where to look in your brief for the information you are asked to give.

Any format, as long as it presents the essential elements of a case in an organized fashion, can be used. Experience, however, has led *Casenotes* to develop and utilize the following format because of its logical flow and universal applicability.

NATURE OF CASE: This is a brief statement of the legal character and procedural status of the case (e.g., "Appeal of a burglary conviction").

There are many different alternatives open to a litigant dissatisfied with a court ruling. The key to determining which one has been used is to discover *who is asking this court for what.*

This first entry in the brief should be kept as *short as possible.* The student should use the court's terminology if the student understands it. But since jurisdictions vary as to the titles of pleadings, the best entry is the one that apprises the student of who wants what in this proceeding, not the one that sounds most like the court's language.

CONCISE RULE OF LAW: A statement of the general principle of law that the case illustrates (e.g., "An acceptance that varies any term of the offer is considered a rejection and counteroffer").

Determining the rule of law of a case is a procedure similar to determining the issue of the case. Avoid being fooled by red herrings; there may be a few rules of law mentioned in the case excerpt, but usually only one is *the* rule with which the casebook editor is concerned. The techniques used to locate the issue, described below, may also be utilized to find the rule of law. Generally, your best guide is simply the chapter heading. It is a clue to the point the casebook editor seeks to make and should be kept in mind when reading every case in the respective section.

FACTS: A synopsis of only the essential facts of the case, i.e., those bearing upon or leading up to the issue.

The facts entry should be a short statement of the events and transactions that led one party to initiate legal proceedings against another in the first place. While some cases conveniently state the salient facts at the beginning of the decision, in other instances they will have to be culled from hiding places throughout the text, even from concurring and dissenting opinions. Some of the "facts" will often be in dispute and should be so noted. Conflicting evidence may be briefly pointed up. "Hard" facts must be included. Both must be *relevant* in order to be listed in the facts entry. It is impossible to tell what is relevant until the entire case is read, as the ultimate determination of the rights and liabilities of the parties may turn on something buried deep in the opinion.

The facts entry should never be longer than one to three *short* sentences.

It is often helpful to identify the role played by a party in a given context. For example, in a construction contract case the identification of a party as the "contractor" or "builder" alleviates the need to tell that that party was the one who was supposed to have built the house.

It is always helpful, and a good general practice, to identify the "plaintiff" and the "defendant." This may seem elementary and uncomplicated, but, especially in view of the creative editing practiced by some casebook editors, it is sometimes a difficult or even impossible task. Bear in mind that the *party presently* seeking something from this court may not be the plaintiff, and that sometimes only the cross-claim of a defendant is treated in the excerpt. Confusing or misaligning the parties can ruin your analysis and understanding of the case.

ISSUE: A statement of the general legal question answered by or illustrated in the case. For clarity, the issue is best put in the form of a question capable of a "yes" or "no" answer. In reality, the issue is simply the Concise Rule of Law put in the form of a question (e.g., "May an offer be accepted by performance?").

The major problem presented in discerning what is *the* issue in the case is that an opinion usually purports to raise and answer several questions. However, except for rare cases, only one such question is really the issue in the case. Collateral issues not necessary to the resolution of the matter in controversy are handled by the court by language known as *"obiter dictum"* or merely *"dictum."* While dicta may be included later in the brief, it has no place under the issue heading.

To find the issue, the student again asks *who wants what* and then goes on to ask *why did that party succeed or fail in getting it.* Once this is determined, the "why" should be turned into a question.

The complexity of the issues in the cases will vary, but in all cases a single-sentence question should sum up the issue. *In a few cases,* there will be two, or even more rarely, three issues of equal importance to the resolution of the case. Each should be expressed in a single-sentence question.

Since many issues are resolved by a court in coming to a final disposition of a case, the casebook editor will reproduce the portion of the opinion containing the issue or issues most relevant to the area of law under scrutiny. A noted law professor gave this advice: "Close the book; look at the title on the cover." Chances are, if it is Property, the student need not concern himself with whether, for example, the federal government's treatment of the plaintiff's land really raises a federal question sufficient to support jurisdiction on this ground in federal court.

The same rule applies to chapter headings designating sub-areas within the subjects. They tip the student off as to what the text is designed to teach. The cases are arranged in a casebook to show a progression or development of the law, so that the preceding cases may also help.

It is also most important to remember to *read the notes and questions* at the end of a case to determine what the editors wanted the student to have gleaned from it.

HOLDING AND DECISION: This section should succinctly explain the rationale of the court in arriving at its decision. In capsulizing the "reasoning" of the court, it should always include an application of the general rule or rules of law to the specific facts of the case. Hidden justifications come to light in this entry; the reasons for the state of the law, the public policies, the biases and prejudices, those considerations that influence the justices' thinking and, ultimately, the outcome of the case. At the end, there should be a short indication of the disposition or procedural resolution of the case (e.g., "Decision of the trial court for Mr. Smith (P) reversed").

The foregoing format is designed to help you "digest" the reams of case material with which you will be faced in your law school career. Once mastered by practice, it will place at your fingertips the information the authors of your casebooks have sought to impart to you in case-by-case illustration and analysis.

B. BE AS ECONOMICAL AS POSSIBLE IN BRIEFING CASES

Once armed with a format that encourages succinctness, it is as important to be economical with regard to the time spent on the actual reading of the case as it is to be economical in the writing of the brief itself. This does not mean "skimming" a case. Rather, it means reading the case with an "eye" trained to recognize into which "section" of your brief a particular passage or line fits and having a system for quickly and precisely marking the case so that the passages fitting any one particular part of the brief can be easily identified and brought together in a concise and accurate manner when the brief is actually written.

It is of no use to simply repeat everything in the opinion of the court; the student should only record enough information to trigger his or her recollection of what the court said. Nevertheless, an accurate statement of the "law of the case," i.e., the legal principle applied to the facts, is absolutely essential to class preparation and to learning the law under the case method.

To that end, it is important to develop a "shorthand" that you can use to make margin notations. These notations will tell you at a glance in which section of the brief you will be placing that particular passage or portion of the opinion.

Some students prefer to underline all the salient portions of the opinion (with a pencil or colored underliner marker), making marginal notations as they go along. Others prefer the color-coded method of underlining, utilizing different colors of markers to underline the salient portions of the case, each separate color being used to represent a different section of the brief. For example, blue underlining could be used for passages relating to the concise rule of law, yellow for those relating to the issue, and green for those relating to the holding and decision, etc. While it has its advocates, the color-coded method can be confusing and time-consuming (all that time spent on changing colored markers). Furthermore, it can interfere with the continuity and concentration many students deem essential to the reading of a case for maximum comprehension. In the end, however, it is a matter of personal preference and style. Just remember, whatever method you use, underlining must be used sparingly or its value is lost.

For those who take the marginal notation route, an efficient and easy method is to go along underlining the key portions of the case and placing in the margin alongside them the following "markers" to indicate where a particular passage or line "belongs" in the brief you will write:

N   (NATURE OF CASE)
CR   (CONCISE RULE OF LAW)
I   (ISSUE)
HC   (HOLDING AND DECISION, relates to the CONCISE RULE OF LAW behind the decision)
HR   (HOLDING AND DECISION, gives the RATIONALE or reasoning behind the decision)
HA   (HOLDING AND DECISION, APPLIES the general principle(s) of law to the facts of the case to arrive at the decision)

Remember that a particular passage may well contain information necessary to more than one part of your brief, in which case you simply note that in the margin. If you are using the color-coded underlining method instead of margin notation, simply make asterisks or checks in the margin next to the passage in question in the colors that indicate the additional sections of the brief where it might be utilized.

The economy of utilizing "shorthand" in marking cases for briefing can be maintained in the actual brief writing process itself by utilizing "law student shorthand" within the brief. There are many commonly used words and phrases for which abbreviations can be substituted in your briefs (and in your class notes also). You can develop abbreviations that are personal to you and which will save you a lot of time. A reference list of briefing abbreviations will be found elsewhere in this book.

C. USE BOTH THE BRIEFING PROCESS AND THE BRIEF AS A LEARNING TOOL

Now that you have a format and the tools for briefing cases efficiently, the most important thing is to make the time spent in briefing profitable to you and to make the most advantageous use of the briefs you create. Of course, the briefs are invaluable for classroom reference when you are called upon to explain or analyze a particular case. However, they are also useful in reviewing for exams. A quick glance at the fact summary should bring the case to mind, and a rereading of the concise rule of law should enable you to go over the underlying legal concept in your mind, how it was applied in that particular case, and how it might apply in other factual settings.

As to the value to be derived from engaging in the briefing process itself, there is an immediate benefit that arises from being forced to sift through the essential facts and reasoning from the court's opinion and to succinctly express them in your own words in your brief. The process ensures that you understand the case and the point that it illustrates, and that means you will be ready to absorb further analysis and information brought forth in class. It also ensures you will have something to say when called upon in class. The briefing process helps develop a mental agility for getting to the *gist* of a case and for identifying, expounding on, and applying the legal concepts and issues found there. Of most immediate concern, that is the mental process on which you must rely in taking law school examinations. Of more lasting concern, it is also the mental process upon which a lawyer relies in serving his clients and in making his living.

ABBREVIATIONS FOR BRIEFING

acceptance	acp	offer	O
affirmed	aff	offeree	OE
answer	ans	offeror	OR
assumption of risk	a/r	ordinance	ord
attorney	atty	pain and suffering	p/s
beyond a reasonable doubt	b/r/d	parol evidence	p/e
bona fide purchaser	BFP	plaintiff	P
breach of contract	br/k	prima facie	p/f
cause of action	c/a	probable cause	p/c
common law	c/l	proximate cause	px/c
Constitution	Con	real property	r/p
constitutional	con	reasonable doubt	r/d
contract	K	reasonable man	r/m
contributory negligence	c/n	rebuttable presumption	rb/p
cross	x	remanded	rem
cross-complaint	x/c	res ipsa loquitur	RIL
cross-examination	x/ex	respondeat superior	r/s
cruel and unusual punishment	c/u/p	Restatement	RS
defendant	D	reversed	rev
dismissed	dis	Rule Against Perpetuities	RAP
double jeopardy	d/j	search and seizure	s/s
due process	d/p	search warrant	s/w
equal protection	e/p	self-defense	s/d
equity	eq	specific performance	s/p
evidence	ev	statute of limitations	S/L
exclude	exc	statute of frauds	S/F
exclusionary rule	exc/r	statute	S
felony	f/n	summary judgment	s/j
freedom of speech	f/s	tenancy in common	t/c
good faith	g/f	tenancy at will	t/w
habeas corpus	h/c	tenant	t
hearsay	hr	third party	TP
husband	H	third party beneficiary	TPB
in loco parentis	ILP	transferred intent	TI
injunction	inj	unconscionable	uncon
inter vivos	I/v	unconstitutional	unconst
joint tenancy	j/t	undue influence	u/e
judgment	judgt	Uniform Commercial Code	UCC
jurisdiction	jur	unilateral	uni
last clear chance	LCC	vendee	VE
long-arm statute	LAS	vendor	VR
majority view	maj	versus	v
meeting of minds	MOM	void for vagueness	VFV
minority view	min	weight of the evidence	w/e
Miranda warnings	Mir/w	weight of authority	w/a
Miranda rule	Mir/r	wife	W
negligence	neg	with	w/
notice	ntc	within	w/i
nuisance	nus	without prejudice	w/o/p
obligation	ob	without	w/o
obscene	obs	wrongful death	wr/d

TABLE OF CASES

CHAPTER 1
REMEDIES FOR BREACH OF CONTRACT

QUICK REFERENCE RULES OF LAW

1. **The Goals of Contract Damages.** The purpose of awarding damages for breach of contract is to put the plaintiff in as good a position as he would have been in had the defendant kept his contract. (Hawkins v. McGee)

2. **The Goals of Contract Damages.** When a construction contract is defectively performed then the measure of damages is the cost of remedying the defect. (Groves v. John Wunder Co.)

3. **The Goals of Contract Damages.** The measure of damages for a purchaser in a sales contract is the difference between the contract price and the market price at the time and place of delivery. (Acme Mills & Elevator Co. v. Johnson)

4. **The Goals of Contract Damages.** A real estate developer has no action against a defaulting builder if the developer was able to complete the project within the contract price. (Louise Caroline Nursing Home, Inc. v. Dix Construction Corp.)

5. **Limitations on Expectation Damages.** When an aggrieved party receives notice of a major breach by the opposing contacting party then the aggrieved party acquires an immediate duty to reasonably mitigate damages. (Rockingham County v. Luten Bridge Co.)

6. **Limitations on Expectation Damages.** Projected earnings from other employment opportunities only offset damages if the employment is substantially similar to that of which the employee has been deprived. (Parker v. Twentieth Century-Fox Film Corp.)

7. **Limitations on Expectation Damages.** The measure of damages for an aggrieved buyer in a sales contract is the difference between the contract price and the market price at the time and place of delivery. (Missouri Furnace Co. v. Cochran)

8. **Limitations on Expectation Damages.** A seller may recover his lost profit from a sales contract when the buyer defaults on the purchase if the contract market differential measure of damages is inadequate to put the seller in as good a position as performance would have done. (Neri v. Retail Marine Corp.)

9. **Limitations on Expectation Damages.** The injured party may recover either those damages as may reasonably be considered arising naturally from the breach itself or may recover those damages as may reasonably be supposed to have been in contemplation of the parties, at the time they made the contract, as the probable result of a breach of it. (Hadley v. Baxendale)

10. **Limitations on Expectation Damages.** Mental distress damages are not recoverable in an action for breach of an employment contract. (Valentine v. General American Credit, Inc.)

11. **Limitations on Expectation Damages.** When a breach of contract occurs, the law attempts to secure to the injured party the benefit of his bargain, subject to the limitations that the injury was foreseeable and that the amount of damages claimed be measurable with a reasonable degree of certainty and adequately proven. (Freund v. Washington Square Press, Inc.)

12. **Alternative Interests: Reliance and Restitution.** In an action for breach of contract a party can only recover on damages which naturally flow from and are the result of the act complained of. (Chicago Coliseum Club v. Dempsey)

13. **Alternative Interests: Reliance and Restitution.** Partial performance under an otherwise unenforceable contract gives rise to recovery only where the other party was benefited thereby. (Boone v. Coe)

14. **Alternative Interests: Reliance and Restitution.** A subcontractor in a breached construction contract may sue in quantum meruit for services rendered. (United States v. Algernon Blair, Inc.)

15. **Alternative Interests: Reliance and Restitution.** Where labor is performed under a contract for a specified price, the party who fails to perform the whole of the labor contracted for can recover in quantum meruit the value of the labor performed to the degree it is greater than the damage to the other party. (Britton v. Turner)

16. **Alternative Interests: Reliance and Restitution.** Where the deviation was not willful and the structure as built is reasonably adaptable to the desired purpose, the plaintiff may recover for the work performed less its diminished value. (Pinches v. Swedish Evangelical Lutheran Church)

17. **Alternative Interests: Reliance and Restitution.** A party breaching a land sale contract may recover the down payment if he can prove that no damages were inflicted upon the seller at the time of the breach. (Vines v. Orchard Hills, Inc.)

18. **Contractual Controls on the Damage Remedy.** An action on a performance bond will not lie if the bond amount is not related to actual damages. (City of Rye v. Public Service Mut. Ins. Co.)

19. **Contractual Controls on the Damage Remedy.** A contractual limitation of liability on tort claims is enforceable. (Fretwell v. Protection Alarm Co.)

20. **Enforcement in Equity.** Where there is substantial, reliable information as to the monetary value of the subject matter of a breached contract and where specific performance would create harm to the defendant disproportionate to its aid to the plaintiff, specific performance is not available. (Van Wagner Advertising Corp. v. S & M Enterprises)

21. **Enforcement in Equity.** Specific performance is available as a remedy for breach of a long-term supply contract. (Laclede Gas Co. v. Amoco Oil Co.)

22. **Enforcement in Equity.** A court of equity will not grant specific performance in a personal service contract because excessive court entanglement is necessarily involved. (Fitzpatrick v. Michael)

23. **Enforcement in Equity.** Courts of equity will not issue decrees of specific performance where such orders would require extensive supervision by the court. (Northern Delaware Indus. Dev. Corp. v. E.W. Bliss Co.)

HAWKINS v. McGEE

Injured patient (P) v. Surgeon (D)

N.H. Sup. Ct., 84 N.H. 114, 146 A. 641 (1929).

NATURE OF CASE: Action in assumpsit for breach of an alleged warranty.

FACT SUMMARY: McGee (D), a surgeon, performed an unsuccessful operation on Hawkins' (P) hand after having guaranteed to make the hand 100% perfect. Hawkins (P) was awarded damages for pain and suffering and for "what injury he has sustained over and above the injury he had before."

CONCISE RULE OF LAW: The purpose of awarding damages for breach of contract is to put the plaintiff in as good a position as he would have been in had the defendant kept his contract.

FACTS: McGee (D), a surgeon, performed an operation on Hawkins' (P) hand. Before the operation, McGee (D) had repeatedly solicited an opportunity to perform the operation and had guaranteed to make the hand 100% perfect. The operation was not successful, and Hawkins (P) sought to recover on the basis of McGee's (D) warranty. The trial court instructed the jury that Hawkins (P) would be entitled to recover for his pain and suffering and for "what injury he has sustained over and above the injury he had before."

ISSUE: Is the measure of damages for breach of a contract what the defendant contracted to give the plaintiff?

HOLDING AND DECISION: (Branch, J.) Yes. McGee's (D) words, if taken at face value, indicate the giving of a warranty. Coupled with the evidence that McGee (D) repeatedly solicited the opportunity to perform the operation, there is a reasonable basis for a jury to conclude that McGee (D) spoke the words with the intention that they be taken at face value as an inducement for Hawkins' (P) submission to the operation. The jury instruction on damages was erroneous. The purpose of awarding damages is to put a plaintiff in as good a position as he would have been in had the defendant kept his contract. The measure of recovery is what the defendant should have given the plaintiff, not what the plaintiff has given the defendant or otherwise expended. Hence, the measure of Hawkins' (P) damages is the difference between the value of a perfect hand, as promised by McGee (D), and the value of his hand in its present condition. Hawkins' (P) pain is not relevant to this determination. Also, damages might be assessed for McGee's (D) failure to improve the hand, even if there was no evidence that the operation had made it worse.

EDITOR'S ANALYSIS: The measure of damages is the actual loss sustained by reason of the breach, which is the loss of what the promisee would have made if the contract had been performed, less the proper deductions. The plaintiff may recover damages not only for the net gains which were prevented by the breach, but also for expenses incurred in reliance on the defendant's performance of his contract promise. In a proper case, prospective profits which were lost because of the breach are also recoverable.

QUICKNOTES

MONEY DAMAGES - Monetary compensation sought by, or awarded to, a party who incurred loss as a result of a breach of contract or tortious conduct on behalf of another party.

WARRANTY - An assurance by one party that another may rely on a certain representation of fact.

ASSUMPSIT - An oral or written promise by one party to perform or pay another.

NOTES:

GROVES v. JOHN WUNDER CO.
Landowner (P) v. Gravel removing company (D)
Minn. Sup. Ct., 205 Minn. 163, 286 N.W. 235 (1939).

NATURE OF CASE: Action for damages for breach of a construction contract.

FACT SUMMARY: Wunder (D) paid a fee to Groves (P) for the right to remove gravel from Groves' (P) land. The contract provided that after the gravel was removed Wunder (D) would regrade the land which Wunder (D) failed to do. Groves (P) now brings suit for breach of contract.

CONCISE RULE OF LAW: When a construction contract is defectively performed then the measure of damages is the cost of remedying the defect.

FACTS: Groves (P) entered into a contract with John Wunder Co. (D) whereby Wunder (D) paid Groves (P) a fee in consideration of being permitted to remove sand and gravel from Groves (P) property. The contract further provided that after Wunder (D) had completed the removal of the gravel then Wunder (D) would be obligated to regrade the land. Wunder (D) failed to do this whereupon Groves (P) brought suit for breach of contract. The trial court found that Wunder (D) was in breach, however, it only awarded Groves (P) the diminution in value of the land due to the lack of regrading ($15,000) instead of the full cost of regrading. Groves (P) now appeals on the issue of damages.

ISSUE: If a construction contract is defectively performed then is the measure of damages for the owner of the property the cost of remedying the defect?

HOLDING AND DECISION: (Stone, J.) Yes. When a construction contract is defectively performed then the proper measure of damages for the owner of the property is the cost of remedying the defect. In reckoning damages the law aims to give the disappointed promisee what he was promised. In this case Groves was promised regraded land which he did not receive. Groves (P) then is entitled to the cost of such regrading. Reversed.

DISSENT: (Olson, J.) What the parites agreed to was to put the property in shape for general sale. Damages should be the difference between the market value of the property in the condition it was when delivered to and received by Groves (P) and what the market value would have been if the defendant had complied with its terms.

EDITOR'S ANALYSIS: The principal case represents the majority view that in a breach of construction contract the measure of damages is the cost of remedying the defect. The only exception is if major economic waste would occur. In accord is the Restatement of Contracts § 346 which provides that if no major economic waste is involved then the cost of remedying the defect is the amount awarded as compensation for failure to render the promised performance.

QUICKNOTES

RESTITUTION - The return or restoration of what the defendant has gained in a transaction to prevent the unjust enrichment of the defendant.

NOTES:

ACME MILLS & ELEVATOR CO. v. JOHNSON
Wheat buyer (P) v. Wheat seller (D)
Ky. Ct. App., 141 Ky. 718, 133 S.W. 784 (1911).

NATURE OF CASE: Action for damages for breach of a sales contract.

FACT SUMMARY: Johnson (D) contracted to sell a certain amount of wheat to Acme (P) but failed to do so whereupon Acme (P) brought suit for breach of contract.

CONCISE RULE OF LAW: The measure of damages for a purchaser in a sales contract is the difference between the contract price and the market price at the time and place of delivery.

FACTS: Johnson (D) contracted to sell 2,000 bushels of wheat to Acme (P) for $1.03 per bushel, to be delivered on July 29, 1909. Acme (P) supplied Johnson (D) with 1,000 sacks in which to deliver the wheat. On July 13, 1909, Johnson (D) sold his wheat to another mill for $1.16 per bushel. He did not deliver any wheat to Acme (P) on July 29th, on which date the market price of wheat had dropped to $0.975 per bushel. Acme (D) brought suit for breach of contract seeking $240 in damages for nondelivery of the wheat and $80 for the value of the sacks it supplied to Johnson (D). The trial court awarded Acme (P) $80 for the sacks and no more. Acme (P) appealed.

ISSUE: Is the measure of damages for a purchaser in a sales contract the difference between the contract price and the market price at the time and place for delivery?

HOLDING AND DECISION: (Clay, Commr.) Yes. The measure of damages for a purchaser in a sales contract is the difference between the contract price and the market price at the time and place of the delivery. This is the well settled rule. It does not appear that Acme (P) suffered any damage. On the date and at the place of delivery, the price of wheat had dropped to below the price at which Acme (P) had agreed to pay. Acme (P) actually received a benefit of over $0.03 per bushel. Affirmed.

EDITOR'S ANALYSIS: This pre-U.C.C. case represents the majority view that one measure of damages for breach of a sales contract is the difference between the contract price and the market price at the time and place of delivery. The U.C.C. has adopted this measure of damages via § 2-713 but recommends an alternative, that of the purchaser acquiring "cover" (the procurement of substitute goods) via § 2-713 so as to make unquestionably certain the amount of damages involved.

LOUISE CAROLINE NURSING HOME, INC. v. DIX CONSTR. CORP.

Nursing home (P) v. Builder (D)

Mass. Sup. Jud. Ct., 362 Mass 306, 285 N.E.2d 904 (1972).

NATURE OF CASE: Appeal from denial damages in for a breach of contract.

FACT SUMMARY: When Dix Construction (D) failed to compete a construction project, Louise Caroline (P), the developer, sought damages even though it was able to find another contractor who was able to complete the project within the contract price.

CONCISE RULE OF LAW: A real estate developer has no action against a defaulting builder if the developer was able to complete the project within the contract price.

FACTS: Louise Caroline Nursing Home, Inc. (P) contracted with Dix Construction Co. (D) for the latter to build a nursing home. Dix (D) stopped the work prematurely. Louise Caroline (P) was able to engage another builder to complete the project. The work was done within the price specified in the contract. Louise Caroline (P) sued for breach. A special master held no damages to be awardable, and Louise Caroline (P) appealed.

ISSUE: Does a real estate developer have an action against a defaulting builder if the developer was able to complete the project within the contract price?

HOLDING AND DECISION: (Quirico, J.) No. A real estate developer does not have an action against a defaulting builder if the developer was able to complete the project within the contract price. The proper measure of damages when a contractor defaults and the developer finds a substitute to complete the work is the actual cost less the contract price. When the actual price does not exceed the contract price, the developer has not been damaged, and no breach of contract action lies. It is not the purpose of the law to put an aggrieved party to a contract in a better position than he would have been in absent the breach. Here, since Louise Caroline (P) did manage to compete the contract within the contract price, it was not damaged. Affirmed.

EDITOR'S ANALYSIS: The rule stated here only applies when the completed project is substantially the same as the project for which the developer contracted. If the nature of quality of the work is inferior, damages are available, the measure being the likely market value of the contracted-for project and the actual project. This measure of damages can present difficulties of proof, however, and is an issue of fact to be settled by a jury.

NOTES:

ROCKINGHAM COUNTY v. LUTEN BRIDGE CO.
Municipality (P) v. Bridge construction company (D)
35 F.2d 301 (4th Cir. 1929).

NATURE OF CASE: Action for damages for breach of a construction contract.

FACT SUMMARY: Rockingham County (D) contracted with Luten Bridge Co. (P) to construct a bridge. While work was in progress Rockingham (D) wrongfully notified Luten (P) to cease work. However, Luten (P) continued construction for another month.

CONCISE RULE OF LAW: When an aggrieved party receives notice of a major breach by the opposing contacting party then the aggrieved party acquires an immediate duty to reasonably mitigate damages.

FACTS: Rockingham County (D) contracted with the Luten Bridge Co. (P) to construct a bridge. While construction was in progress on the bridge the Commissioners of Rockingham County (D) voted to have the remainder of the bridge completed by another construction firm. Rockingham County (D) then notified Luten (P) to cease work. This order was in breach of the contract between the parties. Luten (P) temporarily ignored the order and continued construction on the bridge for another month. Luten (P) then brought suit for breach of contract. The trial court found that Rockingham County (D) was in breach and awarded Luten (P) costs incurred to the date of the notice of the breach, and its lost profit on the contract but refused to award Luten (P) its costs incurred for the one month's construction after Luten (P) had received notice to cease construction.

ISSUE: Does an aggrieved party have a duty to mitigate damages once the party receives notice of a major breach?

HOLDING AND DECISION: (Parker, J.) Yes. An aggrieved party has a duty to mitigate damages once it receives notice of a major breach by the opposing contracting party. An aggrieved party acquires a responsibility not to cause any unnecessary waste. In this case when Rockingham County (D) notified Luten (P) to cease work, Luten (D) had a duty to cease work even though such notice was wrongful. Any construction work that was done after the notice is considered waste and was done at Luten's (P) own peril. We conclude that Luten (P) is entitled to recover all costs incurred except for the last month's work of construction and may recover its lost profit.

EDITOR'S ANALYSIS: The principal case demonstrates the black letter rule that an aggrieved party has a duty to mitigate damages. This rule has sometimes been called the rule of avoidable consequences. When a party fails to mitigate his damages as in the principal case then the party is precluded from recovering that which was wasted. The principal case is also noteworthy for demonstrating the majority view on damages for an aggrieved contractor which is the recovery of all costs incurred to date plus lost profit.

QUICKNOTES
MITIGATION OF DAMAGES - A plaintiff's implied obligation to reduce the damages incurred by taking reasonable steps to prevent additional injury.

LOST PROFITS - The potential value of income earned or goods which are the subject of the contract; may be used in calculating damages where the contract has been breached.

CONSEQUENTIAL DAMAGES - Monetary compensation that may be recovered in order to compensate for injuries or losses sustained as a result of damages that are not the direct or foreseeable result of the act of a party, but that nevertheless are the consequence of such act and which must be specifically pled and demonstrated.

NOTES:

PARKER v. TWENTIETH CENTURY-FOX FILM CORP.
Actress (P) v. Film company (D)
Sup. Ct. of Cal., 3 Cal. 3d 176, 89 Cal. Rptr. 737, 474 P.2d 689 (1970).

NATURE OF CASE: Appeal from summary judgment in a breach of contract action.

FACT SUMMARY: Parker (P) sued Twentieth (D) for damages resulting from Twentieth's (D) breach of an employment contract with her.

CONCISE RULE OF LAW: Projected earnings from other employment opportunities only offset damages if the employment is substantially similar to that of which the employee has been deprived.

FACTS: Parker (P) was a well known actress who entered into a contract with Twentieth (D) in August 1965 to star in a musical film called "Bloomer Girl." The contract contained many specific clauses, including payment of $53,571.42 per week for fourteen weeks to commence in May 1966, shooting in California. Twentieth (D) decided not to produce "Bloomer Girl" and, as compensation for the broken contract, offered Parker (P) the lead in the western film "Big Country," for the same fee. "Big Country" was scheduled to be shot in Australia. Parker (P) refused the lead in "Big Country" and sued Twentieth (D) for the profits she would have made on her original contract. At trial, Twentieth (D) admitted to the existence of the contract and to its anticipatory breach, but argued that Parker (P) was required to mitigate damages by accepting other work, which she did not by turning down "Big Country." Parker (P) filed a motion for summary judgment which the trial court granted. Twentieth (D) appealed.

ISSUE: Do projected earnings from other employment opportunities offset damages for breach of an employment contract?

HOLDING AND DECISION: (Burke, J.) No. Projected earnings from other employment opportunities only offset damages if the other employment was substantially similar to that of which the employee has been deprived. Generally, there is some duty to mitigate damages by the nonbreaching party. Thus, if an employee is offered a similar job after an employment contract is breached, the projected earnings would offset the damages. In the present case, the two movies offered to Parker (P) were different—one was a musical and one was a western—thereby requiring different types of work. Also, other factors were substantially changed, such as the location of the shoot. Therefore, the offered employment was not substantially similar and the projected earnings cannot be used to offset the damages Twentieth (D) owed for breaching the original contract. Affirmed.

DISSENT: (Sullivan, J.) Summary judgment was not appropriate in this case because the trial court should have carefully examined the kind of work offered. Simply because the work is different does not automatically make it incomparable. New work will always be different in certain respects.

EDITOR'S ANALYSIS: This case demonstrates one type of remedy—the award of money damages. Another type of remedy based on expectations is specific performance. Specific performance is limited to situations in which damages would not adequately protect the parties' expectations.

QUICKNOTES
EXPECTATION DAMAGES - Damages awarded in actions for non-performance of a contract, which are calculated by subtracting the injured party's actual dollar position as a result of the breach from that party's expected dollar position had the breach not occurred.

SPECIFIC PERFORMANCE - An equitable remedy whereby the court requires the parties to perform their obligations pursuant to a contract.

NOTES:

MISSOURI FURNACE CO. v. COCHRAN
Furnace mill (P) v. Coke manufacturer (D)
8 F. 463 (W.D. Pa. 1881).

NATURE OF CASE: Action for breach of a sales contract.

FACT SUMMARY: Missouri Furnace (P) contracted to purchase approximately 36,000 tons of coke from Cochran (D). After partial delivery Cochran refused to make further deliveries whereupon Missouri (P) brought suit for damages.

CONCISE RULE OF LAW: The measure of damages for an aggrieved buyer in a sales contract is the difference between the contract price and the market price at the time and place of delivery.

FACTS: Missouri Furnace Co. (P) contracted to purchase 36,621 tons of coke at $1.20 per ton from Cochran (D). The contract provided that the coke was to be delivered periodically. After 3,765 tons were delivered, Cochran (D) refused to make further deliveries. Two weeks later, when the price of coke had risen, Missouri (P) "covered" by making a substantially similar contract for all of the coke at more than $4.00 per ton. Missouri then brought suit against Cochran (D) for breach of contract and claimed as damages Missouri's "cover" costs. The trial court found Cochran (D) in breach but only awarded as damages the difference between the contract price and the market price at the various times provided for delivery. Missouri now appeals on the issue of damages.

ISSUE: Is the measure of damages for a buyer in a sales contract for nondelivery of goods the difference between the contract price and the market price at the time and place of delivery?

HOLDING AND DECISION: (Acheson, J.) Yes. The measure of damages for a buyer for non delivery of goods in a sales contract is the difference between the contract price and the market price at the time and place of delivery. If a buyer chooses to cover by purchasing replacement goods this may be prima facia evidence of the difference. In fact, however, it is not conclusive. In this case Cochran (D) met his burden of proof in demonstrating that Missouri's "cover" cost was in excess of the market. We conclude then that Missouri (P) is limited to recovering the difference between the contract price and the market price at the various times for delivery.

EDITOR'S ANALYSIS: This pre-U.C.C. case demonstrates the harsh rule against cover. Now under § 2-712 a buyer is permitted to effectuate reasonable cover. In this case Missouri (P) was only awarded a little over $22,000. However, if the U.C.C. had been in effect and the recovery of cover permitted, then Missouri (P) would have been awarded more than $83,000.

NERI v. RETAIL MARINE CORP.
Boat buyer (P) v. Seller (D)
N.Y. Ct. App., 30 N. Y.2d 393. 334 N.Y.S. 2d 165, 285 N.E. 2d 311
(1972).

NATURE OF CASE: Action for breach of a sales contract.

FACT SUMMARY: Neri (P) contracted to purchase a boat from Retail Marine (D). Later Neri (P) wrongfully rescinded the contract and then brought suit for recovery of his deposit. Marine (D) counterclaimed seeking damages for its lost sale.

CONCISE RULE OF LAW: A seller may recover his lost profit from a sales contract when the buyer defaults on the purchase if the contract market differential measure of damages is inadequate to put the seller in as good a position as performance would have done.

FACTS: Neri (P) contracted to purchase a boat from Retail Marine (D). Neri (P) gave a deposit of $4,250 and Marine (D) ordered the boat from the factory. A week later Neri (P) rescinded the contract stating that because he was about to undergo an operation he would be unable to make the payments on the boat. In his rescission Neri (P) requested a refund on his deposit which Marine (D) refused whereupon Neri (P) brought suit for restitution. Marine (D) counterclaimed alleging that they were entitled to damages of $4,250, which included their lost profit on the sale of the boat to another buffer. The trial court held that Marine (D) was only entitled to $500 of its incidental damages - the costs of holding the boat for four months, at which time Marine (D) was able to resell the boat to another purchaser for the same price. On the issue of damages Marine (D) appeals.

ISSUE: May a seller recover his lost profit when a buyer defaults on a purchase contract if the contract market differential measure of damages is inadequate to put the seller in as good a position as performance would have done?

HOLDING AND DECISION: (Gibson, J.) Yes. A seller may recover his lost profit when a buyer defaults on a sales contract if the contract market differential measure of damages is inadequate to put the seller in as good a position as performance would have done. U.C.C. § 2-708(1) provides that the measure of damages for non- acceptance or repudiation by the buyer is the difference between the market price, plus incidentals, at the time and place of tender and the unpaid contract price. U.C.C. § 2-708(2) provides that if U.C.C. § 2-708(1) is inadequate to make the seller whole (to put him in the same position as it the contract had been performed) then the measure is the lost profit on the contract. In this case Marine (D) resold the boat within four months for the same price. Thus U.C.C. § 2-708(1) is inadequate to make the seller whole, and U.C.C. § 2-708(2) would apply, as Marine's (D) real damage

was its lost profit on the contract. We conclude that Marine (D) is entitled to an offset of $2,579 (lost profit) plus $674 in incidental damages against Neri's (P) claim for restitution.

EDITOR'S ANALYSIS: The principal case is an example of the U.C.C. provisions to protect sellers of goods from defaulting purchasers. Here the code gives a specific remedy which does justice for the seller by allowing the seller to recover his lost profit. The principal case is also noteworthy as an illustration of the Codes position on restitution for defaulting purchasers. U.C.C. § 2-718 allows a defaulting purchaser to acquire restitution for money advanced by allowing the defaulting purchaser to recover that money in excess of the seller's damages. Prior to the code a defaulting purchaser was usually remediless.

QUICKNOTES

RESTITUTION - The return or restoration of what the defendant has gained in a transaction to prevent the unjust enrichment of the defendant.

LOST PROFITS - The potential value of income earned or goods which are the subject of the contract; may be used in calculating damages where the contract has been breached.

REPUDIATION - The actions or statements of a party to a contract that evidence his intent not to perform, or to continue performance, of his duties or obligations thereunder.

INCIDENTAL - Subordinate; secondary.

NOTES:

HADLEY v. BAXENDALE
Mill operator (P) v. Carrier (D)
Ct. of Exchequer, 9 Exch. 341 (1854).

NATURE OF CASE: Action for damages for breach of a carrier contract.

FACT SUMMARY: Hadley (P), a mill operator in Gloucester, arranged to have Baxendale's (D) company, a carrier, ship his broken mill shaft to the engineer in Greenwich for a copy to be made. Hadley (P) suffered a £300 loss when Baxendale (D) unreasonably delayed shipping the mill shaft causing the mill to be shut down longer than anticipated.

CONCISE RULE OF LAW: The injured party may recover either those damages as may reasonably be considered arising naturally from the breach itself or may recover those damages as may reasonably be supposed to have been in contemplation of the parties, at the time they made the contract, as the probable result of a breach of it.

FACTS: Hadley (P), a mill operator in Gloucester, arranged to have Baxendale's (D) shipping company return his broken mill shaft to the engineer in Greenwich who was to make a duplicate. Hadley (P) delivered the broken shaft to Baxendale (D) who in consideration for his fee promised to deliver the shaft to Greenwich in a reasonable time. Baxendale (D) did not know that the mill was shut down while awaiting the new shaft. Baxendale (D) was negligent in delivering the shaft within a reasonable time. Reopening of the mill was delayed five days costing Hadley (P) lost profits and paid out wages of £300. Hadley (P) had paid Baxendale (D) £25 to ship the mill shaft. Baxendale (D) paid into court £25 in satisfaction of Hadley's (P) claim. The jury awarded an additional £25 for a total £50 award. Note: The headnote taken from the English reporter and reprinted in the casebook is in error when it states that Hadley's (P) servant told Baxendale (D) the mill was stopped and the shaft must be sent immediately.

ISSUE: Shall damages to be awarded be left to the discretion of the jury?

HOLDING AND DECISION: (Alderson, J.) No. The jury requires a rule for its guidance in awarding damages justly. When a party breaches his contract, the damages he pays ought to be those arising naturally from the breach itself, and, in addition, those as may reasonably be supposed to have been in contemplation of the parties, at the time they made the contract, as the probable result of the breach of it. Therefore, if the special circumstances under which the contract was made were known to both parties, the resulting damages upon breach would be those reasonably contemplated as arising under those communicated and known circumstances. But if the special circumstances were unknown then damages can only be those expected to arise generally from

the breach. Hadley's (P) telling Baxendale (D) that he ran a mill and his mill shaft which he wanted shipped was broken did not notify Baxendale (D) that the mill was shut down. Baxendale (D) could have believed reasonably that Hadley (P) had a spare shaft or that the shaft to be shipped was not the only defective machinery at the mill. Here, it does not follow that a loss of profits could fairly or reasonably have been contemplated by both parties in case of breach. Such a loss would not have flowed naturally from the breach without the special circumstances having been communicated to Baxendale (D).

EDITOR'S ANALYSIS: This case lays down two rules guiding damages. First, only those damages as may fairly and reasonably be considered arising from the breach itself may be awarded. Alternatively, those damages which may reasonably be supposed to have been in contemplation of the parties at the time they made the contract as the probable result of a breach of it may be awarded. The second is distinguished from the first because with the latter, both parties are aware of the special circumstances under which the contract is made. Usually those special circumstances are communicated by the plaintiff to the defendant before the making of the contract. But that is not an absolute condition. If the consequences of the breach are foreseeable, the party who breaches will be liable for the lost profits or expectation damages. Foreseeability and assumption of the risk are ways of describing the bargain. If there is an assumption of the risk, the seller or carrier must necessarily be aware of the consequences. A later English case held that there would be a lesser foreseeability for a common carrier than for a seller as a seller would tend to know the purpose and use of the item sold while the common carrier probably would not know the use of all items it carried. If all loss went on to the seller, this would obviously be an incentive not to enter into contracts. Courts balance what has become a "seller beware" attitude by placing limitations on full recovery. The loss must be foreseeable when the contract is entered into. It cannot be overly speculative. The seller's breach must be judged by willingness, negligence, bad faith, and availability of replacement items. Restatement (First), § 331(2) would allow recovery in the situation in this case under an alternative theory. If the breach were one preventing the use and operation of property from which profits would have been made, damages can be measured by the rental value of the property or by interest on the value of the property. U.C.C. § 2-715(2) allows the buyer consequential damages for any loss which results from general or particular needs of which the seller had reason to know.

Continued on next page.

QUICKNOTES

CONSEQUENTIAL DAMAGES - Monetary compensation that may be recovered in order to compensate for injuries or losses sustained as a result of damages that are not the direct or foreseeable result of the act of a party, but that nevertheless are the consequence of such act and which must be specifically pled and demonstrated.

LOST PROFITS - The potential value of income earned or goods which are the subject of the contract; may be used in calculating damages where the contract has been breached.

EXPECTANCY - The expectation or contingency of obtaining possession of a right or interest in the future.

NOTES:

VALENTINE v. GENERAL AMERICAN CREDIT, INC.
Employee (P) v. Employer (D)
Mich. Sup. Ct., 420 Mich. 256, 362 N.W.2d 628 (1984).

NATURE OF CASE: Appeal of dismissal of an action for damages for breach of contract.

FACTS: Valentine (P) sued for mental distress resulting from a breach of an employment contract.

CONCISE RULE OF LAW: Mental distress damages are not recoverable in an action for breach of an employment contract.

FACTS: Valentine (P) was terminated by General American Credit, Inc. (D). She sued for mental distress allegedly arising out of the termination. She alleged that she had a right to job security that had been violated. The trial court dismissed the suit, and Valentine (P) appealed.

ISSUE: Are mental distress damages recoverable in an action for breach of an employment contract?

HOLDING AND DECISION: (Levin, J.) No. Mental distress damages are not recoverable in an action for breach of an employment contract. Generally speaking, damages for mental anguish are not recoverable in a breach of contract action. Since the obligation to provide job security was contractual, mental anguish damages are not recoverable. The only exception to this rule occurs when the contract is inherently personal, such as breach of a promise to marry. Employment does have a personal element, but the main purpose is economic, not personal. Affirmed.

EDITOR'S ANALYSIS: The rule stated here was once universally recognized. However, the trend has been to recognize breach of an express or implied employment contract as a tort as well as breach of contract. The tort has been characterized as intentional infliction of emotional distress, and also as wrongful termination.

QUICKNOTES

QUASI-CONTRACT - An implied contract created by law to prevent unjust enrichment.

EMOTIONAL DISTRESS - Extreme personal suffering which results in another's conduct and in which damages may be sought.

FREUND v. WASHINGTON SQUARE PRESS, INC.
Author (P) v. Book publisher (D)
N.Y. Ct. App., 34 N.Y.2d 379, 357 N.Y.S.2d 857, 314 N.E.2d 419 (1974).

NATURE OF CASE: Action for damages for breach of contract.

FACT SUMMARY: When Washington Square (D) breached its contract by failing to publish Freund's (P) book, the trial court awarded Freund (P) $10,000 to cover the cost of publishing it himself.

CONCISE RULE OF LAW: When a breach of contract occurs, the law attempts to secure to the injured party the benefit of his bargain, subject to the limitations that the injury was foreseeable and that the amount of damages claimed be measurable with a reasonable degree of certainty and adequately proven.

FACTS: Freund (P) signed an agreement whereby Washington Square (D) was to pay him certain royalties on the sale of his book, which it was obligated to publish in hardbound and paperback editions subject to its right to terminate the agreement within 60 days after submission of the manuscript. Washington Square (D) did not exercise its termination right but nonetheless failed to publish the book. The court that denied Freund's (P) prayer for specific performance set the matter for trial on the issue of money damages. Although Freund (P) argued that his academic promotion had been delayed, that he had lost anticipated royalties, and that it would cost him $10,000 to publish the book himself in hardback, the court allowed recovery only of the $10,000 cost of publishing the book. It denied any recovery for the cost of publishing it in paperback because the proof was conjectural. The appellate division affirmed.

ISSUE: In order to recover damages for breach of contract, must the amount of damages claimed be measurable with a reasonable degree of certainty?

HOLDING AND DECISION: (Rabin, J.) Yes. In allowing recovery for breach of contract, the law attempts to secure to the injured party the benefit of his bargain, subject to the limitations that the injury was foreseeable and that the amount of damages claimed is measurable with a reasonable degree of certainty and adequately proven. It is fundamental that the injured party should not recover more from the breach than he would have gained had the contract been fully performed. Here, an award of the cost of publication would enrich Freund (P) at Washington Square's (D) expense. What Freund (P) bargained for and lost were the royalties he would have been paid, but the amount of royalties he could have expected to receive was not ascertainable with adequate certainty. Thus, only nominal damages are recoverable in this case, and the decision must be so modified. Affirmed as modified.

EDITOR'S ANALYSIS: Restatement (Second) Contracts § 352, Comment a provides: "Courts have traditionally required greater certainty in the proof of damages for breach of contract than in the proof of damages for a tort. . . . The main impact of the requirement of certainty comes in connection with recovery for [lost] profits."

QUICKNOTES

BREACH OF CONTRACT - Unlawful failure by a party to perform its obligations pursuant to contract.

NOMINAL DAMAGES - A small sum awarded to a plaintiff in order to recognize that he sustained an injury that is either slight or incapable of being established.

EXPECTANCY - The expectation or contingency of obtaining possession of a right or interest in the future.

LOST PROFITS - The potential value of income earned or goods which are the subject of the contract; may be used in calculating damages where the contract has been breached.

NOTES:

CHICAGO COLISEUM CLUB v. DEMPSEY
Boxing promoter (P) v. Boxer (D)
Ill. Ct. App., 265 Ill.App. 542 (1932).

NATURE OF CASE: Review of order dismissing action for damages for breach of a written contract.

FACT SUMMARY: When heavyweight champion Dempsey (D) repudiated a written contract with the Chicago Coliseum Club (P) to fight Wills, the Club (P) sued for damages.

CONCISE RULE OF LAW: In an action for breach of contract a party can only recover on damages which naturally flow from and are the result of the act complained of.

FACTS: Chicago Coliseum Club (P) and Dempsey (D) had a written agreement for a public boxing exhibition. The Club (P) incurred expenses in preparation for this event. Dempsey (D) repudiated the contract by letter and refused to carry out his undertaking. Chicago Coliseum Club (P) sued Dempsey (D) in Indiana and was granted a restraining order and an injunction prohibiting Dempsey (D) from fighting without Chicago Coliseum Club's (P) approval. The Club (P) also sued Dempsey (D) for all the expenses it had incurred prior to the signing of the agreement; for expenses incurred in procuring the injunction; for loss of profits; and for other expenses incurred after the signing of the agreement and before Dempsey's (D) breach. The lower court found there was insufficient evidence to prove the damages and dismissed the case. The Club (P) appealed.

ISSUE: In an action for breach of contract, may a party recover on damages which naturally flow from and are the result of the act complained of?

HOLDING AND DECISION: (Wilson, J.) Yes. In an action for breach of contract a party can only recover on damages which naturally flow from and are the result of the act complained of. Therefore, any obligations assumed by the Club (P) prior to the agreement are not changeable to Dempsey (D). Damages for loss of profits are too speculative and are not capable of proof. Furthermore, once Dempsey (D) repudiated the agreement, the Club (P) took steps to procure an injunction at its own risk. However, special expenses incurred after the agreement was entered into and before repudiation, if reasonable, are recoverable. Reversed and remanded for a new trial.

EDITOR'S ANALYSIS: Only wages paid in furtherance of the undertaking of the agreement were allowed by the court in this case. Wages paid to regular officials were treated as overhead expense and were not recoverable. The court applied a reliance rather than an expectancy theory of damages to this case.

QUICKNOTES

BREACH OF CONTRACT - Unlawful failure by a party to perform its obligations pursuant to contract.

LOST PROFITS - The potential value of income earned or goods which are the subject of the contract; may be used in calculating damages where the contract has been breached.

EXPECTANCY - The expectation or contingency of obtaining possession of a right or interest in the future.

REPUDIATION - The actions or statements of a party to a contract that evidence his intent not to perform, or to continue performance, of his duties or obligations thereunder.

NOTES:

BOONE v. COE

Lessee (P) v. Farm owner (D)

Ky. Ct. App., 153 Ky. 233, 154 S.W. 900 (1913).

NATURE OF CASE: Appeal from demurrer to breach of contract action.

FACT SUMMARY: J.F. Coe (D) demurred to the breach of contract complaint on the ground that the alleged agreement was unenforceable under the statute of frauds.

CONCISE RULE OF LAW: Partial performance under an otherwise unenforceable contract gives rise to recovery only where the other party was benefited thereby.

FACTS: Boone (P) and J.T. Coe (P) orally agreed with J.F. Coe (D) to lease his Texas farm for the period of one year from their arrival. It was understood that to do so, they would have to leave their Kentucky homes and travel to Texas with their families and possessions. Once they got there, J.F. Coe (D) agreed to allow them to live in a guest house which he was to construct and to build a barn from materials he was to provide. They would also be allowed to keep a certain percentage of the crops they harvested during their year's lease. In reliance on the agreement, Boone (P) and J.T. Coe (P) traveled to Texas. However, J.F. Coe (D) refused to maintain his end of the bargain. Boone (P) and J.T. Coe (P) brought suit for damages suffered by them in traveling to Texas and back. J.F. Coe (D) demurred, pleading the statute of frauds. His demurrer was granted. Boone (P) and J.T. Coe (P) appealed.

ISSUE: Does partial performance under a contract barred by the statute of frauds give rise to a recovery of damages, where the defendant was not benefited by such performance?

HOLDING AND DECISION: (Clay, Commr.) No. The statute of frauds renders unenforceable both oral contracts to lease real property for a term longer than one year, and such contracts which are not to be performed within one year of the contract's making. Accordingly, oral contracts to lease land for one year, to commence at a future date, such as here presented, falls within the scope of the statute. Unenforceability under the statute means that no suit may be brought on the contract. However, there are exceptions. Partial performance of such a contract, where the defendant is benefited thereby, will give rise to a recovery in restitution, in the amount of the benefit conferred upon the defendant. Unfortunately, in the instant case, J.F. Coe (D) was not benefited by the actions of Boone (P) and J.T. Coe (P) in leaving their homes and traveling to Texas. Therefore, even though they have clearly suffered a loss, it is an uncompensable loss. Affirmed.

EDITOR'S ANALYSIS: There has been much speculation as to why contracts which cannot be performed within one year were included within the scope of the original statute of frauds in 1677.

The authors of the text suggest that the probable reasons for the provision's inclusion, the fallibility of memories, and the death or disability of witnesses, do not necessarily justify the provision. This is because the crucial time factor to be considered is the time lapse between the creation of the contract and trial, rather than that occurring between the contract's creation and its completion.

QUICKNOTES

RESTITUTION - The return or restoration of what the defendant has gained in a transaction to prevent the unjust enrichment of the defendant.

RELIANCE - Dependence on a fact that causes a party to act or refrain from acting.

STATUTE OF FRAUDS - A statute that requires specified types of contracts to be in writing in order to be binding.

NOTES:

UNITED STATES v. ALGERNON BLAIR, INC.

Federal government (P) v. Hospital construction company (D)

479 F.2d 638 (4th Cir. 1973).

NATURE OF CASE: Appeal from denial of damages for breach of contract.

FACT SUMMARY: Coastal (P), a subcontractor, brought suit against Blair (D) for recovery in quantum meruit, after Blair (D) breached its construction contract.

CONCISE RULE OF LAW: A subcontractor in a breached construction contract may sue in quantum meruit for services rendered.

FACTS: Algernon Blair, Inc. (D) contracted with the United States (P) to build a naval hospital. Blair (D) then entered into a contract with Coastal Steel Erectors, Inc. (P), in which Coastal (P) agreed to provide certain subcontracting services. Coastal (P) had provided approximately 28% of the services due under the subcontract when Blair (D) breached the agreement. Coastal (P) then ceased performance and brought suit against Blair (D) in the name of the United States (P) pursuant to the provisions of the Miller Act, 40 U.S.C.A. § 270(a) et seq. The trial court found that Blair (D) had breached the agreement and that $37,000 was still due Coastal (P). However, it also found that Coastal (P) would have lost more than $37,000 by completing the contract. Thus, it awarded no damages. Coastal (P) appealed, seeking recovery in quantum meruit for services already provided.

ISSUE: May a subcontractor recover in quantum meruit for services rendered under a breached construction contract?

HOLDING AND DECISION: (Craven, J.) Yes. It is an accepted principal of law that a party to a contract, upon breach of the other party, may, alternatively, sue on the contract or choose to ignore the contract and sue in quantum meruit for the reasonable value of his performance. This principal has often been applied to construction contracts and should have been applied by the lower court in the instant case. Thus, despite the finding that Coastal (P) would have realized no profit from the completed performance of the contract, it was entitled, upon Blair's (D) breach, to recover in quantum meruit for the reasonable value of the benefits it had already conferred upon Blair (D). Reversed and remanded.

EDITOR'S ANALYSIS: See *Oliver v. Campbell*, 43 Cal. 2d 298, P.2d 15 (1954), where a discharged attorney sought recovery in quantum meruit in excess of the fee provided for by contract. The attorney was discharged after trial, and after a decision had been reached by the court, although not officially rendered. Acknowledging that generally an employee may choose to ignore a breached employment contract and sue in quantum meruit, the court nonetheless held the attorney to be limited to the fees stated in the contract. The ruling was apparently based on the fact that

since the court had virtually made its decision at the time of the discharge, the contract was effectively completed and thus served as a limitation on damages.

QUICKNOTES

QUANTUM MERUIT - Equitable doctrine allowing recovery for labor and materials provided by one party, even though no contract was entered into, in order to avoid unjust enrichment by the benefitted party.

BREACH OF CONTRACT - Unlawful failure by a party to perform its obligations pursuant to contract.

NOTES:

BRITTON v. TURNER

Employee (P) v. Employer (D)

N.H. Sup. Ct., 6 N.H. 481 (1834).

NATURE OF CASE: Appeal from an award of damages in quantum meruit for breach of contract.

FACT SUMMARY: Britton (P) contracted to work for Turner (D) for a period of one year at the end of which he would be paid $120 for his labor, but Britton (P) quit work after 9½ months for which time Turner (D) refused to pay Britton (P).

CONCISE RULE OF LAW: Where labor is performed under a contract for a specified price, the party who fails to perform the whole of the labor contracted for can recover in quantum meruit the value of the labor performed to the degree it is greater than the damage to the other party.

FACTS: Britton (P) contracted to work for Turner for 12 months. At the end of that year, Turner (D) was to pay Britton (P) $120 for his labor. After 9½ months, Britton (P) quit without Turner's (D) consent and without good cause. Turner (D) refused to pay Britton (P) for the time that he did work. Britton (P) brought suit on the contract and in quantum meruit. The trial judge instructed that Britton (P) could receive the value of his work in quantum meruit. The jury returned a verdict of $95 for Britton (P), and Turner (D) appealed.

ISSUE: Where labor is performed under a contract for a specified price, can the party who fails to perform the whole of the labor contracted for recover in quantum meruit the value of the labor performed to the degree it is greater than the damage done to the other party?

HOLDING AND DECISION: (Parker, J.) Yes. Where labor is performed under a contract for a specified price, the party who fails to perform the whole of the labor contracted for can recover in quantum meruit the value of the labor performed to the degree it is greater than the damage done to the other party. The settled rule, which held the opposite, was unfair because one party could receive nearly all of the performance while the other party, upon his breach, would get nothing. Thus, an employer would get more by the breach than he would generally be entitled to if he brought an action for damages. In construction contracts, if a building is built with minor variations from the plan, the owner still receives the benefit of the labor and materials and must pay for their reasonable worth. There is no reason for not applying the same rule to employment contracts. In a contract for labor, the employer, day to day, is continually receiving the benefit of the contract, and upon the employee's breach, he cannot elect to refuse what he has already received. Thus, for the benefit received over the damage done by the employee's breach, the labor actually done and the value received furnish a new consideration upon which the law

raises a promise to pay to the extent of the reasonable worth of such excess. An employee could not recover only when the damage done is greater than the benefit received. Here, Turner (D) did not show that he suffered any damage by the breach at all. Affirmed.

EDITOR'S ANALYSIS: The court in *Britton* also noted that "[t]he technical reasoning, that the performance of the whole labor is a condition precedent, and the right to recover anything dependent upon it—that the contract being entire there can be no apportionment—and that there being an express contract no other can be implied, even upon the subsequent performance of service—is not properly applicable to this species of contract, where a beneficial service has been actually performed; for we have abundant reason to believe that the general understanding of the community is that the hired laborer shall be entitled to compensation for the service actually performed, though he does not continue the entire term contracted for, and such contracts must be presumed to be made with reference to that understanding, unless an express stipulation shows the contrary."

QUICKNOTES

PART PERFORMANCE - Partial performance of a contract, promise or obligation.

QUANTUM MERUIT - Equitable doctrine allowing recovery for labor and materials provided by one party, even though no contract was entered into, in order to avoid unjust enrichment by the benefitted party.

SUBSTANTIAL PERFORMANCE - Performance of all the essential obligations pursuant to an agreement.

NOTES:

PINCHES v. SWEDISH EVANGELICAL LUTHERAN CHURCH

Church builder (P) v. Lutheran church (D)
Conn. Sup. Ct. of Errors, 55 Conn. 183, 10 A. 264 (1887).

NATURE OF CASE: Action to recover the contract price in a construction contract.

FACT SUMMARY: Pinches (P) built a church which had several material defects in the construction.

CONCISE RULE OF LAW: Where the deviation was not willful and the structure as built is reasonably adaptable to the desired purpose, the plaintiff may recover for the work performed less its diminished value.

FACTS: Due to a mutual mistake the ceiling of Swedish Evangelical Lutheran's (D) new church was 2 feet lower than specified in the contract. The windows were shorter and narrower and the seats were narrower than specified. When Pinches (P) demanded payment, the Church (D) refused until the defects were corrected. Pinches (P) brought suit to recover the contract price. The court found that the defects were not willfully done. It found that the Church (D) was currently occupying the building and that it was reasonably fit for the intended use. The court also found that it would cost a great deal of money to rectify the defects. Based on these findings the court held for Pinches (P). It awarded him the contract price less the diminished value of the building with the defects.

ISSUE: May a party to a construction contract refuse to pay for the work defectively performed where the defects cannot be readily cured and the structure may be used for its intended purpose?

HOLDING AND DECISION: (Beardsley, J.) No. Hardship and economic waste make it necessary to temper the rule that the contract cannot recover unless the building conforms to the contract. Where the cost of repair is large and the building is reasonably fit for the intended purpose, the courts will require that the contract price be paid less damages for the diminished value of the structure. The breach was not willful and the defects were caused by mutual mistakes and inadvertence. In such a situation as this, it would be inequitable to allow the Church (D) to retain the benefits of Pinches' (P) labor without paying for it or to require him to spend a large amount to repair the defects. Judgment affirmed.

EDITOR'S ANALYSIS: A plaintiff who is in default may still recover on a contract. He may sue for restitution. His recovery is limited to the value of his services to the defendant. His part performance must provide the defendant with some net benefit. The defendant must have accepted the part performance. If it was not accepted or it was of no benefit to the defendant, the plaintiff cannot recover.

VINES v. ORCHARD HILLS, INC.

Condominium purchaser (P) v. Seller (D)

Conn. Sup. Ct., 181 Conn. 501, 435 A.2d 1022 (1980).

NATURE OF CASE: Appeal of award of damages in action for restitution.

FACT SUMMARY: Vines (P) reneged on a land sale contract after making a down payment, which Orchard Hills, Inc. (D) kept as liquidated damages.

CONCISE RULE OF LAW: A party breaching a land sale contract may recover the down payment if he can prove that no damages were inflicted upon the seller at the time of the breach.

FACTS: Vines (P) contracted to purchase a condominium. He paid $7,800 as a down payment, which was also liquidated damages in the event of a buyer's breach. Shortly thereafter, Vines (P) was transferred to another state and reneged on the contract. Orchard Hills (D) kept the down payment as liquidated damages. Vines (P) sued to recover his down payment. The trial court, finding that the property had substantially appreciated by the time of trial, found the liquidated damages provision an unjust enrichment and ordered Orchard Hills (D) to pay $7,800, plus interest. Orchard Hills (D) appealed.

ISSUE: May a party breaching a land sale contract recover the down payment if he can prove that no damages were inflicted upon the seller at the time of the breach?

HOLDING AND DECISION: (Peters, J.) Yes. A party breaching a land sale contract may recover his down payment if he can prove that no damages were inflicted upon the seller at the time of the breach. At one time, it was generally held that a party breaching a contract could never recover monies paid at the time of execution of the contract. However, more recent cases have recognized this right when to do so will prevent unjust enrichment. Unjust enrichment will inure to the non-defaulting party where it suffers no damages as a result of the breach and, also, is permitted to keep the down payment as liquidated damages. Whether the non-defaulting party was injured by the breach is measured as of the time of the breach, not trial. Since the trial court measured Orchard Hills' (D) damages as of the time of trial, the judgment must be reversed, and the trial court must determine if Orchard Hills (D) had been injured at the time of the breach. Reversed.

EDITOR'S ANALYSIS: Orchard Hills (D) had kept the down payment as liquidated damages pursuant to contract. Liquidated damages have generally been disfavored in contract law, which prefers to compensate for damages in amounts genuinely reflecting a party's actual losses. Nonetheless, liquidated damages

provisions generally will be enforced if, at the time of contract formation, they were reasonably related to foreseeable damages.

QUICKNOTES

LIQUIDATED DAMAGES - An amount of money specified in a contract representing the damages owed in the event of breach.

UNJUST ENRICHMENT - The unlawful acquisition of money or property of another for which both law and equity require restitution to be made.

RESTITUTION - The return or restoration of what the defendant has gained in a transaction to prevent the unjust enrichment of the defendant.

NOTES:

CITY OF RYE v. PUBLIC SERVICE MUT. INS. CO.
Municipality (P) v. Insurance company (D)
N.Y. Ct. App., 34 N.Y. 2d 470, 358 N.Y.S. 2d 391, 315 N.E.2d 458
(1974).

NATURE OF CASE: Appeal from order dismissing action to recover on bond.

FACT SUMMARY: The City of Rye, N.Y. (P) sought to recover a predetermined amount on a bond absent evidence of its actual loss.

CONCISE RULE OF LAW: An action on a performance bond will not lie if the bond amount is not related to actual damages.

FACTS: Several developers contracted with the City of Rye, N.Y. (P) to construct six cooperative apartments. The developers had to post a $100,000 bond to ensure liquidated damages of $200 per day for each day past the projected completion date for the buildings. Five hundred days past that date, the buildings had not been completed. The City (P) brought an action to recover on the bond, which had been issued by Public Service Mut. Ins. Co. (D). The trial court denied the City's (P) motion for summary judgment. The appellate division affirmed, and the New York court of appeals granted review.

ISSUE: Will an action on a performance bond lie if the bond amount is not related to actual damages?

HOLDING AND DECISION: (Breitel, J.) No. An action on a performance bond will not lie if the amount is not related to actual damages. When damages flowing from a breach of contract would be difficult to ascertain, the parties may provide for liquidated damages that reasonably approximate likely actual damages. However, if liquidated damages are so disproportionate as to constitute a penalty, they will not be permitted. Here, there was no evidence that the $200 per day liquidated damages provision was commensurate with actual damages; in fact, there was no convincing evidence that any damages were incurred by the City (P). For these reasons, the liquidated damages provision constituted a penalty and may not be enforced. Affirmed.

EDITOR'S ANALYSIS: The rule stated here is fairly universal. Liquidated damages are allowable, but only if they are commensurate with actual damages. To provide otherwise would constitute a penalty, which would be at odds with contract law's purpose of compensation, not punishment. In addition, it would often violate the rule of contract damages which generally limits recover to that amount which would restore the damaged party, rather than place that party in a better position than he would have been had there been no breach.

QUICKNOTES

LIQUIDATED DAMAGES - An amount of money specified in a contract representing the damages owed in the event of breach.

ACTUAL DAMAGES - Measure of damages necessary to compensate victim for actual injuries suffered.

RESTITUTION - The return or restoration of what the defendant has gained in a transaction to prevent the unjust enrichment of the defendant.

NOTES:

FRETWELL v. PROTECTION ALARM CO.

Homeowners (P) v. Security alarm company (D)

Okla. Sup. Ct., 764 P.2d 149 (1988).

NATURE OF CASE: Review of award of damages for negligence.

FACT SUMMARY: Charged with negligence due to the circumvention of a security system it had installed, Protection Alarm (D) sought to invoke a contractual limitation of liability.

CONCISE RULE OF LAW: A contractual limitation of liability on tort claims is enforceable.

FACTS: Protection Alarm Co. (D) contracted with the Fretwells (P) to install a security system in their home. The agreement contained a disclaimer by Protection (D) insuring the success of its equipment against circumvention but limiting damages should the system fail to $50. At one point burglars managed to shut off the system and were able to steal a significant amount of personal property. The Fretwells (P) sued for negligence, and the jury returned a verdict of over $90,000. The court of appeal affirmed, and the Oklahoma supreme court granted review.

ISSUE: Is a contractual limitation of liability enforceable in a tort action?

HOLDING AND DECISION: (Wilson, J.) Yes. A contractual limitation of liability is enforceable in a tort action. When a contract establishes a duty, any lawful limitations in the contract on that duty may act to limit liability. A limitation on liability is not to be viewed as a punitive type of liquidated damage. They are entirely different creatures, serving different purposes. Liability limitations are not punitive but rather constitute part of the framework of the parties' relationship. Here, even though this is a tort action, it arises out of a contractual relationship. Consequently, the parameters of the relationship are controlled by the contract. The contract provides for a limitation on liability, and this was part of the parties' bargain. It should be enforced. Reversed.

EDITOR'S ANALYSIS: It is something of an axiom in law that a party cannot contract away liability for his own negligence. This is not always true, however, as the instant case demonstrates. When the scope of a party's duty to another is defined by contract, contractual limitations on that duty are valid, with the assumption that each side was aware of its risks and liabilities and that the contracts for price reflected this awareness.

QUICKNOTES

NEGLIGENCE - Conduct falling below the standard of care that a reasonable person would demonstrate under similar conditions.

PUNITIVE DAMAGES - Damages exceeding the actual injury suffered for the purposes of punishment, deterrence and comfort to plaintiff.

NOTES:

VAN WAGNER ADVERTISING CORP. v. S & M ENTERPRISES

Billboard space lessee (P) v. Building owner (D)

N.Y. Ct. App., 67 N.Y.2d 186, 492 N.E.2d 756 (1986).

NATURE OF CASE: Appeal by defendant from award to defendant for breach of contract and appeal by plaintiff from denial of specific performance.

FACT SUMMARY: When S & M (D) purchased a building and wrongfully attempted to terminate a lease of billboard space which S & M's (D) predecessor had made with Van Wagner (P), Van Wagner (P) abandoned the space under protest and sued for specific performance to reinstate the lease.

CONCISE RULE OF LAW: Where there is substantial, reliable information as to the monetary value of the subject matter of a breached contract and where specific performance would create harm to the defendant disproportionate to its aid to the plaintiff, specific performance is not available.

FACTS: Michaels leased for 10 years space on a side of its Manhattan building to Van Wagner (P), and Van Wagner (P) erected a billboard. One month later, S & M (D) purchased the building from Michaels and purported to exercise a termination clause in the lease. Van Wagner (P) abandoned the space under protest and sued S & M (D) for specific performance to reinstate the lease. The trial court determined that S & M (D) had wrongfully terminated the lease but denied Van Wagner (P) specific performance, instead awarding it monetary damages for the period through trial and allowing it to sue for damages in the future if S & M (D) would not reinstate the lease. Both parties appealed, Van Wagner (P) arguing that the property was unique, making monetary damages an inadequate remedy requiring specific performance, S & M (D) arguing that future damages were too speculative and uncertain. The appellate division affirmed, and both parties appealed to the New York court of appeals.

ISSUE: Where there is substantial, reliable information as to the monetary value of the subject matter of a breached contract and where specific performance would create harm to the defendant disproportionate to its aid to the plaintiff, is specific performance available?

HOLDING AND DECISION: (Kaye, J.) No. Where there is substantial, reliable information as to the monetary value of the subject after of a breached contract and where specific performance would create harm to the defendant disproportionate to its aid to the plaintiff, specific performance is not available. To obtain specific performance, the plaintiff must show that monetary damages are inadequate because the subject matter of the contract is unique or because damages are too speculative to be awarded. The subject matter of a contract is unique when there is little reliable information as to its economic value, creating a high

risk that monetary damages will over- or undercompensate the plaintiff. In this case, however, there is an abundance of reliable information on the value of the contract since leases of Manhattan building space for billboard use are very common. Thus, the leased space is not unique, and both parties are wrong in asserting that an estimate of future losses would be too speculative. Furthermore, specific performance is not available since the trial court found that specific performance would inequitably burden S & M (D) by imposing hardship disproportionate to Van Wagner's (P) benefit. Affirmed. [The case was remitted to the trial court to adjust the amount of damages previously awarded and to allow Van Wagner (P) to establish all future damages at once.]

EDITOR'S ANALYSIS: The comment to the Restatement (Second) of Contracts § 360 explains that specific performance of contracts for the sale of land has historically been given special treatment. Land is traditionally considered unique, and monetary damages are considered inadequate compensation for a piece of land which the buyer is said to have chosen for its subjective value to him. Where the buyer has already sold the property to a third party, the "uniqueness" argument does not apply, but courts still find monetary damages inadequate since the buyer may be subject to a lawsuit by the third party unless the buyer can convey the property. Even an aggrieved seller is usually granted specific performance of a land sale contract because the value of land may be too speculative to allow for proof of lost profits, and finding a new buyer for the property may take a long time, especially where there is a dispute over a prior land sale contract.

QUICKNOTES

SPECIFIC PERFORMANCE - An equitable remedy whereby the court requires the parties to perform their obligations pursuant to a contract.

LOST PROFITS - The potential value of income earned or goods which are the subject of the contract; may be used in calculating damages where the contract has been breached.

NOTES:

LACLEDE GAS CO. v. AMOCO OIL CO.
Distributing utility (P) v. Propane supplier (D)
522 F.2d 33 (8th Cir. 1975).

NATURE OF CASE: Appeal from denial of damages or specific performance for breach of contract.

FACT SUMMARY: After Amoco (D) breached a long-term propane supply contract, Laclede (P) sought specific performance of the contract.

CONCISE RULE OF LAW: Specific performance is available as a remedy for breach of a long-term supply contract.

FACTS: A contract existed between Laclede Gas Co. (P) and Amoco Oil Co. (D) for the latter to supply the former with propane on a long-term basis. Laclede (P) had no other long-term propane supply contracts. A dispute arose between Laclede (P) and Amoco (D) as to Amoco's (D) obligations. Amoco (D) eventually abrogated the contract. Laclede (P) sued for specific performance or, in the alternative, damages. The trial court found the contract void and dismissed the suit. Laclede (P) appealed.

ISSUE: Is specific performance available as a remedy for breach of a long-term supply contract?

HOLDING AND DECISION: (Ross, J.) Yes. Specific performance is available as a remedy for breach of a long-term supply contract. (The court first held the contract enforceable and then discussed damages.) While ordering specific performance is within a trial court's discretion, that discretion is limited. When a litigant can show that damages will not make him whole, and that no policy considerations militate against specific performance, it shall be granted. Here, Laclede (P) had no other long-term supply contracts, so no amount of damages could guarantee it a supply of propane. This court does not believe that such a remedy would require onerous court supervision, nor does it believe the contract to be so uncertain as to make specific performance unworkable. This being so, Laclede (P) is entitled to specific performance as a matter of law. Reversed.

EDITOR'S ANALYSIS: Amoco (D) made one additional argument, to which the court gave no consideration. It argued that mutuality of remedy did not exist, and this barred specific performance. At common law in England, authority existed for the proposition that specific performance had to be available to both parties for any party to obtain it. This rule has long since been abandoned.

QUICKNOTES

SPECIFIC PERFORMANCE - An equitable remedy whereby the court requires the parties to perform their obligations pursuant to a contract.

MUTUALITY OF REMEDY - An equitable doctrine that one party to a contract may not have available an equitable remedy if the other party does not have such remedy available.

NOTES:

FITZPATRICK v. MICHAEL
Nurse (P) v. Elderly patient (D)
Md. Ct. App., 177 Md. 248, 9 A.2d 639 (1939).

NATURE OF CASE: Action for specific performance of a personal service contract.

FACT SUMMARY: Michael (D) contracted with Fitzpatrick (P), a nurse, that If Fitzpatrick (P) would take care of Michael (D) in his remaining years then Michael (P) would leave a large bequest to Fitzpatrick (P). Two years later, Michael (D) repudiated the contract whereupon Fitzpatrick (P) brought suit for specific performance.

CONCISE RULE OF LAW: A court of equity will not grant specific performance in a personal service contract because excessive court entanglement is necessarily involved.

FACTS: Michael (D), an elderly man, contracted with Fitzpatrick (P), a practical nurse, that if Fitzpatrick (P) would remain with Michael (D) as a companion and nurse for the rest of Michael's (D) life then Michael (D) in consideration would give Fitzpatrick (P) room and board, a salary of $8 a week plus in his will he would leave Fitzpatrick (P) a life estate in his home and title to his automobiles. Two years later, without explanation, Michael (D) repudiated the contract. Fitzpatrick (P) then brought suit for specific performance of the contract. The trial court refused to give the relief requested.

ISSUE: Will a court of equity grant specific performance in a personal service contract?

HOLDING AND DECISION: (Offutt, J.) No. A court of equity will not grant specific performance in a personal service contract because excessive court entanglement would necessarily be involved. If the relief were granted then this court would be required for an extensive period of time to monitor the quantity and quality of the services to be rendered by Fitzpatrick (P), a task which is completely beyond the scope of the jurisdiction of this court. We conclude that because excessive court entanglement is involved the request for specific performance must be denied.

EDITOR'S ANALYSIS: The principal case represents the majority view that a court of equity will decline to grant specific performance any time excessive court supervision or entanglement is involved. Obviously what is excessive court supervision is a question of fact. In recent years the courts have been more liberal in construing a given set of facts as not involving excessive court supervision. Specific performance is rarely granted in personal service cases.

QUICKNOTES

SPECIFIC PERFORMANCE - An equitable remedy whereby the court requires the parties to perform their obligations pursuant to a contract.

PERSONAL SERVICES CONTRACT - A contract whose bargained-for performance includes specific conduct or activity that must be performed by one party.

COURT OF EQUITY - A court that determines matters before it consistent with principles of fairness and not in strict compliance with rules of law.

NOTES:

NORTHERN DELAWARE IND. DEV. CORP. v. E.W. BLISS CO.

Developer (P) v. Mill refurbisher (D)
Del. Ct. Ch., 245 A.2d 431 (1968).

NATURE OF CASE: Suit seeking specific performance.

FACT SUMMARY: Northern Delaware Industrial Development Corp. (P) retained E. W. Bliss Co. (D) to refurbish a steel mill. Although construction lagged behind schedule, Bliss (D) refused to hire extra workers as required by the contract.

CONCISE RULE OF LAW: Courts of equity will not issue decrees of specific performance where such orders would require extensive supervision by the court.

FACTS: Northern Delaware Industrial Development Corp. (P) entered into a contract with E. W. Bliss Co. (D) by the terms of which the latter agreed to refurbish a steel mill. A work proposal prepared by a subcontractor of Bliss (D) provided that additional workers would be hired to comprise a night shift during part of the construction period, and this work proposal was incorporated into the contract. When construction schedules lagged and Bliss (D) refused to hire additional workers, Northern (P) sought a court order requiring Bliss (D) to hire the added personnel.

ISSUE: Should a court order specific performance of the terms of a contract calling for the completion of a vast and complex construction project?

HOLDING AND DECISION: (Marvel, V.C.) No. A court of equity will not issue a decree of specific performance where such an order would require extensive supervision by the court. Although the parties seem to agree that there was a covenant to hire additional workers, it would be impractical for the court to supervise the carrying out of a massive and complex construction project such as the one herein involved. Therefore, specific performance will not be ordered. Northern (P) may instead seek relief in the form of damages.

ON REARGUMENT: Northern (P) claims that it (P) does not seek to make the court the supervisor of a complex construction project, but merely desires an order compelling Bliss (D) to perform the ministerial act of hiring added personnel. However, this motion for reargument must be denied in view of the rule that personal services contracts may not be specifically enforced because of the impracticality of enforcing an order according that relief.

EDITOR'S ANALYSIS: In refusing to decree specific performance, courts frequently cite the inconvenience of having to perform the supervisory function necessary to insure compliance with the order for specific performance. However, the problem of supervision need not present an insurmountable obstacle to the enforcement of a decree for specific performance. The court could, for instance, appoint a referee or master who would be charged with the responsibility of insuring compliance. Courts resort to the practice of appointing specified individuals to carry out judicial orders in other contexts, and no reason appears why decrees of specific performance could not be implemented in like fashion.

QUICKNOTES

SPECIFIC PERFORMANCE - An equitable remedy whereby the court requires the parties to perform their obligations pursuant to a contract.

COURT OF EQUITY - A court that determines matters before it consistent with principles of fairness and not in strict compliance with rules of law.

NOTES:

CHAPTER 2
GROUNDS FOR ENFORCING PROMISES

QUICK REFERENCE RULES OF LAW

1. **Formality.** An oral promise to donate money is unenforceable. (Congregation Kadimah Toras-Moshe v. DeLeo)

2. **Exchange Through Bargain.** Forbearance from a lawful act at the request of another is sufficient consideration for a contract. (Hamer v. Sidway)

3. **Exchange Through Bargain.** Mere love and affection do not constitute sufficient consideration to compel performance of an entirely executory contract. (Fischer v. Union Trust Co.)

4. **Exchange Through Bargain.** Mere inadequacy of consideration will not void a contract. (Batsakis v. Demotsis)

5. **Exchange Through Bargain.** Forbearance to sue on a claim is not sufficient consideration when the claim itself is illegal. (Duncan v. Black)

6. **Exchange Through Bargain.** One who volunteers information to another to the other's benefit has not formed a contract. (Martin v. Little, Brown & Co)

7. **Promises Grounded in the Past.** A moral obligation is insufficient as consideration for a promise. (Mills v. Wyman)

8. **Promises Grounded in the Past.** A moral obligation is a sufficient consideration to support a subsequent promise to pay where the promisor has received a material benefit. (Webb v. McGowin)

9. **Reliance on a Promise.** To be legally enforceable an executory promise must be supported by sufficient, bargained for consideration. (Kirksey v. Kirksey)

10. **Reliance on a Promise.** The acceptance of a charitable subscription by the trustees of the charity implies a promise on their part to execute the work contemplated and to carry out the purposes for which the subscription was made. (Allegheny College v. National Chautauqua County Bank)

11. **Reliance on a Promise.** A promise which the promisor should reasonably expect to induce action or forbearance of a definite and substantial character on the part of the promisee and which does induce such action or forbearance is binding if injustice can be avoided only by enforcement of a promise. (East Providence Credit Union v. Geremia)

12. **Reliance on a Promise.** Specific performance of a parol contract to convey land is decreed in favor of the vendee who has performed his part of the contract, when a failure or refusal to convey would operate as a fraud upon him. (Seavey v. Drake)

13. **Reliance on a Promise.** A contract of "permanent employment" is terminable at will by either party unless additional compensation in the form of an economic benefit is rendered by the employee to the employer. (Forrer v. Sears, Roebuck & Co.)

14. **Reliance on a Promise.** Promissory estoppel may not be used to defeat a Statute of Frauds defense to an asserted oral employment contract. (Stearns v. Emery-Waterhouse Co.)

15. **Reliance on a Promise.** One who by his language or conduct leads another to do what he would not otherwise have done shall not subject such person to loss or injury by disappointing the expectation upon which he acted. (Goodman v. Dicker)

16. **Reliance on a Promise.** When a subsequent oral agreement which has been made to change and alter the terms of the written lease is not supported by a lawful consideration, it is wholly ineffective. (Levine v. Blumenthal)

17. **Promises of Limited Commitment.** The fact that a contract has a condition precedent to its formation does not make the contract too indefinite to be enforceable. (Obering v. Swain Roach Lumber Co.)

18. **Promises of Limited Commitment.** While an express promise may be lacking, the whole writing may be instinct with an obligation—an implied promise—imperfectly expressed so as to form a valid contract. (Wood v. Lucy, Lady Duff-Gordon)

19. **Promises of Limited Commitment.** A contractual condition calling for the subjective satisfaction of a party imposes a duty of good faith in the exercise of the party's discretion and is not illusory. (Omni Group, Inc. v. Seattle-First National Bank)

20. **Promises of Limited Commitment.** Output contracts are valid and any indefiniteness or mutuality is supplied by a "good-faith requirement" implied by the U.C.C. into such contracts. (Feld v. Henry S. Levy & Sons, Inc.)

21. **Promises of Limited Commitment.** An employer's general right to terminate the services of an employee hired for an unlimited term is limited by public policy. (Sheets v. Teddy's Frosted Foods, Inc.)

CONGREGATION KADIMAH TORAS-MOSHE v. DELEO
Temple (P) v. Estate administrator (D)
Mass. Sup. Jud. Ct., 405 Mass. 365, 540 N.E. 2d 691 (1989).

NATURE OF CASE: Appeal from dismissal of action for damages for breach of contract.

FACT SUMMARY: Congregation Kadimah Toras-Moshe (P) sought to enforce a decedent's oral promise to donate money to it.

CONCISE RULE OF LAW: An oral promise to donate money is unenforceable.

FACTS: During the course of a terminal illness, a decedent promised to donate $25,000 to Congregation Kadimah Toras-Moshe (P). The decedent did not complete the gift before his death. When Deleo (D) the estate's administrator, refused to give over the money, the Congregation (P) sued, having already incorporated the sum into its budget. The trial court dismissed, and the judicial state supreme court granted review.

ISSUE: Is an oral promise to donate money enforceable?

HOLDING AND DECISION: (Liacos, J.) No. An oral promise to donate money is unenforceable. A gratuitous promise to do or give something to another, without any benefit accruing to the promisor, lacks the element of consideration, and therefore no contract has been entered. Justifiable detrimental reliance may constitute consideration. Here, however, the mere incorporation of the $25,000 into the Congregation's (P) budget was insufficient to create an estoppel. As there was no consideration or basis for an estoppel here, the promise was unenforceable. Affirmed.

EDITOR'S ANALYSIS: In a sense, an attempt to enforce an oral promise after the promissor's death would be very much like attempting to enforce an oral will, a situation wide open to fraudulent claims. This approach is rejected in almost all jurisdictions. Due to serious proof problems with oral wills, virtually all states require wills to be written and witnessed.

QUICKNOTES

ORAL PROMISE - An oral declaration of a person's intention to do or refrain from doing an act that, by itself, is not legally binding.

CONSIDERATION - Value given by one party in exchange for performance, or a promise to perform, by another party.

HAMER v. SIDWAY
Nephew (P) v. Uncle (D)
N.Y. Ct. App., 124 N.Y. 538, 27 N.E. 256 (1891).

NATURE OF CASE: Action for breach of a performance contract.

FACT SUMMARY: Story Sr. requested that if his nephew (P) refrained from using tobacco, alcohol, and other things until he was 21 years old then Sr. would give his nephew (P) $5,000. The nephew (P) performed as requested however his uncle's estate (D) refused to make payment whereupon the nephew (P) brought suit.

CONCISE RULE OF LAW: Forbearance from a lawful act at the request of another is sufficient consideration for a contract.

FACTS: William Story Sr. promised his nephew (P), William Story Jr., that if the nephew (P) retrained from drinking, using tobacco, swearing and playing cards or billiards for money until he became 21 years of age then William Story Sr. would pay him a sum of $5,000. The nephew (P) assented thereto and fully performed the conditions involved. The nephew (P) then made a claim against his now deceased uncle's estate (D). The executor Sidway (D) refused the claim whereupon the nephew (P) brought suit for breach of contract. The trial court gave judgment for the nephew (P) and the executor appeals.

ISSUE: Is forbearance from a lawful act at the request of another party sufficient consideration for a contract?

HOLDING AND DECISION: (Parker, J.) Yes. Forbearance from a lawful act at the request of another party is sufficient consideration for a contract. A valuable consideration in the eyes of the law may consist either in some right, interest, profit or benefit accruing to the one party, or some forbearance, detriment, loss or responsibility given, suffered or undertaken by the other party. Courts will not ask whether the thing promised does in fact benefit the promisee or a third party or is of any substantial value to anyone. It is enough that something is promised, done, forborne or suffered by the party to whom the promise is made as consideration for the promise made to him. In this case the nephew (P) received a detriment by refraining from certain acts which he had a right to engage in such as using tobacco. This abstention is sufficient in the eyes of the law to be valuable consideration. We conclude that the nephew (P) performed as required under the contract therefore he has a right to full payment of the $5,000.

EDITOR'S ANALYSIS: It is immaterial whether the forbearance would have been undertaken regardless of the promise. Binding oneself to a particular course of conduct is sufficient. It is also immaterial whether the promisee actually receives a benefit in return. It is presumed that the detriment undertaken is sufficient consideration. Similarly, the promise to go to college is sufficient consideration to enforce a promise. 19 Wash. 258, 69 Md. 199.

QUICKNOTES

CONSIDERATION - Value given by one party in exchange for performance, or a promise to perform, by another party.

FORBEARANCE - Refraining from doing something that one has the legal right to do.

NOTES:

FISCHER v. UNION TRUST CO.
Administrator of father's estate (D) v. Daughter (P)
Mich. Sup. Ct., 138 Mich. 612, 101 N.W. 852 (1904).

NATURE OF CASE: Suit to enforce a promise contained in a deed.

FACT SUMMARY: Fischer deeded realty to his daughter (P), agreeing to pay off the mortgages on the property. He failed to do so, and she sued his administrator (D).

CONCISE RULE OF LAW: Mere love and affection do not constitute sufficient consideration to compel performance of an entirely executory contract.

FACTS: Prior to his death, William Fischer deeded certain property to his daughter (P), a mental incompetent. The deed contained a promise that he would pay off two mortgages on the property. At the time of the transfer Bertha (P), the daughter, gave Fischer $1, which had been handed her by one of her brothers. She then gave the deed to a brother for safekeeping. William Fischer died without paying off the mortgages. One of the mortgages was eventually foreclosed and was satisfied out of a portion of the property that had been conveyed to Bertha (P). In order to enforce Fischer's promise to discharge the mortgages, Bertha (P) brought this action against Union Trust Co. (D) as administrator of Fischer's estate and was awarded judgment.

ISSUE: May an individual's affection for a loved one constitute sufficient consideration to support a deed of valuable real estate and a promise to pay off all encumbrances against the property?

HOLDING AND DECISION: (Grant, J.) No. Mere love and affection do not constitute sufficient consideration to compel performance of a purely executory contract. Although Bertha (P) paid her father the sum of $1, it is obvious from the circumstances that the grantor's actual motivation for the conveyance was his love and affection for his daughter (P). No matter how laudable his intentions may have been, it would be contrary to common sense to hold that either Fischer's feelings toward Bertha (P) or her payment of a dollar were adequate consideration for the promise to which Bertha (P) seeks to bind his estate. Therefore, the judgment in favor of Bertha (P) must be reversed.

EDITOR'S ANALYSIS: Courts of law do not, as a rule, evaluate the adequacy of any consideration which passes between the parties. Courts of equity, however, may refuse to enforce a contract unless consideration of approximately equivalent value has passed. Sham, token, or moral consideration cannot support a contract either at law or in equity, since anything which purports to constitute consideration must have some measurable value, however minute.

BATSAKIS v. DEMOTSIS
Lender (P) v. Borrower (D)
Tex. Ct. Civ. App., 226 S.W.2d 673 (1949).

NATURE OF CASE: Action to recover on promissory note.

FACT SUMMARY: Batsakis (P) loaned Demotsis (D) 500,000 drachmae (which, at the time, had a total value of $25 in American money) in return for Demotsis' (D) promise to repay $2,000 in American money.

CONCISE RULE OF LAW: Mere inadequacy of consideration will not void a contract.

FACTS: During World War II, Batsakis (P), a Greek resident, loaned Demotsis (D), also a Greek resident, the sum of 500,000 drachmae which at the time had a distressed value of only $25 in American money. In return, Demotsis (D), eager to return to the United States, signed an instrument in which she promised to repay Batsakis (P) $2,000 of American money. When Demotsis (D) refused to repay, claiming that the instrument was void at the outset for lack of adequate consideration, Batsakis (P) brought an action to collect on the note, and recovered a judgment for $750 (which, at the time, after the war, reflected the rising value of drachmae), plus interest. Batsakis (P) appealed on the ground that he was entitled to recover the stated sum of the note—$2,000—plus interest.

ISSUE: Will mere inadequacy of consideration void a contract?

HOLDING AND DECISION: (McGill, J.) No. Only where the consideration for a contract has no value whatsoever will the contract be voided. A plea of want of consideration amounts to a contention that the instrument never became a valid obligation in the first instance. As a result, mere inadequacy of consideration is not enough. Here, the trial court obviously placed a value on the consideration—the drachmae—by deeming it to be worth $750. Thus, the trial court felt that there was consideration of value for the original transaction. Furthermore, the 500,000 drachmae was exactly what Demotsis (D) bargained for. It may not have been a good bargain, but she nonetheless agreed to repay Batsakis (P) $2,000. Accordingly, Batsakis (P) is entitled to recover $2,000, and not just $750, plus interest.

EDITOR'S ANALYSIS: Official Comment (e) to the Restatement (Second) of Contracts, § 81, states "gross inadequacy of consideration may be relevant in the application of other rules, (such as) . . . lack of capacity, fraud, duress, undue influence or mistake." Section 234 provides for the avoidance of a contract which, at the time it is made, contains an unconscionable term. The Official Comment (c) to this section states that "gross disparity in the values exchanged . . . may be sufficient ground, without more, for denying specific performance."

QUICKNOTES

CONSIDERATION - Value given by one party in exchange for performance, or a promise to perform, by another party.

LEGAL DETRIMENT - The relinquishment of rights or conduct to which one is entitled to, as consideration for a binding contract.

SPECIFIC PERFORMANCE - An equitable remedy whereby the court requires the parties to perform their obligations pursuant to a contract.

NOTES:

DUNCAN v. BLACK
Cotton buyer (P) v. Seller (D)
Mo. Ct. App., 324 S.W.2d 483 (1959).

NATURE OF CASE: Action for collection of a promissory note.

FACT SUMMARY: Black (D) agreed to sell to Duncan (P) a certain allotment of cotton each year for a number of years. Two years later a dispute arose as to the amount of the allotment. Duncan (P) threatened legal action and Black (D) settled by giving Duncan (P) a $1,500 promissory note. Duncan (P) now sues to collect on the note.

CONCISE RULE OF LAW: Forbearance to sue on a claim is not sufficient consideration when the claim itself is illegal.

FACTS: Black (D) contracted to sell to Duncan (P) a certain allotment of cotton each year for a number of years. The allotment was set up in conjunction with the Federal Allotment System, a system of quotas set up to prevent the overproduction of cotton. Two years later a dispute arose between the parties as to the exact amount of the allotment. Duncan (P) threatened to take legal action whereupon Black (D) agreed to settle the dispute by executing a $1,500 promissory note. Thereafter, Black (D) learned that if he would have given the extra amount to Duncan (P) as claimed by him, this would have exceeded the quota under the allotment system and therefore have been illegal. Based on this Black (D) refused to make payments under the note whereupon Duncan (D) brought suit for its collection. The trial court gave judgment to Black (D).

ISSUE: Is forbearance to sue on a claim sufficient consideration when the claim itself is illegal?

HOLDING AND DECISION: (Ruark, J.) No. Forbearance to sue on a claim is not sufficient consideration when the claim itself is illegal. The settlement of a claim based on a contract which is against public morals or public policy or which is inherently illegal or which is in direct violation of the statutes cannot form the basis of consideration for a valid compromise settlement, for the reason that "the wrong done is against the state and the state only can forgive it." We conclude then that the attempt here to transfer the allotment was the attempt to do that which was clearly contrary to the Federal Allotment System, and being illegal as such, it did not constitute a consideration which the law can recognize. We must therefore leave the parties where we have found them. Affirmed.

EDITOR'S ANALYSIS: To be deemed adequate consideration the claim must be susceptible of being legally enforced. It is immaterial whether the claim could have been won at trial so long as the party asserting it believed a valid claim existed. The rationale is the judicial encouragement of and deference to settlement agreements. They will be upheld in the interest of promoting binding settlement agreements. This purpose is not served by enforcing illegal or patently specious claims.

QUICKNOTES

FORBEARANCE - Refraining from doing something that one has the legal right to do.

CONSIDERATION - Value given by one party in exchange for performance, or a promise to perform, by another party.

NOTES:

MARTIN v. LITTLE, BROWN AND CO.
Book publisher (P) v. Rival (D)
Pa. Sup. Ct., 304 Pa. Super. 424, 450 A.2d 984 (1981).

NATURE OF CASE: Appeal from demurrer to action for damages for breach of contract.

FACT SUMMARY: Martin (P) gratuitously informed Little, Brown and Co. (D) about an act of plagiarism and then demanded compensation.

CONCISE RULE OF LAW: One who volunteers information to another to the other's benefit has not formed a contract.

FACTS: Martin (P) sent a letter to Little, Brown and Co. (D), informing it that one of their books had been plagiarized, offering to send evidence thereof. Little, Brown (D) requested that he do so, and Martin (P) did. When Martin (D) discovered that Little, Brown (D) was taking action on the information, he demanded one third of whatever Little, Brown (D) recovered from the offending publisher. Little, Brown (D) denied any such agreement had been made. At no time had Martin (P) conditioned the provision of information on any compensation. Little, Brown (D) successfully demurred to Martin's (P) complaint, and Martin (P) appealed.

ISSUE: Has one who volunteered information to another to the other's benefit formed a contract?

HOLDING AND DECISION: (Wieand, J.) No. One who volunteers information to another to the other's benefit has not formed a contract. A true contract has not been formed, as the requisite offer-acceptance has not occurred. An implied-in-fact contract arises when the actions of the parties demonstrate a contract-like relationship in the absence of a genuine contract. Such a situation does not occur when one party performs gratuitously, as Martin (P) did here. Finally, a quasi-contract arises in cases of unjust enrichment, where restitution would be just. Again, the law is that volunteers have no right to restitution. The evidence here is that Martin (P) was never anything other than a volunteer, and, therefore, no contract of any type was formed. Affirmed.

EDITOR'S ANALYSIS: The rule stated here is fairly universal. Those who volunteer their services without recompense have no right to unilaterally demand payment therefore after the fact. It seems rather obvious that Martin (P) did not handle his transaction properly.

QUICKNOTES

QUASI-CONTRACT - An implied contract created by law to prevent unjust enrichment.

UNJUST ENRICHMENT - The unlawful acquisition of money or property of another for which both law and equity require restitution to be made.

RESTITUTION - The return or restoration of what the defendant has gained in a transaction to prevent the unjust enrichment of the defendant.

NOTES:

MILLS v. WYMAN
Caretaker (P) v. Mother of patient (D)
Mass. Sup. Jud. Ct., 20 Mass. (3 Pick.) 207 (1825).

NATURE OF CASE: Action on appeal to recover upon alleged promise.

FACT SUMMARY: Mills (P) took care of Wyman's (D) son without being requested to do so and for so doing was promised compensation for expenses arising out of the rendered care by Wyman (D). Wyman (D) later refused to compensate Mills (P).

CONCISE RULE OF LAW: A moral obligation is insufficient as consideration for a promise.

FACTS: Mills (P) nursed and cared for Levi Wyman the son of Wyman (D). Upon learning of Mills' (P) acts of kindness towards his son, Wyman (D) promised to repay Mills (P) his expenses incurred in caring for Levi Wyman. Later, Wyman (D) refused to compensate Mills (P) for his expenses. Mills (P) filed an action in the court of common pleas where the defendant Wyman was successful in obtaining a nonsuit against Mills (P). Mills (P) appeals.

ISSUE: Is a moral obligation sufficient consideration for a promise?

HOLDING AND DECISION: (Parker, J.) No. It is said a moral obligation is a sufficient consideration to support an express promise, however, the universality of the rule cannot be supported, therefore, there must be some other pre-existing obligation which will suffice as consideration.

EDITOR'S ANALYSIS: In cases such as this one, the nearly universal holding is that the existing moral obligation is not a sufficient basis for the enforcement of an express promise to render the performance that it requires. The general statement is that it is not sufficient consideration for the express promise. The difficulties and differences of opinion involved in the determination of what is a moral obligation are probably much greater than those involved in determining the existence of a legal obligation. This tends to explain the attitude of the majority of courts on the subject and justifies the generally stated rule.

QUICKNOTES

MORAL CONSIDERATION - An inducement to enter a contract that is not enforceable at law, but is made based on a moral obligation and may enforceable in order to prevent unjust enrichment on the part of the promisor.

WEBB v. McGOWIN
Conscientious worker (P) Grateful pedestrian (D)
Ala. Ct. App., 27 Ala. App. 82, 168 So. 196 (1935).

NATURE OF CASE: Action on appeal to collect on a promise.

FACT SUMMARY: Webb (P) saved the now deceased J. McGowin from grave bodily injury or death by placing himself in grave danger and subsequently suffering grave bodily harm. J. McGowin, in return, promised Webb (P) compensation. McGowin's executors (D) now refuse to pay the promised compensation.

CONCISE RULE OF LAW: A moral obligation is a sufficient consideration to support a subsequent promise to pay where the promisor has received a material benefit.

FACTS: Webb (P), while in the scope of his duties for the W. T. Smith Lumber Co., was clearing the floor, which required him to drop a 75-lb. pine block from the upper floor of the mill to the ground. Just as Webb (P) was releasing the block, he noticed J. McGowin below and directly under where the block would have fallen. In order to divert the fall of the block, Webb (P) fell with it, breaking an arm and leg and ripping his heel off. The fall left Webb (P) a cripple and incapable of either mental or physical labor. In return for Webb's (P) act, J. McGowin promised to pay Webb (P) $15 every two weeks for the rest of Webb's (P) life. J. McGowin paid the promised payments until his death eight years later. Shortly after J. McGowin's death, the payments were stopped and Webb (P) brought an action against N. McGowin (D) and J.F. McGowin (D) as executors of J. McGowin's estate for payments due him. The executors (D) of the estate were successful in obtaining a nonsuit against Webb (P) in the lower court. Webb (P) appeals.

ISSUE: Was the moral obligation to compensate as promised sufficient consideration?

HOLDING AND DECISION: (Bricken, J.) Yes. It is well settled that a moral obligation is a sufficient consideration to support a subsequent promise to pay where the promisor has received a material benefit, although there was no original duty or liability resting on the promisor.

CONCURRENCE: (Samford, J.) If the benefit is material and substantial, and was to the person of the promisor rather than to his estate, it is within the class of material benefits which he has the privilege of recognizing and compensating either by an executed payment or an executed promise to pay.

PETITION FOR REHEARING: If the benefit was material and substantial, and was to the person of the promisor rather than to his estate, it is within the class of material benefits which he has the privilege of recognizing and compensating either by an executed payment or an executory promise to pay. When the compensation is not only for the benefits which the promisor received, but also for the injuries either to the property or person of the promisee by reason of the services rendered, it fits within the above general rule recognizing that more than a moral benefit is involved. The rehearing is denied.

EDITOR'S ANALYSIS: In most cases where the moral obligation is asserted, the court feels that the promise ought not be enforced; instead of going into the uncertain field of morality the court chooses to rely upon the rule that moral obligation is not a sufficient consideration. On the other hand, in cases where the promise is one which would have been kept by most citizens, and the court feels that enforcement is just, a few courts will enforce the promise using the *Webb v. McGowin* rule. In general, the *Webb v. McGowan* rule is the minority rule and the *Mills v. Wyman* the majority rule.

QUICKNOTES
MORAL CONSIDERATION - An inducement to enter a contract that is not enforceable at law, but is made based on a moral obligation and may enforceable in order to prevent unjust enrichment on the part of the promisor.

EXECUTORY PROMISE - A promise to perform an action that has not yet been performed.

MATERIAL BENEFIT - An advantage gained by entering into a contract that is essential to the performance of the agreement and without which the contract would not have been entered into.

NOTES:

KIRKSEY v. KIRKSEY
Sister (P) v. Brother (D)
Ala. Sup. Ct., 8 Ala. 131 (1845).

NATURE OF CASE: Action to recover damages for breach of a promise.

FACT SUMMARY: Kirksey (D) promised "Sister Antillico" (P) a place to raise her family "If you come down and see me."

CONCISE RULE OF LAW: To be legally enforceable an executory promise must be supported by sufficient, bargained for consideration.

FACTS: Kirksey (D) wrote to "Sister Antillico" (P) a letter containing the following clause: "If you will come down and see me, I will let you have a place to raise your family." "Sister Antillico" (P) moved sixty miles to Kirksey's (D) residence where she remained for over two years. Kirksey (D) then required her to leave although her family was not yet " raised." "Sister Antillico" (P) contends that the loss which she sustained in moving was sufficient consideration to support Kirksey's (D) promise to furnish her with "a place" until she could raise her family.

ISSUE: Is a promise on the condition "If you will come down and see me" given as a bargained exchange for the promisee's "coming down and seeing" the promisor?

HOLDING AND DECISION: (Ormond, J.) No. Such a promise is a promise to make a gift. Any expenses incurred by the promisee in "coming down and seeing" are merely conditions necessary to acceptance of the gift. In this case Kirksey (D) did not appear to be bargaining either for "Sister Antillico's" presence or for her sixty-mile move. Instead, Kirksey (D) merely wished to assist her out of what he perceived as a grievous and difficult situation.

EDITOR'S ANALYSIS: This well-known case demonstrates the court's insistence on finding a bargained-for exchange before it will enforce an executory promise. A promise to make a gift is generally not legally binding until it is executed. Compare Williston's famous hypothetical in which a benevolent man says to a tramp: "If you go around the corner to the clothing shop there, you may purchase an overcoat on my credit." This hypo highlights the conceptual problem of the present case in that it is unreasonable to construe the walk around the corner as the price of the promise, yet it is a legal detriment to the tramp to make the walk. Perhaps a reasonable (though not conclusive) guideline is the extent to which the happening of the condition will benefit the promisor. The present case might be decided differently today under the doctrine of promissory estoppel which had not yet been developed in 1845.

QUICKNOTES

DONATIVE PROMISE- A promise to make a gift.

EXECUTORY PROMISE - A promise to perform an action that has not yet been performed.

PROMISSORY ESTOPPEL - A promise that is enforceable if the promisor should reasonably expect that it will induce action or forbearance on the part of the promisee, and does in fact cause such action or forbearance, and it is the only means of avoiding injustice.

NOTES:

ALLEGHENY COLLEGE v. NATIONAL CHAUTAUQUA COUNTY BANK

College (P) v. Bank (D)

N.Y. Ct. App., 246 N.Y. 369, 159 N.E. 173 (1927).

NATURE OF CASE: Appeal from dismissal of a complaint for breach of contract.

FACT SUMMARY: National (D), Johnston's executor, refused to pay the balance of a charitable subscription which Johnston made to Allegheny's (P) endowment fund but later repudiated after paying a portion of it to Allegheny (P).

CONCISE RULE OF LAW: The acceptance of a charitable subscription by the trustees of the charity implies a promise on their part to execute the work contemplated and to carry out the purposes for which the subscription was made.

FACTS: In response to a campaign by Allegheny (P) to increase its endowment fund, Johnston pledged $5,000 to become due 30 days after her death and to be paid by her executor. The money was to be added to the endowment fund or used to educate students preparing for the ministry, and, if the latter, the fund was to be called the "Mary Yates Johnston Memorial Fund." Before her death, Johnston paid Allegheny (P) $1,000 of the pledge which Allegheny (P) set aside as a scholarship fund for students preparing for the ministry. Later, Johnston notified Allegheny (P) that she repudiated the pledge. Thirty days after death, when National (D), Johnston's executor, failed to pay the balance, Allegheny (P) brought this action for breach. National (D) argued that no consideration was given for the promise. Allegheny (P) appealed a judgment for National (D) upon dismissal of its complaint.

ISSUE: Does the acceptance of a charitable subscription by the trustees of the charity imply a promise on their part to execute the work contemplated and to carry out the purposes for which the subscription was made?

HOLDING AND DECISION: (Cardozo, J.) Yes. The acceptance of a charitable subscription by the trustees of the charity implies a promise on their part to execute the work contemplated and to carry out this purpose for which the subscription was made. While charitable subscriptions are unenforceable if given without consideration, when subscriptions have been in question, courts have found consideration where general contract law would have said it was absent. Also, the doctrine of promissory estoppel has been adopted as the equivalent of consideration in connection with charitable subscriptions. In this case, traditional consideration could be found without resorting to promissory estoppel. Allegheny (P), by accepting part of the pledge, was required to apply the money as conditioned but it did not have to fulfill all conditions until all of the pledge was paid. The duty assumed by Allegheny (D) "to perpetuate the name of the founder of the memorial is sufficient in itself to give validity to the subscription within the rules that define consideration for a promise of that order." When Allegheny (P) as promisee subjected itself to such a duty at the implied request of Johnston as promisor, the result was creation of a bilateral contract. Reversed.

DISSENT: (Kellogg, J.) Johnston offered the sum as a gift. Even if one strains to find a contract, there was never an acceptance because not all acts were performed. Also, the donation was not to take effect until death, but by her death, the offer was withdrawn.

EDITOR'S ANALYSIS: Though the facts as recited in this case do not make it clear, apparently, Johnston repudiated her pledge because Allegheny (P) did not immediately create a fund in her name upon payment of the $1,000. Allegheny (P) only established a nameless fund. To this J. Cardozo said that Johnston would have had grounds to repudiate the pledge had Allegheny (P) announced the fund as coming from an anonymous donor, but Allegheny (P) said nothing as to the source and was held not to be obligated to do so until the whole pledge was paid. As for this case, Corbin commented, "The implied promise of the trustees is said to be a sufficient consideration for the subscriber's promise. By such an implied promise, the trustees may sometimes be assuming duties that were not already incumbent upon them as trustees, but this does not necessarily show that the transaction was a bargaining transaction." Corbin, Contracts, 1 vol. ed., § 198.

QUICKNOTES

CONSIDERATION - Value given by one party in exchange for performance, or a promise to perform, by another party.

REPUDIATION - The actions or statements of a party to a contract that evidence his intent not to perform, or to continue performance, of his duties or obligations thereunder.

NOTES:

EAST PROVIDENCE CREDIT UNION v. GEREMIA
Lender (P) v. Borrower (D)
R.I. Sup. Ct., 103 R.I. 597, 239 A.2d 725 (1968).

NATURE OF CASE: Action to recover damages for breach of a promise.

FACT SUMMARY: East Providence (P) made a promise to its mortgagor, Geremia (D), to pay his insurance premium; the promise was not kept and Geremia (D) suffered detriment as a result.

CONCISE RULE OF LAW: A promise which the promisor should reasonably expect to induce action or forbearance of a definite and substantial character on the part of the promisee and which does induce such action or forbearance is binding if injustice can be avoided only by enforcement of a promise.

FACTS: Geremia (D) borrowed money from East Providence (P) and gave his note in return, secured by a mortgage on his car. The mortgage required Geremia (D) to keep his car insured but stipulated that if Geremia (D) failed to pay the insurance premium, East Providence (P) could pay the premium and add the amount to Geremia's (D) outstanding loan. A premium subsequently became overdue and Geremia (D), low on funds, called East Providence (P) which promised to pay the premium. However, for some reason, and unknown to Geremia (D) East Providence (P) did not pay the premium and the insurance policy was cancelled by the insurer. When the car was later damaged and the insurer would not pay, East Providence (P) brought this action against Geremia (D) for the balance of the loan. Geremia (D) counterclaimed for damages resulting from breach of East Providence's (P) promise to pay the insurance premium.

ISSUE: Will the doctrine of promissory estoppel enforce a mortgagee's promise to pay an insurance premium where the mortgagor relies on that promise and suffers detriment because of its breach?

HOLDING AND DECISION: (Kelleher, J.) Yes. The conditions precedent for the invocation of the doctrine of promissory estoppel are as follows: (1) Was there a promise which the promisor should reasonably expect to induce action or forbearance of a definite and substantial character on the part of the promisee? (2) Did the promise induce such action or forbearance? (3) Can injustice be avoided only by enforcement of the promise? With respect to the instant case, each of these questions may be answered in the affirmative. The promissory estoppel doctrine is thus applicable and reliance by the promisee [Geremia (D)] to his detriment provides a substitute for consideration. While promissory estoppel was originally recognized and most often used in charitable subscription cases, it now enjoys a much wider application as an ever increasing number of courts have felt the need for a remedy to alleviate the plight of those who suffer a serious injustice as a result of their good faith reliance on the unfilled promises of others.

EDITOR'S ANALYSIS: Note that the court also holds that East Providence's (P) promise was not gratuitous but was supported by consideration in that East Providence (P) would have received interest on the money which it used to pay Geremia's (D) premium. Thus, the greater part of the opinion regarding the doctrine of promissory estoppel is technically dictum. As a generalized doctrine, promissory estoppel is a twentieth century innovation although it has ancient roots. It has been extracted from a number of decisions in which the courts sought to do justice but which were difficult to explain in terms of consideration. Because of its heritage, promissory estoppel has been subject to some doctrinal confusion. For example, the present court refers to reliance as a "substitute" for consideration. Other courts have said that the reliance serves as consideration. It is probably best to straightforwardly admit that promissory estoppel is an exception to the rule requiring consideration for the enforcement of a promise. And perhaps the Restatement Second's liberalization of the doctrine as it was exposed in the original Restatement of Contracts is one step down a long road toward a general abolition of the consideration requirement as it is now understood.

QUICKNOTES

PROMISSORY ESTOPPEL - A promise that is enforceable if the promisor should reasonably expect that it will induce action or forbearance on the part of the promisee, and does in fact cause such action or forbearance, and it is the only means of avoiding injustice.

CONSIDERATION - Value given by one party in exchange for performance, or a promise to perform, by another party.

FORBEARANCE - Refraining from doing something that one has the legal right to do.

LEGAL DETRIMENT - The relinquishment of rights or conduct to which one is entitled to, as consideration for a binding contract.

NOTES:

SEAVEY v. DRAKE
Only son (P) v. Father's estate (D)
N.H. Sup. Ct., 62 N.H. 393 (1882).

NATURE OF CASE: Action in equity for specific performance of a parol agreement of land.

FACT SUMMARY: Seavey (P), the only son of Drake's (D) estate, was given land by his father on which he built a house and barn but to which he never received a deed.

CONCISE RULE OF LAW: Specific performance of a parol contract to convey land is decreed in favor of the vendee who has performed his part of the contract, when a failure or refusal to convey would operate as a fraud upon him.

FACTS: Seavey (P) alleged that in 1860 his father, owning a tract of land and wishing to assist his only son, gave him a portion of the land which Seavey (P) accepted and took possession. Later, Seavey's (P) father gave him an additional strip of land adjoining the first gift tract. Seavey (P) spent $3,000 to build a dwelling, barn, and stables and to make other improvements. The father died in 1880 without ever having given Seavey (P) a deed. He sought to enforce the parol agreement of land against Drake (D), his father's executor. Drake (D) moved to dismiss on the ground that the parol agreement was without consideration and executory.

ISSUE: Will specific performance of a parol contract to convey land be decreed in favor of the vendee who has performed his part of the contract, when a failure or refusal to convey would operate as a fraud upon him?

HOLDING AND DECISION: (Smith, J.) Yes. Specific performance of a parol contract to convey land is decreed in favor of the vendee who has performed his part of the contract, when a failure or refusal to convey would operate as a fraud upon him. While at law the statute of frauds would not allow an action upon a contract for the transfer of land not in writing, equity, when there has been part performance, will remove the bar of the statute. This is done upon the ground that it is a fraud for the vendor to insist upon the absence of a written instrument when he has permitted the contract to be partly executed. Consideration is found in Seavey's (P) having been induced to enter the land and make expenditures for improvements. Judgment for Seavey (P).

EDITOR'S ANALYSIS: Cases involving gifts of land usually arise in family situations and involve both noncompliance with the statute of frauds as well as absence of consideration. Besides the rationale seen above for awarding an equitable remedy, courts have also relied on an analogy from the law of gifts, whereby the entry upon the land and the making of improvements thereon are treated as being the same as physical delivery of a chattel. The view taken by the court in *Seavy* has been criticized for applying a different definition of consideration then in equity. Modern decisions enforcing oral promises to give land now rest on promissory estoppel theory.

QUICKNOTES

RELIANCE - Dependence on a fact that causes a party to act or refrain from acting.

STATUTE OF FRAUDS - A statute that requires specified types of contracts to be in writing in order to be binding.

PAROL CONTRACT - An oral contract that may be offered to contradict the terms of an existing, written agreement.

NOTES:

FORRER v. SEARS, ROEBUCK & CO.
Employee (P) v. Employer (D)
Wis. Sup. Ct., 36 Wis. 2d 388, 153 N.W.2d 587 (1967).

NATURE OF CASE: Action in promissory estoppel for damages.

FACT SUMMARY: Forrer (P) sought damages from Sears (D) arising out of a breach of a promise of "permanent employment."

CONCISE RULE OF LAW: A contract of "permanent employment" is terminable at will by either party unless additional compensation in the form of an economic benefit is rendered by the employee to the employer.

FACTS: Forrer (P) was employed at Sears (D) for 18 years when he left in 1963, due to ill health. He then bought and operated a farm. Shortly thereafter, agents of Sears (D) persuaded Forrer (P) to return to Sears (D) on a part-time basis. After several months, the store manager offered Forrer (P) a "permanent," full-time position, if he would agree to give up his farming work. Forrer(P) agreed and sold his farm, mostly at a loss. On June 1, 1965, four months after he began working full-time, Forrer (P) was discharged without cause from Sears (D). He brought suit in promissory estoppel for damages arising out of the alleged breach of promise. Sears' (D) demurrer was granted, and Forrer (P) appealed.

ISSUE: Does the termination of an employee under a contract for permanent employment give rise to a right of recovery?

HOLDING AND DECISION: (Heffernan, J.) No. A case for promissory estoppel is made out where it is shown (1) that the promisor induced a certain action of forbearance on the part of the promisee; (2) that he should have expected such action or forbearance to result from his promise; and (3) that an injustice can be avoided only by enforcement of the promise. Although the first two elements of promissory estoppel are clearly established here, the third one is not. That is because the term "permanent employment" is commonly understood to mean a contract of employment terminable at will by either party. The difficulties which would arise from a literal interpretation of the term "permanent employment" are manifest. As such, Sears (D) discharged its obligation when it hired Forrer (P) on a full-time basis. The subsequent termination does not constitute a breach of promise. An exception to the general rule occurs where an employee has conferred an economic benefit upon his employee other than a mere rendering of services. In such a case, the contract may no longer be deemed terminable at will by the employer. However, no such economic benefit is evident in the instant case. Therefore, the general principal that a contract of permanent employment is terminable at will by either party applies. Affirmed.

EDITOR'S ANALYSIS: The principle of promissory estoppel, which is raised in the *Forrer* case, in actuality provides for a sort of substitute for consideration, when valid consideration is lacking. The principle appears in many different areas of law. For example, see California Civil Code § 2090, which provides that a carrier who begins performance without consideration must continue the performance unless he restores the other party to the position he was in before performance was begun. In that situation, the carrier's partial performance substitutes for valid consideration and helps create a contract.

QUICKNOTES
PROMISSORY ESTOPPEL - A promise that is enforceable if the promisor should reasonably expect that it will induce action or forbearance on the part of the promisee, and does in fact cause such action or forbearance, and it is the only means of avoiding injustice.

FORBEARANCE - Refraining from doing something that one has the legal right to do.

CONSIDERATION - Value given by one party in exchange for performance, or a promise to perform, by another party.

NOTES:

STEARNS v. EMERY-WATERHOUSE CO.
Employee (P) v. Employer (D)
MN. Sup. Jud. Ct., 596 A.2d 72 (1991).

NATURE OF CASE: Appeal from award of damages for breach of contract.

FACT SUMMARY: Sterns (P) relied on promissory estoppel to defeat the Statute of Frauds defense asserted by Emery-Waterhouse (D) to his action for breach of an oral employment contract.

CONCISE RULE OF LAW: Promissory estoppel may not be used to defeat a Statute of Frauds defense to an asserted oral employment contract.

FACTS: Sterns (P) had been a long-term employee of Sears Roebuck. Hildreth, president of Emery-Waterhouse Co. (D), induced him to come to work for Emery (D). He was employed there for two years but was eventually laid off. No employment contract had ever been signed. Stearns (P) sued for breach of an alleged oral employment contract. Emery (D) raised a Statute of Frauds defense. The trial court awarded damages, and Emery (D) appealed.

ISSUE: May promissory estoppel be used to defeat a Statute of Frauds defense to an action for breach of an asserted oral employment contract?

HOLDING AND DECISION: (Roberts, J.) No. Promissory estoppel may not be used to defeat a Statute of Frauds defense to an action for breach of an asserted oral employment contract. The purpose of the Statute of Frauds is to prevent fraudulent claims of obligations arising from unprovable oral agreements. In the context of employment, it is too easy for a disgruntled former employee to allege some sort of employment agreement and then allege detrimental reliance thereon as a basis for enforcing it. When an employer, by clear and convincing evidence, effects a deceit upon an employee, quantum meruit or equitable estoppel may lie to provide a remedy. However, the Statute of Frauds commands that the focus remain upon the employer's conduct, not the employee's reliance. Here, all Sterns (P) was able to show was reliance upon Hildreth's (D) supposed assertions. This was insufficient to defeat the statute. Reversed.

EDITOR'S ANALYSIS: Promissory estoppel is generally utilized in the context of contract formation. It is a legitimate substitute for consideration. The Statute of Frauds is an entirely different matter from contract formation, being more evidentiary in nature. While some courts do allow promissory estoppel to defeat a statute of frauds defense, most do not.

QUICKNOTES

PROMISSORY ESTOPPEL - A promise that is enforceable if the promisor should reasonably expect that it will induce action or forbearance on the part of the promisee, and does in fact cause such action or forbearance, and it is the only means of avoiding injustice.

STATUTE OF FRAUDS - A statute that requires specified types of contracts to be in writing in order to be binding.

QUANTUM MERUIT - Equitable doctrine allowing recovery for labor and materials provided by one party, even though no contract was entered into, in order to avoid unjust enrichment by the benefitted party.

NOTES:

GOODMAN v. DICKER
Franchise representative (D) v. Franchise applicant (P)
169 F.2d 684 (D.C. Cir. 1948).

NATURE OF CASE: Action for damages for breach of a contract for granting of a franchise.

FACT SUMMARY: Dicker (P) made certain expenditures after applying for an Emerson radio and phonograph franchise in the District of Columbia upon the inducement of an Emerson representative, Goodman (D). While Goodman (D) had represented that the franchise would be granted and radios would be delivered, no franchise was approved.

CONCISE RULE OF LAW: One who by his language or conduct leads another to do what he would not otherwise have done shall not subject such person to loss or injury by disappointing the expectation upon which he acted.

FACTS: Dicker (P) was encouraged by Goodman (D) a local representative for Emerson Radio and Phonograph Co. to apply for an Emerson dealer franchise for the District of Columbia. Dicker (P) was induced by Goodman's (D) representations to make certain expenditures including hiring salesmen and soliciting orders. Dicker (P) was told by Goodman (D) that the franchise application had been accepted and would be granted plus an initial delivery of radios was on the way. None were delivered and the franchise was not granted.

ISSUE: Was Goodman (D) estopped from denying the existence of a contract by reason of his statements and conduct upon which Dicker (P) relied to his detriment?

HOLDING AND DECISION: (Proctor, J.) Yes. Dicker (P) justifiably relied upon Goodman's (D) statement and conduct. Even though under a formal franchise agreement, a franchise would have been terminable at will and would have imposed no duty on the manufacturer, this is a defense inconsistent with the assurance that a franchise would be granted. Justice and fair dealing require that one who acts to his detriment on the faith of conduct such as seen here should be protected by estopping the party whose conduct is responsible from alleging anything opposite to the natural consequences of his course of conduct. Expenses of $1,150 expended in preparation for doing business are recoverable. However, the $350 loss of profits on the undelivered radios is not recoverable as it was not a loss incurred in reliance upon the assurance of a dealer franchise.

EDITOR'S ANALYSIS: Goodman's (D) promise is enforced because there was justifiable reliance by Dicker (P). The one who desires the franchise assumes more of a risk because had the radios been delivered, the franchise would have been granted and then become terminable at will. Good faith by the party offering the franchise is required by the court so that negotiations may be conducted with a sense of fair play. The appeals court apparently did not want to award $350 loss of profits to a business that really had not started - it may be a simple desire on the court's part to avoid speculation. The loss of profits was probably considered to have been covered by the award of reliance damages so that any award of loss of profits damages would have put Dicker (P) in a better position than had a franchise been granted. If it had been proven that Goodman (D) did not deal in good faith, expectation profits could then be awarded.

QUICKNOTES

DETRIMENTAL RELIANCE - Action by one party, resulting in loss, that is based on the conduct or promises of another.

RELIANCE DAMAGES - The injury suffered by a party to a breached contract as the result of that party's dependence on the agreement.

NOTES:

LEVINE v. BLUMENTHAL

Landlord (P) v. Store owner (D)

N.J. Sup. Ct., 117 N.J.L. 23, 186 A. 457 (1936).

NATURE OF CASE: Appeal from a judgment ordering recovery of unpaid balance on a written lease.

FACT SUMMARY: When Blumenthal (D) failed to make full payment on a written lease agreement, landlord Levine (P) sued to recover the unpaid balance due on the rent.

CONCISE RULE OF LAW: When a subsequent oral agreement which has been made to change and alter the terms of the written lease is not supported by a lawful consideration, it is wholly ineffective.

FACTS: Blumenthal (D) leased store premises from Levine (P) in order to operate a retail women's apparel shop. The two-year lease called for an increase in rent for the second year. Blumenthal (D) notified Levine (P) that because business was down they would not be able to pay the higher rent for the second year. Levine (P) allowed Blumenthal (D) to remain under the same rent until business improved. After the lease expired, Levine (P) sued to collect the last month's rent and the unpaid balance due on the increased rent for the second year as per the written lease agreement. Blumenthal (D) argued that a subsequent oral agreement had been made to change the terms of the written lease, or, in the alternative, that an accord and satisfaction had been reached. The court granted Levine (P) a judgment for the balance due under the lease, and Blumenthal (D) appealed.

ISSUE: Is a subsequent oral agreement which has been made to change and alter the terms of the written lease effective when not supported by a lawful consideration?

HOLDING AND DECISION: (Heher, J.) No. When a subsequent oral agreement which has been made to change and alter the terms of the written lease is not supported by a lawful consideration, it is wholly ineffective. To be valid, the subsequent agreement must rest upon a new and independent consideration. An act or forbearance required by a legal duty owing to the promisor that is neither doubtful nor the subject of reasonable dispute is not sufficient consideration. The new consideration must consist of something which the debtor was not legally bound to do or give. A new consideration is also essential to the validity of an accord and satisfaction. Affirmed.

EDITOR'S ANALYSIS: The legal-duty rule was also known as the doctrine of *Foakes v. Beer*. It was extended to apply far beyond money debts for which part payment is made or promised. Modern statutes limit the doctrine, and the Uniform Commercial Code has replaced the necessity for new consideration by a test of "good faith" for all contract modifications.

OBERING v. SWAIN-ROACH LUMBER CO.
Contract breaker (D) v. Lumber company (P)
Ind. Ct. App., 86 Ind. App. 632, 155 N.E. 712 (1927).

NATURE OF CASE: Action for breach of a land sales contract.

FACT SUMMARY: Swain Lumber (P) contracted with Obering (D) that if Swain (P) were able to purchase certain land then Swain (P) would resell the land to Obering (D). Swain (P) made the purchase, tendered the deed to Obering (D), who refused to purchase whereupon Swain (P) brought suit.

CONCISE RULE OF LAW: The fact that a contract has a condition precedent to its formation does not make the contract too indefinite to be enforceable.

FACTS: Henry Buhner owned a certain tract of land which the Swain-Roach Lumber Co. (P) desired to purchase because of the timber there. Obering (D), a relative of Buhner also desired to purchase the land for use as a farm. Henry Buhner died and the executor of the estate announced that he was considering selling the land. Swain-Roach (P) and Obering (D) then entered into a contract that if the land were offered for sale then Swain-Roach (P) would purchase the land and then immediately sell the land to Obering (D). Swain-Roach would reserve the right to remove timber for four years after the sale to Obering (D). The land was offered for sale, Swain-Roach (P) purchased the land but when it tendered the deed to Obering (D), Obering (D) refused to accept the tender. Swain (P) then brought suit for specific performance. Obering (D) defends pleading that the contract was too indefinite because of the condition precedent and therefore it was not enforceable.

ISSUE: If a contract has a condition precedent to its formation does this fact make the contract too indefinite to be enforceable?

HOLDING AND DECISION: (Remy, J.) No. The fact that a contract has a condition precedent to its formation does not make the contract too indefinite to be enforceable. So long as the condition is not illusory and is established in good faith then the existence of the condition in and of itself is not a bar to the enforcement of the contract in a court of equity. In this case the condition was satisfied because the property was offered for sale, and there are no facts to indicate that the parties did not act in good faith. Therefore, we conclude that the contract is sufficiently definite to be enforceable. Affirmed.

EDITOR'S ANALYSIS: Generally when one pleads for specific performance in a court of equity he must plead that the contract had definite and certain terms. Under the majority view, a condition precedent to the formation of the contract does not destroy the definiteness of the contract so long as the condition is not based on the unfettered discretion of the promisor. The most common situation is where the condition is based on some external happening beyond the control of the promisor. In *Obering*, the condition precedent occurred and the contract became binding at that point.

QUICKNOTES
CONDITION PRECEDENT - The happening of an uncertain occurrence, which is necessary before a particular right or interest may be obtained or an action performed.

NOTES:

WOOD v. LUCY, LADY DUFF-GORDON
Clothing marketer (P) Fashion designer (D)
N.Y. Ct. App., 222 N.Y. 88, 118 N.E. 214 (1917).

NATURE OF CASE: Action for damages for breach of a contract for an exclusive right.

FACT SUMMARY: Wood (P) in a complicated agreement received the exclusive right for one year, renewable on a year-to-year basis if not terminated by 90-day notice, to endorse designs with Lucy's (D) name and to market all her fashion designs for which she would receive one half the profits derived. Lucy (D) broke the contract by placing her endorsement on designs without Wood's (P) knowledge.

CONCISE RULE OF LAW: While an express promise may be lacking, the whole writing may be instinct with an obligation—an implied promise—imperfectly expressed so as to form a valid contract.

FACTS: Lucy (D), a famous-name fashion designer, contracted with Wood (P) that for her granting to him an exclusive right to endorse designs with her name and to market and license all of her designs, they were to split the profits derived by Wood (P) in half. The exclusive right was for a period of one year, renewable on a year-to-year basis and terminable upon 90-days' notice. Lucy (D) placed her endorsement on fabrics, dresses, and millinery without Wood's (P) knowledge and in violation of the contract. Lucy (D) claims that the agreement lacked the elements of a contract as Wood (P) allegedly is not bound to do anything.

ISSUE: If a promise may be implied from the writing even though it is imperfectly expressed, is there a valid contract?

HOLDING AND DECISION: (Cardozo, J.) Yes. While the contract did not precisely state that Wood (P) had promised to use reasonable efforts to place Lucy's (D) endorsement and market her designs, such a promise can be implied. The implication arises from the circumstances. Lucy (D) gave an exclusive privilege and the acceptance of the exclusive agency was an acceptance of its duties. Lucy's (D) sole compensation was to be one-half the profits resulting from Wood's (P) efforts. Unless he gave his efforts, she could never receive anything. Without an implied promise, the transaction could not have had such business efficacy as they must have intended it to have. Wood's (P) promise to make monthly accountings and to acquire patents and copyrights as necessary showed the intention of the parties that the promise has value by showing that Wood (P) had some duties. The promise to pay Lucy (D) half the profits and make monthly accountings was a promise to use reasonable efforts to bring profits and revenues into existence.

EDITOR'S ANALYSIS: A bilateral contract can be express, implied in fact, or a little of each. The finding of an implied promise for the purpose of finding sufficient consideration to support an express promise is an important technique of the courts in order to uphold agreements which seem to be illusory and to avoid problems of mutuality of obligation. This is the leading case on the subject. It is codified in U.C.C. § 2-306 (2) where an agreement for exclusive dealing in goods imposes, unless otherwise agreed, an obligation to use best efforts by both parties.

QUICKNOTES
IMPLIED PROMISE - A promise inferred by law from a document as a whole and the circumstances surrounding its implementation.

BILATERAL CONTRACT - An agreement pursuant to which each party promises to undertake an obligation, or to forbear from acting, at some time in the future.

NOTES:

OMNI GROUP, INC. v. SEATTLE-FIRST NATIONAL BANK
Landbuyer (P) v. Seller (D)
Wash. Ct. App., 32 Wash. App. 22, 645 P.2d 727 (1982).

NATURE OF CASE: Appeal from the denial of enforcement of a contract for the sale of realty.

FACT SUMMARY: The Clarks (D) contended that by making their contractual obligations subject to a satisfactory engineer's and architect's feasibility report, Omni (P) rendered its promise to purchase the Clarks' (D) land illusory and the contract unenforceable.

CONCISE RULE OF LAW: A contractual condition calling for the subjective satisfaction of a party imposes a duty of good faith in the exercise of the party's discretion and is not illusory.

FACTS: Omni (P) signed an earnest money agreement to purchase the Clarks' (D) land. The agreement provided that Omni's (P) performance was subject to its receiving a satisfactory engineer's and architect's feasibility report concerning the land's development potential. Subsequently, Omni (P) notified the Clarks (D) it would forgo the study. After further negotiations, the Clarks (D) refused to go through with the transaction, and Omni (P) sued for breach of contract. The Clarks (D) defended on the basis that by making its performance conditional upon receipt of a satisfactory feasibility report, Omni (P) rendered its promise illusory, and, therefore, the contract lacked consideration and was unenforceable. The trial court entered judgment for the Clarks (D), and Omni (P) appealed.

ISSUE: Does a contract condition calling for a party's satisfaction with the performance of an act render that party's promise to perform illusory and the contract unenforceable?

HOLDING AND DECISION: (James, J.) No. A contract condition which requires a party's satisfaction with the performance of an act imposes on that party the duty to exercise his judgment, concerning whether the performance is satisfactory, in good faith. In this case, Omni's (P) acceptance of the feasibility report was not left to its unfettered discretion. It was bound to act in good faith in either accepting it or rejecting it. Therefore, the promise was not illusory; it supplied sufficient consideration for the Clarks' (D) promise to sell, and a valid contract was formed. Reversed.

EDITOR'S ANALYSIS: This case illustrates the requirement of good faith in contracts calling for the satisfaction of a party as a condition precedent to his obligations under the contract. This requirement exists where the performance must meet the subjective satisfaction of the party. In such a case, some courts allow evidence of the unreasonableness of the rejection of performance to show a lack of good faith. The good faith rule is codified in Restatement Second, Contracts, §254, and is derived from the Case of *Devoine Co. v. International Co.*, 136 A. 37 (Md. 1927).

QUICKNOTES

EARNEST MONEY - A payment made by a buyer to a seller to evidence the intent to fulfill the obligations of a contract to purchase property.

ILLUSORY PROMISE - A promise that is not legally enforceable because performance of the obligation by the promisor is completely within his discretion.

NOTES:

FELD v. HENRY S. LEVY & SONS, INC.
Breadcrumb buyer (P) v. Breadcrumb seller (D)
37 N.Y.2d 466, 373 N.Y.S.2d 102, 335 N.E.2d 320 (1975).

NATURE OF CASE: Action for breach of contract.

FACT SUMMARY: Levy (D) agreed to sell all breadcrumbs produced by it to Feld (P).

CONCISE RULE OF LAW: Output contracts are valid and any indefiniteness or mutuality is supplied by a "good-faith requirement" implied by the U.C.C. into such contracts.

FACTS: Levy and Sons (D) agreed to sell all breadcrumbs produced by it to Feld (P) for one year. The contract was automatically renewable except upon six months' written notice by either party. Levy (D) ceased making breadcrumbs because the price was too low. Feld (P) sued for breach of contract and Levy (D) alleged that since it was not producing breadcrumbs, it had not breached the contract.

ISSUE: Must parties to an outputs contract deal with each other in good faith?

HOLDING AND DECISION: (Cooke, J.) Yes. Output contracts are valid. They are not indefinite and do not lack mutuality of obligation. Under the U.C.C., there is a requirement of good faith read into such contracts and both parties must deal with each other fairly and according to commercial standards. Under U.C.C. § 2-306(2), a seller is obligated to use his best efforts to supply the buyer under an output contract. It is implied that both parties will diligently attempt to honor their commitments for the full term of the contract. Whether Levy (D) ceased production in good faith is a question of fact which must be resolved other than in a motion for summary judgment. We remand for a hearing on the parties' good faith.

EDITOR'S ANALYSIS: The party who is determining what output is necessary to operate his factory or business is under a duty of good faith also. It cannot take advantage of price fluctuations to either stockpile goods prior to the expiration of the contract or to resell to other manufacturers at a profit. *Matter of United Cigar Stores Co. of America*, 8 F.Supp. 243 (D.C.) Requirements must be based on reasonably foreseeable needs.

QUICKNOTES
MUTUALITY OF OBLIGATION - Requires that both parties to a contract are bound or else neither is bound.

SHEETS v. TEDDY'S FROSTED FOODS, INC.

Employee (P) v. Employer (D)

Conn. Sup. Ct., 179 Conn. 471, 427 A.2d 385 (1980).

NATURE OF CASE: Action for damages for wrongful discharge.

FACT SUMMARY: Sheets (P) claimed his discharge from Teddy's (D) was in retaliation for his bringing statutory violations to his employer's attention.

CONCISE RULE OF LAW: An employer's general right to terminate the services of an employee hired for an unlimited term is limited by public policy.

FACTS: Sheets (P) was employed by Teddy's Frozen Foods (D) as quality control director under a contract of limited duration. In that capacity, Sheets (P) began to notice that the quality of Teddy's (D) food products was deviating from the standards listed on its labels. Such deviations were in violation of the Connecticut Uniform Food, Drug and Cosmetic Act. Sheets (P) informed Teddy's (D) management of the product deviations and several months later he was terminated. Sheets (P) brought suit against Teddy's (D), alleging that his termination was wrongful in that it was in violation of public policy as expressed in the Food, Drug and Cosmetic Act. Teddy's (D) moved to strike the complaint as legally insufficient, noting that the employment contract involved in the case was terminable at will by either party. The trial court granted the motion to strike, and Sheets (P) appealed.

ISSUE: May limits be imposed on an employer's general right to terminate an employee hired for an unlimited term?

HOLDING AND DECISION: (Peters, J.) Yes. An employer does not have to show just cause underlying his decision to terminate an employee. However, where an employee can demonstrate a clearly improper motive for his dismissal, then a cause of action may be set out. A dismissal motive which is in violation of public policy shall be deemed a "clearly improper" reason for termination. In the instant case, Sheets' (P) job, as quality control director, involved in large part his making sure the company complied with state labelling and quality laws. Such laws were enacted to protect the public health and safety. Thus, Sheets' (P) dismissal for pointing out noncompliance with those laws was clearly contradictory to public policy. Accordingly, Sheets (P) has set out a valid cause of action for the recovery of damages. Reversed.

DISSENT: (Cotter, J.) The majority overextends the principle of "retaliatory firing" to cover situations, such as presented here, which are of marginal value to the public interest. In so doing, it has taken a step which will greatly impair the right of employers to hire and fire employees as they see fit.

EDITOR'S ANALYSIS: The principle espoused in the Sheets case is analogous to that found in landlord-tenant law which provides that although a landlord may terminate the relationship under a month-to-month lease (provided he gives the requisite notice) for no reason whatsoever, he may not do so for the wrong reason. See generally *Green v. Superior Court*, 10 Cal. 3d 616, 517 P.2d 1168 (1974). Thus, in many jurisdictions, "retaliatory" evictions; i.e., eviction proceedings commenced after a tenant has informed the authorities of code violations by the landlord, are not permitted.

QUICKNOTES

RETALIATORY DISCHARGE - The firing of an employee in retribution for an act committed against the employer's interests.

NOTES:

CHAPTER 3
THE MAKING OF AGREEMENTS

QUICK REFERENCE RULES OF LAW

1. **Mutual Assent.** The secret feelings, intentions or beliefs of a party will not affect the formation of a contract in which their words and acts indicate that they intended to enter into a binding agreement. (Embry v. Hargadine, McKittrick Dry Goods Co.)

2. **Mutual Assent.** Testimony as to the subjective opinions of a party regarding a contract may be admitted so long as suitable jury instructions counteracting any prejudicial effect such testimony might have are given. (Kabil Developments Corp v. Mignot)

3. **Mutual Assent.** An employer in an otherwise at-will employment may be bound by policies set forth in an employee manual. (McDonald v. Mobil Coal Producing, Inc.)

4. **Mutual Assent.** A general letter informing others that a merchant has a product for sale may not constitute an offer that binds the merchant upon acceptance. (Moulton v. Kershaw)

5. **Mutual Assent.** A real estate lease provision calling for the renewal of the lease at a rental to be agreed upon is unenforceable due to its omission of a material term. (Joseph Martin, Jr. Delicatessen v. Schumacher)

6. **Mutual Assent.** Parties who have made their pact "subject to" a later definitive agreement have manifested an intent not to be bound. (Empro Mfg. Co. v. Ball-Co Mfg., Inc.)

7. **Mutual Assent.** Under § 90 of the Restatement of Contracts, "a promise which the promisor should reasonably expect to induce action or forbearance of a definite and substantial character on the part of the promisee and which does induce such action or forbearance is binding if injustice can be avoided only by enforcement of the promise." (Wheeler v. White)

8. **Mutual Assent.** Where neither party knows or has reason to know of the ambiguity or where both know or have reason to know, the ambiguity is given the meaning that each party intended it to have. (Raffles v. Wichelhaus)

9. **Control Over Contract Formation.** An offer to give away a prize contingent upon performance of an act is enforceable by one doing the act. (Cobaugh v. Klick-Lewis, Inc.)

10. **Control Over Contract Formation.** Where the offeror merely suggests a permitted method of acceptance, other methods of acceptance are not precluded. (Allied Steel & Conveyors, Inc. v. Ford Motor Co.)

11. **Control Over Contract Formation.** In case of doubt it is presumed that an offer invites the formation of a bilateral rather than a unilateral contract. (Davis v. Jacoby)

12. **Control Over Contract Formation.** An offer to enter into a unilateral contract may be withdrawn at any time prior to performance of the act requested to be done. (Petterson v. Pattberg)

13. **Control Over Contract Formation.** A contractual offer may be accepted by performance if a unilateral contract is involved. (Brakenbury v. Hodgkin)

14. **Precontractual Obligation.** When an option contract under seal provides for nominal consideration by one party, a failure by that party to provide that consideration will not invalidate the agreement. (Thomason v. Bescher)

15. Precontractual Obligation. The doctrine of promissory estoppel shall not be applied in cases where there is an offer for exchange as the offer is not intended to become a promise until a consideration is received. (James Baird Co. v. Gimbel Bros.)

16. Precontractual Obligation. Reasonable reliance on a promise binds an offeror even if there is no other consideration. (Drennan v. Star Paving Co.)

17. Precontractual Obligation. A promise which the promisor should reasonably expect to induce action or forbearance of a definite and substantial character on the part of the promisee and which does induce such action or forbearance is binding where injustice can be avoided only by enforcement. (Hoffman v. Red Owl Stores, Inc.)

18. Conduct Concluding a Bargain. A counter-offer is a rejection of the original offer and terminates it. (Livingstone v. Evans)

19. Conduct Concluding a Bargain. A contract between merchants may be created even though the acceptance contains different terms than the offer. (Idaho Power Co. v. Westinghouse Electric Corp.)

20. Conduct Concluding a Bargain. A buyer accepts goods when, after an opportunity to inspect, he fails to make an effective rejection. (ProCD, Inc. v. Zeidenberg)

21. Conduct Concluding a Bargain. An acceptance is effective when it is posted even though a subsequent rejection is actually received before the acceptance. (Morrison v. Thoelke)

22. Conduct Concluding a Bargain. Silence may constitute acceptance in appropriate cases. (Hobbs v. Massasoit Whip Co.)

23. Conduct Concluding a Bargain. In the absence of contrary legislation, the court may decline to recognize the relationship of an unmarried couple living together as giving rise to an implied-in-law contract regarding their earnings and assets or the personal services which each may render. (Morone v. Morone)

24. The Effects of Adopting a Writing. An oral agreement is permitted to vary from a written contract only if it is collateral in form, does not contradict express or implied conditions of the written contract, and consists of terms which the parties could not reasonably have been expected to include in the written contract. (Mitchill v. Lath)

25. The Effects of Adopting a Writing. For an oral term to be inconsistent with a writing, thereby barring its admission as evidence under the parol evidence rule, it must be contradictory to an express provision contained in the writing. (Hatley v. Stafford)

26. The Effects of Adopting a Writing. An oral condition to a written agreement may be proven so long as it in no way contradicts the express terms of the writing. (Long Island Trust Co. v. International Inst. for Packaging Educ., Ltd.)

27. The Effects of Adopting a Writing. An action in fraud may be based on a promise, even when the promise itself cannot be enforced under the law of contracts. (Lipsit v. Leonard)

28. The Effects of Adopting a Writing. A party who has executed a contract containing a merger clause and a provision disclaiming all prior representations may not successfully claim reliance on such representations. (LaFazia v. Howe)

EMBRY v. HARGADINE, McKITTRICK DRY GOODS CO.
Employee (P) v. Employer (D)
Mo. Ct. App., 127 Mo. App. 383, 105 S.W. 777 (1907).

NATURE OF CASE: Action to enforce renewal of employment contract.

FACT SUMMARY: Embry (P) was allegedly rehired by Hargadine-McKittrick (D) after his employment contract had expired. Hargadine-McKittrick (D) denied the rehiring.

CONCISE RULE OF LAW: The secret feelings, intentions or beliefs of a party will not affect the formation of a contract in which their words and acts indicate that they intended to enter into a binding agreement.

FACTS: Embry (P) was working for Hargardine-McKittrick (D) under a written employment contract. After its expiration, Embry (P) approached McKittrick and demanded a new contract or he would immediately quit. According to Embry (P), McKittrick agreed to rehire him. Embry (P) was terminated in February of the next year. He brought suit to recover the amount due him under the contract. McKittrick swore that the conversation never took place and that Embry (P) had not been rehired. The judge instructed the jury that even if the conversation occurred as related by Embry (P), to form a contract both parties must have intended to enter into a binding agreement. The jury found against Embry (P). He appealed on the basis that the judge's instruction was incorrect. That if McKittrick conveyed by word and deed his intent to rehire Embry (P), a binding contract was formed regardless of McKittrick's secret intention.

ISSUE: Will a hidden, undisclosed intention affect the formation of a contract?

HOLDING AND DECISION: (Goode, J.) No. If the other party reasonably relies on the promise, an undisclosed intention will not affect the formation of a binding contract. Therefore, the trial judge's instructions were erroneous. If the jury reasonably believed that McKittrick (D) had promised to rehire Embry (P), it is immaterial whether McKittrick (D) meant his promise or not. It is obvious that Embry (P) believed a valid contract had been formed because he remained on the job. His reliance was reasonable since McKittrick (D) was the president of the company and had the authority to rehire him. Therefore, the case must be remanded for a new trial since it cannot be determined on what basis the jury found for McKittrick (D). The same holding applies where a reasonable person would interpret the meaning of a conversation as the formation of a binding contract. The fact that McKittrick (D) did not intend to rehire Embry (P) is immaterial if the natural interpretation of the conversation is that he was being rehired. Again McKittrick's (D) undisclosed intent is immaterial.

EDITOR'S ANALYSIS: In order to analyze the manifest intentions of the parties, there are several standards of interpretation which may be applied to their words. First, there is the general accepted meaning of the terms used. Then there is the meaning of the term according to trade or custom. Finally, there is the meaning the parties may have assigned to the term in the course of past dealings. By utilizing these methods, a court attempts to determine what the parties thought they were doing and to give affect to their legitimate expectations.

QUICKNOTES

INTENT TO CONTRACT - The unequivocal manifestation by a party wishing to enter into a contract to be legally bound by the agreement.

COURSE OF DEALING - Previous conduct between two parties to a contact which may be relied upon to interpret their actions.

NOTES:

KABIL DEVELOPMENTS CORP. v. MIGNOT

Construction developer (P) v. Helicopter service company (D)
Or. Sup. Ct., 279 Or. 151, 566 P.2d 505 (1977).

NATURE OF CASE: Appeal from award of damages in breach of contract suit.

FACT SUMMARY: The jury awarded Kabil (P) damages arising out of Mignot's (D) breach of a contract to provide helicopter service, although Mignot (D) argued that there had never been a contract in the first place.

CONCISE RULE OF LAW: Testimony as to the subjective opinions of a party regarding a contract may be admitted so long as suitable jury instructions counteracting any prejudicial effect such testimony might have are given.

FACTS: Kabil (P) negotiated orally with Mignot (D) regarding Mignot's (D) provision of helicopter service for an upcoming construction project. Kabil (P) contended that a contractual agreement between the parties was reached. Mignot (D) argued that an agreement was not reached. When Mignot (D) failed to provide the helicopters, Kabil (P) brought suit for breach of contract. During the resulting trial, testimony of Kabil's (P) vice president, Munroe, regarding his feeling that a contract had been reached, was admitted into evidence over Mignot's (D) objection that such testimony had no bearing upon whether a contract had, in fact, been mutually agreed upon. The jury subsequently rendered a verdict in favor of Kabil (P), and Mignot (D) appealed.

ISSUE: May testimony as to subjective opinions of a party regarding a contract be entered into evidence in a jury trial?

HOLDING AND DECISION: (Linde, J.) Yes. It is true that the law in Oregon requires an objective showing of an agreement between parties to a contract. As such, the subjective opinions of one of those parties, in and of themselves, have no bearing on the actual existence or terms of a contract. However, such opinions may bear on that party's behavior as perceived by the other party. That perception is a vital factor in determining whether a contract has been formed. Accordingly, testimony as to the subjective opinions of a party regarding a contract may be admitted into evidence so long as care is taken to instruct the jury on the meaning of the testimony in accordance with applicable law. The record reflects that the jury was suitably instructed in the instant case. Affirmed.

EDITOR'S ANALYSIS: In the case of *New York Trust Co. v. Island Oil and Transport Co.*, 34 F.2d 655 (2nd Cir.1929), Judge Learned Hand commented on the notion that the words creating a contract must be objectively explicit: "... contracts depend upon the meaning which the law imputes to the utterances, not upon what the parties actually intended; but, in ascertaining what meaning to impute, the circumstances in which the words are used are always relevant and usually indispensable ... [T]he form of utterance chosen is never final; it is always possible to show that the parties did not intend to perform what they said they would, as, for example, that the transaction was a joke."

QUICKNOTES

MUTUAL ASSENT - A requirement of a valid contract that the parties possess a mutuality of assent as manifested by the terms of the agreement and not by a hidden intent.

INTENT TO CONTRACT - The unequivocal manifestation by a party wishing to enter into a contract to be legally bound by the agreement.

NOTES:

McDONALD v. MOBIL COAL PRODUCING, INC.

Employee (P) v. Employer (D)

Wy. Sup. Ct., 820 P.2d 986 (1991).

NATURE OF CASE: Appeal from summary judgment dismissing wrongful termination action.

FACT SUMMARY: Mobil Coal (D) provided an employee manual which provided, among other things, certain procedures for employee disciplining.

CONCISE RULE OF LAW: An employer in an otherwise at-will employment may be bound by policies set forth in an employee manual.

FACTS: When McDonald (P) came to work at Mobil Coal Producing, Inc., he was given a manual explaining Mobil's (D) work environment. The manual set forth, among other things, a progressive schedule of disciplining procedures, up to and including termination. The manual also stated that Mobil (D) recognized a fundamental obligation to be considerate to employees. The manual also contained, in its general introductory section, a disclaimer that the manual was not to be construed as an employment contract. At one point, rumors began circulating that accusations of harassment had been made against McDonald (P). Supervisors told him not to worry about it. He was then summarily fired. He sued for wrongful termination. The trial court dismissed, ruling that the disclaimer precluded any alteration in traditional at-will employment. McDonald (P) appealed.

ISSUE: May an employer in an otherwise at-will employment be bound by policies set forth in an employee manual?

HOLDING AND DECISION: (Golden, J.) Yes. An employer in an otherwise at-will employment may be bound by policies set forth in an employee manual. When an employer provides a manual which sets forth assertions that certain policies and procedures have been adopted, an employee may rely on such assertions. It is possible for an employer to circumvent this situation by way of a disclaimer; however, that disclaimer must be conspicuous. Here, it was buried in a lengthy passage, which precluded its effectiveness. Thus, the disclaimer cannot be given effect and a triable issue of fact existed as to whether the procedures set forth in the manual, along with McDonald's (P) supervisors' assertions, constituted an employment agreement with respect to termination procedures. This being so, summary judgment was inappropriate and the case must be remanded for trial. Reversed and remanded.

CONCURRENCE: (Macy, J.) It appears clear that Mobil (D) led McDonald (P) to rely on its stated termination procedures.

DISSENT: (Thomas, J.) The language in the disclaimer could not have been clearer that no agreement or contract had been created.

DISSENT: (Cardine, J.) It is clear that Mobil (D) never intended to make a contract, and no outward manifestation of intent to do so existed. Because of this, no contract could possibly have been formed incorporating the manual.

EDITOR'S ANALYSIS: It is often stated in contract law that there must be a "meeting of the minds" for a contract to be formed. This is not always so, as this case illustrates. When a party reasonably believes that the other party asserts to a contractual provision, the fact that the other party actually does not intend to be so bound will not be an assertable defense to a breach of contract claim; the intention not to be bound must be made known in some fashion that will be recognizable by the other side.

QUICKNOTES

MUTUAL ASSENT - A requirement of a valid contract that the parties possess a mutuality of assent as manifested by the terms of the agreement and not by a hidden intent.

BREACH OF CONTRACT - Unlawful failure by a party to perform its obligations pursuant to contract.

AT-WILL EMPLOYMENT - The rule that an employment relationship is subject to termination at any time, or for any cause, by an employee or an employer in the absence of a specific agreement otherwise.

NOTES:

MOULTON v. KERSHAW
Salt buyer (P) v. Salt dealer (D)
Wis. Sup. Ct., 59 Wis. 316, 18 N.W. 172 (1884).

NATURE OF CASE: Appeal from order overruling demurrer to breach of contract complaint.

FACT SUMMARY: Kershaw (D) circulated a letter informing Moulton (P), among others, that he had salt to sell.

CONCISE RULE OF LAW: A general letter informing others that a merchant has a product for sale may not constitute an offer that binds the merchant upon acceptance.

FACTS: Kershaw (D), a salt dealer, mailed a letter to Moulton (P), among others, informing him that he had salt to sell in certain quantities. Moulton (P) responded with a letter requesting shipment of 2,000 barrels of salt. Kershaw (D) declined to accept the order. Moulton (P) sued for breach. The trial court overruled Kershaw's (D) demurrer. Kershaw (D) appealed.

ISSUE: Does a general letter informing others that a merchant has a product for sale necessarily constitute an offer therefor, binding the merchant upon acceptance?

HOLDING AND DECISION: (Taylor, J.) No. A general letter informing others that a merchant has a product for sale may not constitute an offer that binds the merchant upon acceptance. For a communication to be an offer, there must be a manifestation that the offeror intends to enter into a binding agreement. Such manifestation can be found in language to that effect or specificity in the terms of the offer. However, a general, informational communication should not, in itself, be considered an offer. To so hold would inject a large element of uncertainty into contractual relations. Here, Kershaw's (D) communication was of a general, informational nature: it contained no words such as "offer" and it was not specific as to terms. It should therefore not have been construed as an offer. Reversed.

EDITOR'S ANALYSIS: It is something of a maxim in contract law that there must be a "meeting of the minds" for a contract to be formed. This is not necessarily true, as objective behavior without an actual subjective intent can constitute an offer or an acceptance. However, it seems clear that this was not the case here.

QUICKNOTES

OFFER - A proposed promise to undertake performance of an action, or to refrain from acting, that is to become binding upon acceptance by the offeree.

MUTUAL ASSENT - A requirement of a valid contract that the parties possess a mutuality of assent as manifested by the terms of the agreement and not by a hidden intent.

JOSEPH MARTIN, JR. DELICATESSEN v. SCHUMACHER

Store lessor (P) v. Lessee (D)

N.Y. Ct. App., 52 N.Y.2d 105, 436 N.Y.S.2d 247, 417 N.E.2d 541 (1981).

NATURE OF CASE: Appeal from denial of specific enforcement.

FACT SUMMARY: Schumacher (D) sought to enforce a lease provision which stated that the lease may be renewed at a rental "to be agreed upon."

CONCISE RULE OF LAW: A real estate lease provision calling for the renewal of the lease at a rental to be agreed upon is unenforceable due to its omission of a material term.

FACTS: Schumacher (D) leased a store from Martin (P) for a five-year term at a specified rental. A clause in the lease provided that Schumacher (D), as tenant, was entitled to renew the lease for an additional five-year term at a rental "to be agreed upon." Schumacher (D) gave timely notice of his desire to exercise his privilege of renewal, and Martin (P) responded that the price would be $900 a month, almost double the current rent. Schumacher (D) hired an appraiser who placed the fair market value of the store at $545 a month. Schumacher (D) then filed suit for specific performance. Martin (P) brought a separate eviction action and the trial court ruled in his favor, holding that the lease provision was only an agreement to agree and therefore unenforceable. On appeal, the court expressly overruled an established line of precedents and held that Schumacher (D) should be able to prove whether a binding agreement by the parties was intended. Martin (P) appealed.

ISSUE: May a real estate lease provision calling for the renewal of the lease at a rental to be agreed upon, be specifically enforced?

HOLDING AND DECISION: (Fuchsberg, J.) No. It is a well settled principle of law that a court may enforce a contract only where the terms of that contract are sufficiently certain and specific. Otherwise, a court would be forced to impose its own conception of what the parties should or might have agreed upon, rather than attempting to implement the bargain actually made. Accordingly, definiteness and specificity as to material matters is the essence of contract law. For that reason, a mere agreement to agree on a material term in the future without any details as to the methods of ascertaining that term cannot be enforced, since the court, rather than the parties, would be creating the agreement. A real estate lease which provides for a renewal term at a rental to be agreed upon is nothing more than an agreement to agree and, hence, cannot be enforced due to its omission of a material term. Reversed.

CONCURRENCE: (Meyer, J.) While the majority was correct in its decision in the instant case, it goes too far in suggesting that such a lease provision would never be enforceable.

DISSENT IN PART: (Jasen, J.) Although the renewal clause was unenforceable due to its uncertainty, Schumacher (D) should have been able to prove his entitlement to renewal of the lease on other grounds.

EDITOR'S ANALYSIS: The difficulty courts have in enforcing contracts which are left incomplete by the parties is illustrated by the case of *Ansorge v. Kane*, 244 N.Y. 395 (1927). The parties had agreed on a sale of land and had specified the price and the amount which was to be paid in cash up front. The manner of the deferred payments was "to be agreed upon." When the seller reneged, the buyer sought specific performance. In denying the remedy, the court held that an agreement to agree upon such a material term as contract payments rendered the contract unenforceable. However, the court stated that had the contract been absolutely silent regarding the payments, rather than saying they would be as agreed upon, the contract could have been enforced using reasonable and customary payment terms.

QUICKNOTES

SPECIFIC PERFORMANCE - An equitable remedy whereby the court requires the parties to perform their obligations pursuant to a contract.

MATERIAL TERMS OF CONTRACT - A fact without the existence of which a contract would not have been entered.

NOTES:

EMPRO MANUFACTURING CO. v. BALL-CO MANUFACTURING, INC.

Manufacturing company (P) v. Manufacturing company (D)

870 F.2d 423 (7th Cir. 1989).

NATURE OF CASE: Appeal of dismissal of action for breach of contract.

FACT SUMMARY: Empro (P) contended that a letter of intent had the effect of binding Ball-Co (P).

CONCISE RULE OF LAW: Parties who have made their pact "subject to" a later definitive agreement have manifested an intent not to be bound.

FACTS: Empro (P) and Ball-Co (D) signed a letter of intent containing the general provisions of the sale of Ball-Co's (D) assets to Empro (P), which proposed to pay $2.4 million, with $650,000 to be paid on closing and a 10-year promissory note for the remainder. The letter stated, "Empro's [P] purchase shall be subject to the satisfaction of certain conditions precedent to closing including, but not limited to," the definitive Asset Purchase Agreement and, among five other conditions, "with the approval of the shareholders and board of directors of Empro [P]." The sticking point for the deal turned out to be the security for Empro's (P) promissory note. When Ball-Co (D) started negotiating with someone else, Empro (P) sued, contending that the letter of intent bound Ball-Co (D) to sell only to Empro (P). The trial court dismissed, and Empro (P) appealed.

ISSUE: Have parties who have made their pact "subject to" a later definitive agreement manifested an intent not to be bound?

HOLDING AND DECISION: (Easterbrook, J.) Yes. Parties who have made their pact "subject to" a later agreement have manifested an intent not to be bound. Contract law gives effect to parties' wishes, but these must be expressed openly. Intent in contract law is measured objectively rather than subjectively and must be determined solely from the language used when no ambiguity in its terms exists. Parties may decide for themselves whether the results of preliminary negotiations bind them, but they do this through their words. "Subject to a definitive agreement" appears twice in the letter. The letter also recites, twice, that it contains the "general terms and conditions," implying that each side retained the right to make additional demands. The fact that Empro (P) listed as a condition that its own shareholders and board of directors had to approve the deal showed an intent not to be bound. Letters of intent and agreements in principle often, as here, do no more than set the stage for negotiations on details which may or may not be ironed out. Approaching agreement by stages is a valuable method of doing business because it allows parties to agree on the basics without bargaining away their privilege to disagree on specifics. Ball Co. (D) did not intend to be bound by its letter of intent. Affirmed.

EDITOR'S ANALYSIS: Compare this situation with one where the parties have agreed that their agreement is to be reduced to writing and signed by both of them. If the agreement is sufficient to be deemed to be a contract and one party withdraws before the signing, there can be no contract if the parties have clearly stated that they do not intend to be bound until the writing is signed. The second circuit, in *Winston v. Mediafare Entertainment Corporation*, 777 F.2d 78, 80 (2d Cir., 1985), has set forth the following factors to determine whether the parties intend to be bound before the document is fully executed: "(1) whether there has been an express reservation of the right not to be bound in the absence of a writing; (2) whether there has been partial performance of the contract; (3) whether all of the terms of the alleged contract have been agreed upon; and (4) whether the agreement at issue is the type of contract that is usually committed to writing."

QUICKNOTES

OFFER - A proposed promise to undertake performance of an action, or to refrain from acting, that is to become binding upon acceptance by the offeree.

INTENT TO CONTRACT - The unequivocal manifestation by a party wishing to enter into a contract to be legally bound by the agreement.

MUTUAL ASSENT - A requirement of a valid contract that the parties possess a mutuality of assent as manifested by the terms of the agreement and not by a hidden intent.

NOTES:

WHEELER v. WHITE
Landowner (P) v. Construction financer (D)
Tex. Sup. Ct., 398 S.W.2d 93 (1965).

NATURE OF CASE: Suit for damages.

FACT SUMMARY: After White (D) promised to finance the construction of a new building on Wheeler's (P) land, Wheeler (P) demolished the older building on such site.

CONCISE RULE OF LAW: Under § 90 of the Restatement of Contracts, "a promise which the promisor should reasonably expect to induce action or forbearance of a definite and substantial character on the part of the promisee and which does induce such action or forbearance is binding if injustice can be avoided only by enforcement of the promise."

FACTS: White (D) contracted with Wheeler (P) to finance the construction of a new building upon Wheeler's (P) land. After signing this contract, White (D) urged Wheeler (P) to demolish the old building present on the site. After Wheeler (P) demolished the old building, White (D) refused to finance a new one. Thereupon, Wheeler (P) brought an action against White (D) for damages. Wheeler (P) alleged that White (D) had breached the contract agreement. Wheeler (P) further pleaded, in the alternative, that if the contract was not sufficiently definite, then White (D) was estopped from asserting such insufficiency. After judgment for White (D), Wheeler (P) appealed.

ISSUE: Is a promise which creates no legal contractual obligation nevertheless enforceable if it induces reasonable detrimental reliance on the part of the promisee?

HOLDING AND DECISION: (Smith, J.) Yes. Under § 90 of the Restatement of Contracts, "a promise which the promisor should reasonably expect to induce action or forbearance of a definite and substantial character on the part of the promisee and which does induce such action or forbearance is binding if injustice can be avoided only by enforcement of the promise." This section states the doctrine of "promissory estoppel" which is basically defensive in that it estops a promisor from denying the enforceability of a promise which has induced reasonable reliance. Here, the promise by White (D) was not sufficiently definite to create a contractual obligation. However, such promise did reasonably and foreseeably induce substantial, detrimental reliance on the part of Wheeler (P). As such, it is binding. Reversed.

CONCURRENCE: (Greenhill, J.) Although the contract here is not definite enough to be specifically enforced, it is "sufficiently definite to support an action for damages."

EDITOR'S ANALYSIS: This case points up the general acceptance of the "promissory estoppel" doctrine, as embodied in Restatement (First), as a standard substitute for consideration. Compare the provisions of Restatement (First) in Wheeler with these of Restatement (Second), § 90. Under § 90 of Restatement (Second), "any" promise (i.e. not just a gratuitous promise) which causes a mere "change in position" (i.e. not substantial detriment) is sufficient to give rise to application of the doctrine of promissory estoppel.

QUICKNOTES
PROMISSORY ESTOPPEL - A promise that is enforceable if the promisor should reasonably expect that it will induce action or forbearance on the part of the promisee, and does in fact cause such action or forbearance, and it is the only means of avoiding injustice.

FORBEARANCE - Refraining from doing something that one has the legal right to do.

NOTES:

RAFFLES v. WICHELHAUS
Cotton seller (P) v. Cotton buyer (D)
Ct. of Exchequer, 2 Hurlstone and Coltman 906 (1864).

NATURE OF CASE: Action for damages for breach of a contract for the sale of goods.

FACT SUMMARY: Raffles (P) contracted to sell cotton to Wichelhaus (D) to be delivered from Bombay at Liverpool on the ship "Peerless." Unknown to the parties was the existence of two different ships carrying cotton, each named "Peerless" arriving at Liverpool from Bombay, but at different times.

CONCISE RULE OF LAW: Where neither party knows or has reason to know of the ambiguity or where both know or have reason to know, the ambiguity is given the meaning that each party intended it to have.

FACTS: Raffles (P) contracted to sell Wichelhaus (D) 125 bales of Surrat cotton to arrive from Bombay at Liverpool on the ship "Peerless." Wichelhaus (D) was to pay 17¼ pence per pound of cotton within an agreed upon time after the arrival of the goods in England. Unknown to the parties, there were two ships called "Peerless" each of which was carrying cotton from Bombay to Liverpool. One ship was to sail in October by Wichelhaus (D) for delivery of the goods while Raffles (P) had expected the cotton to be shipped on the "Peerless" set to sail in December. As Wichelhaus (D) could not have the delivery he expected, he refused to accept the later delivery.

ISSUE: Did a latent ambiguity arise showing that there had been no meeting of the minds, hence, no contract?

HOLDING AND DECISION: (Per curiam) Yes. While the contract did not show which particular "Peerless" was intended, the moment it appeared two ships called "Peerless" were sailing from Bombay to Liverpool with a load of cotton, a latent ambiguity arose, and parol evidence was admissible for the purpose of determining that both parties had intended a different "Peerless" to be subject in the contract. When there is an ambiguity, it is given the meaning that each party intended it to have. However, if different meanings were intended there is no contract if the ambiguity relates to a material term. Consequently, there was no meeting of the minds, and no binding contract.

EDITOR'S ANALYSIS: When there is no integration of the contract, the standard for its interpretation is the meaning that the party making the manifestation should reasonably expect the other party to give it, i.e., a standard of reasonable expectation. This case illustrates an exception to this rule. Where there is an ambiguity, if both parties give the same meaning to it, there is a contract. If the parties each give a different meaning to the ambiguity, then there is no contract as occurred here. The ambiguity struck at a material term as payment was to be made within an agreed upon time after delivery. The parties could not even agree on the time of delivery. The other exception occurs when one party has reason to know of the ambiguity and the other does not, so it will bear the meaning given to it by the latter, that is the party who is without fault. Note that under U.C.C. § 2-322, delivery "exship", it would make no difference which ship would be carrier of the goods and the case would have gone the other way. However, Restatement (First) § 71 would appear to follow the general rule of the present case.

QUICKNOTES

AMBIGUITY - Language that is capable of more than one interpretation.

MUTUAL ASSENT - A requirement of a valid contract that the parties possess a mutuality of assent as manifested by the terms of the agreement and not by a hidden intent.

MATERIAL TERMS OF CONTRACT - A fact without the existence of which a contract would not have been entered.

NOTES:

COBAUGH v. KLICK-LEWIS, INC.
Golf player (P) v. Car dealer (D)
Pa. Super. Ct., 385 Pa. Super. 587, 561 A.2d 1248 (1989).

NATURE OF CASE: Appeal from judgment awarding damages for breach of contract.

FACT SUMMARY: Klick-Lewis (D), a car dealer, reneged on a pledge to give away a car to a golfer who scored an ace, a feat achieved by Cobaugh (P).

CONCISE RULE OF LAW: An offer to give away a prize contingent upon performance of an act is enforceable by one doing the act.

FACTS: Cobaugh (P) was playing in a golf tournament. At the tee of the ninth hole was situated a car bearing a sign that it would be given to anyone making a hole in one on that hole. In fact, the car had been placed there for a tournament two days prior and had not been removed. Cobaugh (P) aced the hole and demanded the car. Klick-Lewis, Inc. (D), the dealer who had placed the car, refused to deliver. Cobaugh (P) sued for breach. The trial court granted Cobaugh's (P) motion for summary judgment, and Klick-Lewis (D) appealed.

ISSUE: Is an offer to give away a prize contingent upon performance of an act enforceable by one doing the act?

HOLDING AND DECISION: (Wieand, J.) Yes. An offer to give away a prize contingent upon performance of an act is enforceable by one doing the act. An offer is a manifestation of a willingness to enter into a bargain and to be bound by the terms of the bargain if the offer is accepted. An offer can call for acceptance either by a promise to do an act or by an act itself. When the offer calls for acceptance by doing an act, it becomes enforceable upon the doing of that act. Such a contract does not fail for lack of consideration because performing the act in question constitutes consideration. Here, Klick-Lewis (D) manifested an intent to award a car to one acing the ninth hole. Cobaugh (P) accepted the offer by doing so. That Klick-Lewis (D) had made a mistake by leaving the car there is immaterial. It is the objective manifestation of an intent to make an offer, not any subjective intent to the contrary, that controls. A contract was, therefore, formed. Affirmed.

DISSENT: (Popovich, J.) Scoring a hole in one is such a fortuitous event that the "contract" found valid by the court relates to gambling and is, therefore, unenforceable.

EDITOR'S ANALYSIS: This case illustrates the unilateral contract. Most contracts are bilateral, meaning a contract involves an exchange of promises of future performance. A unilateral contract involves an exchange of a promise and present performance.

QUICKNOTES

UNILATERAL CONTRACT - An agreement pursuant to which a party agrees to act, or to forbear from acting, in exchange for performance on the part of the other party.

INTENT TO CONTRACT - The unequivocal manifestation by a party wishing to enter into a contract to be legally bound by the agreement.

NOTES:

ALLIED STEEL & CONVEYORS, INC. v. FORD MOTOR CO.

Machinery seller (D) v. Buyer (P)

277 F.2d 907 (6th Cir. 1960).

NATURE OF CASE: Action for indemnification against damages awarded for personal injuries in a prior suit.

FACT SUMMARY: Hankins, an employee of Allied (D), was injured during performance of Allied's (D) contract with Ford (P) before Allied (D) had formally accepted the contract as per terms of Ford's (P) offer.

CONCISE RULE OF LAW: Where the offeror merely suggests a permitted method of acceptance, other methods of acceptance are not precluded.

FACTS: Ford (P) submitted to Allied (D) an agreement for the purchase of machinery which provided: "This purchase order agreement is not binding until accepted. Acceptance should be executed on acknowledgment copy which should be returned to buyer." Accompanying this agreement was a separate form requiring Allied (D) to assume full responsibility for the negligence of both its own and Ford's (P) employees in connection with Allied's (D) installation of the machinery. Allied (D) began installation prior to executing and returning the agreement in November, and in September its employee Hankins had sustained injuries as a result of the negligence of a Ford (P) employee. Allied (D) contends that it was not bound by the indemnification provision at the time of Hankin's injury since the contract was not in effect prior to its formal acceptance of Ford's (P) offer in November.

ISSUE: If an offeror requests acceptance by return promise, may the offeree accept instead by undertaking performance?

HOLDING AND DECISION: (Miller, J.) Yes, if the offeror was merely suggesting a permitted method of acceptance. The court held that the words "should be" executed and returned were such a suggestion, and that Ford (P) was not prescribing an exclusive manner of acceptance. In the latter instance, an attempt by Allied (D) to accept by undertaking performance would not create a contract. But where acceptance by return promise is only a suggested rather than an exclusive method, the offeree may also accept by undertaking the performance called for by the contract with the offeror's knowledge and consent. In such a case, the undertaking of performance operates as a promise to render a complete performance. Affirmed.

EDITOR'S ANALYSIS: This holding may at first seem contrary to *White v. Corlies and Tift*, in that it permits acceptance by performance even where a return promise is requested, while the White holding required a return promise despite omission of any required method of acceptance. The crucial factor, however, is notification of acceptance to the offeror. In *White v. Corlies and Tift*, the court was concerned lest the offeror find himself indebted for a performance without any means of learning whether his offer had been accepted. In *Allied v. Ford*, the court is careful to limit acceptance by performing, stating that it must be undertaken with the offeror's "knowledge, consent and acquiescence." In addition, it felt that the offeree who had performed with the offeror's consent, leading the offeror to believe a contract had been formed, "should not be allowed to assert an actual intent at variance with the meaning of his acts."

QUICKNOTES

ACCEPTANCE - Assent to the specified terms of an offer, resulting in the formation of a binding agreement.

INDEMNIFICATION - Reimbursement for losses sustained or security against anticipated loss or damages.

NOTES:

DAVIS v. JACOBY
Niece (P) v. Distant nephews (D)
Cal. Sup. Ct., 1 Cal.2d 370, 34 P.2d 1026 (1934).

NATURE OF CASE: Action for specific performance of an alleged contract to make a will.

FACT SUMMARY: Whitehead invited the Davis' (P) to help him with his business affairs and to look after his sick wife; the Davis' (P) accepted by letter, but before they could move down, Whitehead killed himself.

CONCISE RULE OF LAW: In case of doubt it is presumed that an offer invites the formation of a bilateral rather than a unilateral contract.

FACTS: Mr. Whitehead, whose health, as well as his business, was ailing, invited by means of a series of letters his wife's niece, Mrs. Davis (P), and her husband (P), to settle their affairs in Canada and to come and stay with him and his wife. The two families were very close and the Whiteheads regarded Mrs. Davis (P) as their daughter. In one letter, Mr. Whitehead stated that if Mr. Davis (P) could help him with his failing business, and if Mrs. Davis (P) would look after his sick wife, Mrs. Davis (P) "will inherit everything." This letter further asked, "Will you let me hear from you as soon as possible." The Davis' (P) immediately dispatched a letter in which they accepted Mr. Whitehead's offer, and started to pack their belongings. Mr. Whitehead again wrote a letter in which he acknowledged receipt of the Davis' (P) acceptance. Before the Davis' (P) could leave, Mr. Whitehead committed suicide. The Davis' (P) nonetheless came down and tended after Mrs. Whitehead until her death. It was not until that point that the Davis' (P) realized that Mr. Whitehead had failed to make a will in their favor and had instead left all his property to some distant nephews (D). In an action brought by the Davis' (P) for specific enforcement of the alleged contract to make a will, the trial court ruled that Mr. Whitehead's offer was one to enter into a unilateral contract and since they had not performed prior to his death the Davis' (P) acceptance by letter was ineffective.

ISSUE: Will an ambiguous offer be interpreted as inviting the formation of a bilateral, rather than a unilateral, contract?

HOLDING AND DECISION: Yes. In case of doubt, it is presumed that an offer invites the formation of a bilateral contract by an acceptance amounting in effect to a promise by the offeree to perform what the offer requests, rather than the formation of one or more unilateral contracts by actual performance on the part of the offeree. A bilateral contract is favored since it immediately and fully protects the expectations of both parties. Mr. Whitehead's offer was one to enter into a bilateral contract since the facts suggest that he wanted only a promise to perform and not performance. The parties, being very close, were not dealing at arm's length. Mr. Whitehead was looking to the Davis' (P) for assurance and peace of mind. He had asked for a reply. When an offer has indicated the mode and means of acceptance, an acceptance in accordance with that mode or means is binding on the offeror. Finally, since the offer contemplated a service which could not be fully performed until after his death—caring for Mrs. Whitehead—he had to rely on the Davis' (P) promise. Consequently, specific performance should be granted.

EDITOR'S ANALYSIS: U.C.C. § 2-206(1) provides: "Unless otherwise unambiguously indicated by the language or circumstances, (a) an offer to make a contract shall be construed as inviting acceptance in any manner . . . reasonable in the circumstances; (b) an order or other offer to buy goods for prompt or current shipment shall be construed as inviting acceptance either by a prompt promise to ship or by the prompt or current shipment of . . . goods."

QUICKNOTES

BILATERAL CONTRACT - An agreement pursuant to which each party promises to undertake an obligation, or to forbear from acting, at some time in the future.

ACCEPTANCE - Assent to the specified terms of an offer, resulting in the formation of a binding agreement.

UNILATERAL CONTRACT - An agreement pursuant to which a party agrees to act, or to forbear from acting, in exchange for performance on the part of the other party.

NOTES:

PETTERSON v. PATTBERG
Executor (P) v. Holder of mortgage (D)
N.Y. Ct. App., 248 N.Y. 86, 161 N.E. 428 (1928).

NATURE OF CASE: Action for breach of contract.

FACT SUMMARY: Pattberg (D) offered to discount the mortgage on J. Petterson's estate on the condition that it be paid on a certain date. Pattberg (D) then sold the mortgage before Petterson (P), as executor of the estate, had paid him.

CONCISE RULE OF LAW: An offer to enter into a unilateral contract may be withdrawn at any time prior to performance of the act requested to be done.

FACTS: Pattberg (D) held a mortgage on property belonging to J. Petterson's estate. Petterson (P) was executor of that estate. Pattberg (D) offered to discount the amount of the mortgage on the condition that it be paid on a certain date. Before that date Petterson (P) went to Pattberg's (D) home and offered to pay him the amount of the mortgage. Pattberg (D) told Petterson (P) that he had already sold the mortgage to a third person.

ISSUE: Can an offer to enter into a unilateral contract be withdrawn prior to performance of the act requested to be done?

HOLDING AND DECISION: (Kellogg, J.) Yes. An offer to enter into a unilateral contract may be withdrawn at any time prior to performance of the act requested to be done. Here, Pattberg's (D) offer proposed to Petterson (P) the making of a unilateral contract, the gift of a promise (to discount the mortgage) in exchange for the performance of an act (payment by a certain date). Pattberg (D) was free to revoke his offer any time before Petterson (P) accepted by performing the act. He revoked the offer by informing Petterson (P) that he had sold the mortgage. An offer to sell property may be withdrawn before acceptance without any formal notice to the person to whom the offer is made. It is sufficient if that person has actual knowledge that the person who made the offer has done some act inconsistent with the continuance of the offer, such as selling the property to a third person.

DISSENT: (Lehman, J.) Until the act requested was performed, Pattberg (D) had the right to revoke his offer. However, he could not revoke it after Petterson (P) had offered to make the payment.

EDITOR'S ANALYSIS: Other facts in Petterson which do not appear in the opinion may have influenced the court. The trial record shows that Pattberg (D) was prevented from testifying as to a letter sent to J. Petterson, in which the offer was revoked. The record also suggests that Petterson (P) knew of the sale of the mortgage. Note, 1928, 14 Cornell L.Q. 81. The Restatement of Contracts, Second, provides, "Where an offer invites an offeree to accept by rendering performance, an option contract is created when the offeree begins performance." Actual performance is necessary. Preparations to perform, though they may be essential to performance, are not enough. However, they may constitute justifiable reliance sufficient to make the offeror's promise binding under § 90.

QUICKNOTES

REVOCATION - The cancellation or withdrawal of some authority conferred or an instrument drafted, such as the withdrawal of a revocable contract offer prior to the offeree's acceptance.

UNILATERAL CONTRACT - An agreement pursuant to which a party agrees to act, or to forbear from acting, in exchange for performance on the part of the other party.

NOTES:

BRACKENBURY v. HODGKIN

Daughter (P) v. Mother (D)

Me. Sup. Jud. Ct., 116 Me. 399, 102 A. 106 (1917).

NATURE OF CASE: Action for specific performance.

FACT SUMMARY: Mrs. Hodgkin (D) promised her daughter (P) and her daughter's husband (P) that if they would take care of her, then she would leave them her farm. The couple (P) complied. However, disputes arose and Mrs. Hodgkin (D) ordered them off the farm.

CONCISE RULE OF LAW: A contractual offer may be accepted by performance if a unilateral contract is involved.

FACTS: Mrs. Hodgkin (D), a widower, wrote a letter to her daughter and her husband that if they would leave Missouri, move to Maine and take care of her and her farm, then she (D) would leave the farm to them (P). The couple (P) accepted the offer by giving up their home in Missouri, moving to Maine and taking care of Mrs. Hodgkin (D) and her farm. Later, disputes between the parties arose with the culmination that Mrs. Hodgkin (D) ordered the couple (P) off the farm. The couple (P) brought an action for specific performance.

ISSUE: May an offer be accepted by performance?

HOLDING AND DECISION: (Cornish, J.) Yes. A contractual offer may be accepted by performance. In this case Mrs. Hodgkin (D) made an offer via her letter. The offer was for a unilateral contract (promise for an act). Mrs. Hodgkin (D) was promising that if the couple (P) perform by taking care of her then she (D) would give the farm to the couple (P). The couple (P) accepted the offer by their performance. We conclude that there is a binding contract and that specific performance is a proper remedy.

EDITOR'S ANALYSIS: The principal case illustrates the majority rule that in a unilateral contract when an offeree begins performance the offeror is estopped from revoking the offer or from interfering with the offeree's performance. Many theories have been advanced for this proposition including that there is an ipso facto bilateral contract or that there is equitable estoppel. Restatement of Contracts § 45 subscribes to the theory that there is a firm offer while Restatement of Contracts (Second) § 45 employs the theory of an option contract once the offeror knows that the offeree has begun substantial performance.

QUICKNOTES

SPECIFIC PERFORMANCE - An equitable remedy whereby the court requires the parties to perform their obligations pursuant to a contract.

UNILATERAL CONTRACT - An agreement pursuant to which a party agrees to act, or to forbear from acting, in exchange for performance on the part of the other party.

REVOCATION - The cancellation or withdrawal of some authority conferred or an instrument drafted, such as the withdrawal of a revocable contract offer prior to the offeree's acceptance.

OPTION CONTRACT - A contract pursuant to which a seller agrees that property will be available for the buyer to purchase at a specified price and within a certain time period.

NOTES:

THOMASON v. BESCHER
Timber buyer (P) v. Timber seller (D)
N.C. Sup. Ct., 176 N.C. 622, 97 S.E. 654 (1918).

NATURE OF CASE: Appeal from judgment decreeing specific performance.

FACT SUMMARY: Thomason (P) and Bescher (D) entered into an option contract under seal which involved the payment of nominal consideration by Thomason (P), which he failed to provide.

CONCISE RULE OF LAW: When an option contract under seal provides for nominal consideration by one party, a failure by that party to provide that consideration will not invalidate the agreement.

FACTS: Bescher (D), in consideration of $1 payable by Thomason (P), gave the latter an option to later purchase certain timber for $6,000. The contract was placed under seal. Thomason (P) never paid the dollar. When he was ready to exercise the option, Bescher (D) refused to accept. Thomason (P) sued for specific performance. The court so ordered, and Bescher (D) appealed.

ISSUE: When an option contract under seal provides for nominal consideration by one party, will a failure by that party to provide that consideration invalidate the agreement?

HOLDING AND DECISION: (Hoke, J.) No. When an option contract under seal provides for nominal consideration by one party, a failure by that party to provide that consideration will not invalidate the agreement. It is the rule that a seal placed on a contract provides the evidence of solemnity that usually is given by consideration. Consequently, unless the equities of a given case dictate otherwise, a contract under seal will not fail for lack of consideration. Here, the only failure on Thomason's (P) part was a failure to pay a nominal consideration, and the sealing of the contract cures this minor fault. Affirmed.

EDITOR'S ANALYSIS: The seal, even when it was given its greatest respect, was never a complete substitute for consideration. Few jurisdictions would consider it to be a valid replacement for substantial consideration. Today, most states no longer give any significance to the seal.

QUICKNOTES

OPTION CONTRACT - A contract pursuant to which a seller agrees that property will be available for the buyer to purchase at a specified price and within a certain time period.

NOMINAL CONSIDERATION - Consideration that is so insignificant that it does not represent the actual value received from the agreement.

NOTES:

JAMES BAIRD CO. v. GIMBEL BROS.
Contractor (P) v. Linoleum supplier (D)
64 F.2d 344 (2d Cir. 1933).

NATURE OF CASE: Action for breach of a contract for the sale of goods.

FACT SUMMARY: Gimbel (D) offered to supply linoleum to various contractors who were bidding on a public construction contract. Baird (P), relying on Gimbel's (D) quoted prices, submitted a bid and later the same day received a telegraphed message from Gimbel (D) that its quoted prices were in error. Baird's (P) bid was accepted.

CONCISE RULE OF LAW: The doctrine of promissory estoppel shall not be applied in cases where there is an offer for exchange as the offer is not intended to become a promise until a consideration is received.

FACTS: Gimbel (D) having heard that bids were being taken for a public building had an employee obtain the specifications for linoleum required for the building and submitted offers to various possible contractors including Baird (P) of two prices for linoleum depending upon the quality used. The offer was made in ignorance of a mistake as to the actual amount of linoleum needed causing Gimbel's (D) prices to be about half the actual cost. The offer concluded as follows: "If successful in being awarded this contract, it will be absolutely guaranteed, . . . and . . . we are offering these prices for reasonable (sic) prompt acceptance after the general contract has been awarded." Baird (P) received this on the 28th, the same day on which Gimbel (D) discovered its mistake, and telegraphed all contractors of the error, but the communication was received by Baird (P) just after Baird (P) submitted its lump sum bid relying on Gimbel's (D) erroneous prices. Baird's (P) bid was accepted on the 30th. Baird (P) received Gimbel's (D) written confirmation of the error on the 31st but sent an acceptance despite this two days later. Gimbel (D) refused to recognize a contract.

ISSUE: Shall the doctrine of promissory estoppel be applied in cases where there is an offer for exchange if the offer is not intended to become a promise until a consideration is received?

HOLDING AND DECISION: (Hand, J.) No. The doctrine of promissory estoppel shall not be applied in cases where there is an offer for exchange as the offer is not intended to become a promise until a consideration is received. Looking at the language of Gimbel's (D) offer, Gimbel's (D) use of the phrase "if successful in being awarded this contract" clearly shows Gimbel's (D) intent of not being bound simply by a contractor relying or acting upon the quoted prices. This is reinforced by the phrase " . . . prompt acceptance after the general contract has been awarded." No award had been made at the time and reliance on the prices cannot be said to be an award of the contract. Had a relying contractor been awarded the contract and then repudiated it, Gimbel (D) would not have had any right to sue for breach, nor could Gimbel (D) have gone against his estate if the relying contractor had gone bankrupt. The contractors could have protected themselves by insisting on a contract guaranteeing the prices before relying upon them. The court will not strain to find a contract in aid of one who fails to protect himself. The theory of promissory estoppel is not available as it is appropriate in donative or charitable cases where harsh results to the promisee arising from the promisor's breaking his relied-upon promise are to be protected against. However, an offer for an exchange, either being an act or another promise, is not meant to become a promise until a consideration is received. Here, the linoleum was to be delivered for the contractor's acceptance, not his bid. An option contract has not arisen as it is clear from the language of the offer that Gimbel (D) had no intention of assuming a one-sided obligation.

EDITOR'S ANALYSIS: Later cases have held the doctrine of promissory estoppel not to be as narrow. The majority of courts which have considered the issue hold that justifiable detrimental reliance on an offer renders it irrevocable. Naturally, the contractor must have something upon which to justifiably rely. The court in its decision notes that Restatement § 90 follows its view. However, Restatement (Second) § 90 has expanded the section so as to enlarge its scope according to the more modern viewpoint. It must be shown that the offeror foresaw that his promise would reasonably induce forbearance or action. The first inkling of this doctrine probably arose in the well-known *Hamer v. Sidway*, 27 N.E. 256, 1 89 1, where an uncle promised to pay his nephew $5,000 for refraining from the use of liquor, swearing, and other activities until his 21st birthday, and reached full maturity in Mr. J. Traynor's decision in *Drennan v. Star Paving Company*, 51 Cal. 2d 409, 333 P. 2d 757, 1958. Generally, this case is a good example of the manner in which the court will examine the words and actions of the parties in order to determine their intent and, hence, the existence of a contract. It appears that Gimbel (D) could have used the defense of unilateral mistake based upon a clerical error as seen in *M. F. Kemper Construction Co. v. City of Los Angeles*, 235 P. 2d 7, 1951.

QUICKNOTES

UNILATERAL MISTAKE - Occurs when only one party to an agreement makes a mistake and is generally not a basis for relief by rescission or reformation.

PROMISSORY ESTOPPEL - A promise that is enforceable if the promisor should reasonably expect that it will induce action or forbearance on the part of the promisee, and does in fact cause such action or forbearance, and it is the only means of avoiding injustice.

CONSIDERATION - Value given by one party in exchange for performance, or a promise to perform, by another party.

RELIANCE - Dependence on a fact that causes a party to act or refrain from acting.

DRENNAN v. STAR PAVING CO.
General contractor (P) v. Paving company (D)
Cal. Sup. Ct., 51 Cal. 2d 409, 333 P.2d 757 (1958).

NATURE OF CASE: Appeal of an award of damages for breach of contract.

FACT SUMMARY: Drennan (P) sued Star (D) to recover damages when Star (D) could not perform the paving work at the price quoted in its subcontracting bid.

CONCISE RULE OF LAW: Reasonable reliance on a promise binds an offeror even if there is no other consideration.

FACTS: In formulating a bid to the Lancaster School District, Drennan (P), a general contractor, solicited bids for subcontracting work. Star (P), a paving company, submitted the lowest paving bid, and Drennan (P) used that bid in formulating its bid to the school district. Using Star's (D) subcontracting bid of $7,131.60, Drennan (P) was awarded the general contract. Star (D) then told Drennan (P) that it made a mistake and could not do the work for less than $15,000. Star (D) refused to do the work, and Drennan (P) found a substitute company that did the work for $10,948.60. Drennan (P) sued Star (D) for the difference, claiming that Drennan (P) had reasonably relied on Star's (D) offer. Star (D) claimed that it had made a revocable offer. The trial court ruled in favor of Drennan (P) on the grounds of promissory estoppel, and Star (D) appealed.

ISSUE: Does reasonable reliance on a promise bind the offeror if there no other consideration?

HOLDING AND DECISION: (Traynor, J.) Yes. Reasonable reliance on a promise binds the offeror even if there is no other consideration. Section 90 of the Restatement of Contracts provides that when a promise is made that induces action or forbearance of the promisee, the promissor is bound if injustice would result from nonenforcement. In the case of a unilateral offer, the offeror is bound to the promise if it produces reasonable reliance. Star (D) made a promise to Drennan (P) of a certain price. Star's (D) bid was the lowest, and Drennan (P) reasonably relied on it in formulating its bid and winning the contract. As a result, Drennan (P) was obligated to do the work at the price quoted and even had to put up a bond. Star (D) should have known such a result would occur if Star's (D) bid was accepted. The absence of consideration is not fatal to Star's (D) initial promise, as Drennan (P) substantially changed its position in reliance on Star (D). Injustice can only be avoided by the enforcement of Star's (D) subcontracting promise. Affirmed.

EDITOR'S ANALYSIS: Such reasonable reliance cases are often called firm offers. Firm offers can sometimes be implied promises to hold an offer open and have received criticism on the grounds that one party (the subcontractor) is bound while the other party (the general contractor) is not. Nonetheless, the modern trend is to enforce such promises.

QUICKNOTES
PROMISSORY ESTOPPEL - A promise that is enforceable if the promisor should reasonably expect that it will induce action or forbearance on the part of the promisee, and does in fact cause such action or forbearance, and it is the only means of avoiding injustice.

RELIANCE - Dependence on a fact that causes a party to act or refrain from acting.

CONSIDERATION - Value given by one party in exchange for performance, or a promise to perform, by another party.

NOTES:

HOFFMAN v. RED OWL STORES, INC.
Franchise purchaser (P) v. Supermarket (D)
Wis. Sup. Ct., 26 Wis. 2d 683, 133 N.W.2d 267 (1965).

NATURE OF CASE: Cross-appeals of award of damages in an action promissory estoppel.

FACT SUMMARY: After the Hoffmans (P) took certain actions in reliance on promises made by Red Owl (D) during negotiations for a Red Owl (D) franchise, Red Owl (D) increased the amount of capital required as an investment, causing Hoffman (P) to break off negotiations and file suit.

CONCISE RULE OF LAW: A promise which the promisor should reasonably expect to induce action or forbearance of a definite and substantial character on the part of the promisee and which does induce such action or forbearance is binding where injustice can be avoided only by enforcement.

FACTS: Relying on assurances by Red Owl (D) that Hoffman (P) would be set up in a Red Owl (D) supermarket franchise, Hoffman (P) obtained an option on the site Red Owl (D) selected for a new store. With continuing assurances from Red Owl (D) that everything was ready to go, the Hoffmans (P) sold their assets, which included their business (a grocery) and a bakery building and rented a house near the site for the new store. Despite the fact that Red Owl (D) knew the Hoffmans (P) had only $18,000 to invest, Red Owl (D) increased the amount of required capital to a total of $34,000. The Hoffmans (P) terminated negotiations and filed an action based on promissory estoppel, arguing that Red Owl (D) should reasonably have known that they would have relied on Red Owl's (D) promise since they had taken definite steps to prepare for opening the store. The jury awarded the Hoffmans (P) damages of $20,000. The trial court, on Red Owl's (D) motion, set aside the award of $16,735 for the sale of the grocery and ordered a new trial on that issue. Red Owl (D) appealed, and the Hoffmans (P) cross-appealed.

ISSUE: Is a promise which the promisor should reasonably expect to induce action or forbearance of a definite and substantial character on the part of the promisee and which does induce such action or forbearance binding where injustice can be avoided only by enforcement?

HOLDING AND DECISION: (Currie, J.) Yes. A promise which the promisor should reasonably expect to induce action or forbearance of a definite and substantial character on the part of the promisee and which does induce such action or forbearance is binding where injustice can be avoided only by enforcement. Red Owl's (D) promises induced the Hoffmans (P) to sell off their assets on the promise that they would be in their new store by fall and that this was the last step necessary to have the deal go through. Injustice

would result here if the Hoffmans (P) were not granted some relief because of the failure of Red Owl (D) to keep its promises which induced them to act to their detriment. However, the damages should not exceed the loss caused by the change of position. Because this was a promissory estoppel action, not one for breach of contract, any award of damages does not have to be the exact amount of the loss. It only need be an amount that is just under the circumstances. Justice does not require that the damages awarded should exceed any actual loss sustained measured by the difference between the sales price (of the grocery) and the fair market value. The trial court properly ordered a new trial on the issue of damages. Affirmed.

EDITOR'S ANALYSIS: Originally the doctrine of promissory estoppel was invoked as a substitute for consideration rendering a gratuitous promise enforceable as a contract. However, the Restatement of Contracts § 90 does not impose the requirement that the promise giving rise to the cause of action must be so comprehensive in scope as to meet the requirements of an offer that would ripen into a contract if accepted by the promisee. The court deemed it a mistake to regard an action grounded on promissory estoppel as the equivalent of a breach of contract action.

QUICKNOTES

PROMISSORY ESTOPPEL - A promise that is enforceable if the promisor should reasonably expect that it will induce action or forbearance on the part of the promisee, and does in fact cause such action or forbearance, and it is the only means of avoiding injustice.

CONSIDERATION - Value given by one party in exchange for performance, or a promise to perform, by another party.

FORBEARANCE - Refraining from doing something that one has the legal right to do.

NOTES:

LIVINGSTONE v. EVANS
Buyer of land (P) v. Seller (D)
Alberta Sup. Ct., 4 D.L.R. 769 (1925).

NATURE OF CASE: Action for specific performance.

FACT SUMMARY: Livingstone (P) submitted a counter-offer which Evans (D) rejected. Livingstone (P) then unsuccessfully attempted to accept the original offer.

CONCISE RULE OF LAW: A counter-offer is a rejection of the original offer and terminates it.

FACTS: Evans (D) offered to sell land to Livingstone (P) for $1,800. Livingstone (P) telegraphed that he would offer $1,600 or the lowest price. Evans (D) telegraphed back " cannot reduce price". Livingstone (P) immediately wired an acceptance. Evans (D) refused to enter into a written contract or to convey the land alleging that his original offer was rejected by Livingstone's (P) counter-offer and could not be revived without an acceptance of the offer in Livingstone's (P) second telegram.

ISSUE: May the original offer be unilaterally accepted once a counter-offer has been submitted?

HOLDING AND DECISION: (Walsh, J.) No. A counter-offer is a rejection of the original offer. It states a new contract which the original offeror is then free to accept or reject. If he rejects it, the other party cannot then unilaterally accept the original offer. He, in effect, makes a new offer at the original terms, which the original offeror is then free to accept or reject. Here, Evans (D) rejected it. However, this does not end the inquiry herein. Evans' (D) telegram "cannot reduce price" is a reaffirmation of the original offer and demonstrates an intent to be bound by it. It re-establishes the original offer and Livingstone's (P) acceptance forms a binding contract. Specific performance is therefore granted. Judgment for Livingstone (P).

EDITOR'S ANALYSIS: Courts, to ameliorate the harshness of the "mirror image" rule, that the acceptance must exactly match the terms of the offer, found that some acceptances were binding where there was a mere inquiry whether the offeror would accept some other terms. *Stevenson v. McLean*, 5 O.B.D. 346. For example, "I accept but would like payment to be due 30 days after delivery." Courts would generally find that this was an unequivocal acceptance of the offer with a request for the addition of another term.

QUICKNOTES
REJECTION - The refusal to accept the terms of an offer.

COUNTEROFFER - A statement by the offeree which has the legal effect of rejecting the offer and of proposing a new offer to the offeror.

SPECIFIC PERFORMANCE - An equitable remedy whereby the court requires the parties to perform their obligations pursuant to a contract.

MIRROR-IMAGE RULE - The common law rule that for acceptance to be effective the offeree must accept each and every term of the offer.

NOTES:

IDAHO POWER CO. v. WESTINGHOUSE ELECTRIC CORP.
Utility company (P) v. Electrical equipment seller (D)
596 F.2d 924 (9th Cir. 1979).

NATURE OF CASE: Appeal from dismissal of breach of contract action.

FACT SUMMARY: Idaho Power (P) sought recovery from Westinghouse (D) for damages caused by defective machinery, although Westinghouse's (D) price quote had included a disclaimer for liability for damage resulting from a malfunction.

CONCISE RULE OF LAW: A contract between merchants may be created even though the acceptance contains different terms than the offer.

FACTS: Idaho Power (P) sent an inquiry to Westinghouse (D) regarding the sale of a regulator. Westinghouse (D) responded with a form quoting a selling price and other terms and conditions, including a disclaimer of liability for any damages resulting from the equipment's malfunction. Idaho Power (P) then sent an order form for the regulator. The form provided that its terms and conditions constituted the basis of the agreement and "superseded all previous agreements." The form contained additional terms regarding shipping, but did not discuss Westinghouse's (D) liability. Shortly after the regulator was installed, it failed, causing a fire which damaged other machinery. Idaho Power (P) sued for damages and Westinghouse (D) moved to dismiss on the basis of its disclaimer. The court dismissed the complaint, and Idaho Power (P) appealed, contending that the contract terms were contained in its order form which did not limit Westinghouse's (D) liability.

ISSUE: Can a contract be created between merchants where the acceptance contains different terms than the offer?

HOLDING AND DECISION: (Wright, J.) Yes. U.C.C. § 2-207 controls this case. It provides that a contract between merchants is created, even though the acceptance contains different terms than the offer, unless acceptance is expressly made conditional on assent to the different terms. The latter provision has been narrowly construed by the courts. Therefore, the statement in Idaho Power's (P) order form that the terms contained therein superseded all prior agreements is not sufficient to have the order deemed a counteroffer rather than an acceptance. Furthermore, although Idaho Power's (P) acceptance contained some different terms, it did not discuss Westinghouse's (D) liability. As such, the statement that it superseded all previous agreements would not serve to negate the disclaimers of liability found in Westinghouse's (D) original offer. Accordingly, the disclaimers apply to the suit brought by Idaho Power (P), and the suit was properly dismissed. Affirmed.

EDITOR'S ANALYSIS: The modern rule of acceptance between merchants, as discussed in the principal case, is quite different from the common law rule of acceptance, set out in the Restatement of Contracts § 60: "A reply to an offer, though purporting to accept it, which adds qualifications or requires performance of conditions, is not an acceptance but is a counter-offer." This rule, sometimes known as the mirror-image rule of acceptance, is gradually losing vitality in most American jurisdictions.

QUICKNOTES

MIRROR-IMAGE RULE - The common law rule that for acceptance to be effective the offeree must accept each and every term of the offer.

BATTLE OF THE FORMS - Refers to the exchange of forms, pursuant to a contract for the sale of goods, between a buyer and seller.

NOTES:

ProCD, INC. v. ZEIDENBERG
Software manufacturer (P) v. Purchaser (D).
86 F.3d 1477 (7th Cir. 1996).

NATURE OF CASE: Appeal from an order in favor of defendant in a case alleging breach of the terms of a shrinkwrap or end-user license.

FACT SUMMARY: When Zeidenberg (D), a customer, bought and then resold the data compiled on its CD-ROM software disk, ProCD (P) sued for breach of contract.

CONCISE RULE OF LAW: A buyer accepts goods when, after an opportunity to inspect, he fails to make an effective rejection.

FACTS: ProCD (P) compiled information from over 3,000 telephone directories into a computer database which it sold on CD-ROM disks. Every box containing the disks declared that the software came with restrictions stated in an enclosed license. This license, which was encoded on the CD-ROM disks as well as printed in the manual, and which appeared on a user's screen every time the software ran, limited use of the application program and listings to non-commercial purposes. Zeidenberg bought a ProCD (P) software package but decided to ignore the license and to resell the information in the database. Zeidenberg (D) also made the information from ProCD's (P) database available over the Internet for a price, through his corporation. ProCD (P) sued for breach of contract. The district court found that placing the package of software on the shelf was an "offer," which the customer "accepted" by paying the asking price and leaving the store with the goods. A contract includes only those terms which the parties have agreed to and one cannot agree to secret terms. Thus, the district court held that buyers of computer software need not obey the terms of shrinkwrap licenses. Such licenses were found to be ineffectual because their terms did not appear on the outsides of the packages. ProCD (P) appealed.

ISSUE: Does a buyer accept goods when, after an opportunity to inspect, he fails to make an effective rejection?

HOLDING AND DECISION: (Easterbrook, J.) Yes. A buyer accepts goods when, after an opportunity to inspect, he fails to make an effective rejection under §2-602 of the Uniform Commercial Code. A vendor, as master of the offer, may invite acceptance by conduct, and may propose limitations on the kind of conduct that constitutes acceptance. ProCD (P) proposed a contract that a buyer would accept by using the software after having an opportunity to read the license at leisure. Zeidenberg (D) did this, since he had no choice when the software splashed the license across his computer screen and would not let him proceed without indicating acceptance. The license was an ordinary contract accompanying the sale of products and was therefore governed by the common law of contracts and the Uniform Commercial Code. Transactions in which the exchange of money precedes the communication of detailed terms are common. Buying insurance or buying a plane ticket are two common examples. ProCD (P) extended an opportunity to reject if a buyer should find the license terms unsatisfactory. Zeidenberg (D) inspected the package, tried out the software, learned of the license, and did not reject the goods. Reversed and remanded.

EDITOR'S ANALYSIS: The sale of information contained in computer databases presented new challenges to courts. Some courts found that the sale of software was the sale of services, rather than of goods. This case treated the sale of software as a sale of goods governed by Article 2 of the U.C.C.

QUICKNOTES

CD-ROM - Compact disc - read only memory.

INSPECTION OF GOODS - The examination of goods, which are the subject matter of a contract for sale, for the purpose of determining whether they are satisfactory.

REJECTION - The refusal to accept the terms of an offer.

SHRINKWRAP LICENSE - Terms of restriction packaged inside a product.

U.C.C. § 2-602 - Provides that a rejection after an opportunity to inspect may be effective unless the buyer manifests acceptance in the manner invited by the offeror.

NOTES:

MORRISON v. THOELKE
Seller of land (P) v. Buyer (D)
Fla. Dist. App. Ct., 155 So.2d 889 (1963).

NATURE OF CASE: Action to quiet title.

FACT SUMMARY: After mailing an acceptance, Morrison (P) informed Theolke (D) that the offer was being rejected, the rejection being received before the acceptance.

CONCISE RULE OF LAW: An acceptance is effective when it is posted even though a subsequent rejection is actually received before the acceptance.

FACTS: Theolke (D) offered to purchase land from Morrison (P). Morrison (P) agreed, had a deed made out, and mailed it to Theolke (D). Prior to receipt of the deed by Theolke (D). Morrison (P) used a faster means to reject the offer, the rejection having reached Theolke (D) before the acceptance. Theolke (D) had the deed recorded and tendered the purchase price alleging that a valid contract had been entered into by them. Morrison (P) sued to quiet title alleging that an acceptance was not valid until received and could be withdrawn by the prior receipt of a rejection. Theolke (D) alleged that the acceptance was binding upon posting.

ISSUE: Is an acceptance binding upon posting?

HOLDING AND DECISION: (Allen, J.) Yes. While courts are split over this fact, we find that an acceptance is valid upon posting and may not thereafter be recalled. We find that the act of posting effectively places the acceptance beyond the control of the party and is an effective point at which to find a contract has been formed. We feel that such a holding is consistent with modern business practices and serves the best interest of both parties to the contract and the community in general. Having posted the acceptance, a valid contract was formed. Judgment for Theolke (D).

EDITOR'S ANALYSIS: Jurisdictions are split over this issue. Those holding that an acceptance is valid only when received focus on several different factors: 1) the acceptance could be retrieved prior to delivery, 2) there is no reason to bind the acceptor prior to the offeror learning of the contract, 3) the risk of any loss should be on the person choosing the method of communication. If an acceptance is received prior to an earlier mailed rejection, the Restatement, Second, § 39 would give effect to the acceptance though this rule is also in dispute among the various jurisdictions.

QUICKNOTES

MAILBOX RULE - Common law rule that acceptance of an offer is binding upon dispatch at which time an enforceable contract is formed so long as it complies with the requirements for acceptance.

ACCEPTANCE - Assent to the specified terms of an offer, resulting in the formation of a binding agreement.

REJECTION - The refusal to accept the terms of an offer.

NOTES:

HOBBS v. MASSASOIT WHIP CO.
Eel skin seller (P) v. Whip manufacturer (D)
Mass. Sup. Jud. Ct., 158 Mass. 194, 33 N.E. 495 (1893).

NATURE OF CASE: Action for breach of contract.

FACT SUMMARY: Hobbs (P) sent Massasoit Whip Co. (D) eel skins which it retained until they were subsequently destroyed.

CONCISE RULE OF LAW: Silence may constitute acceptance in appropriate cases.

FACTS: Hobbs (P) sent eel skins to Massasoit Whip Co. (D). Massasoit (D) retained the skins but never used them. There was no contract between the parties, and Massasoit (D) never formally accepted the skins. The skins were subsequently destroyed, and Hobbs (P) sued for their value. At trial, Hobbs (P) introduced evidence that he had previously sent skins to Massasoit (D) under similar circumstances on four or five occasions. They had always been accepted and paid for by Massasoit (D) so long as they were at least 22 inches long. Massasoit (D) alleged that mere silence cannot create a contract, and no duty can be created requiring Massasoit (D) to respond or return the skins.

ISSUE: Where appropriate, can silence by one party be deemed an acceptance?

HOLDING AND DECISION: (Holmes, J.) Yes. Under appropriate circumstances, silence alone may constitute an acceptance, and a valid contract is formal. A prior course of dealings may render silence an acceptance. Here, receipt of the skins and their retention, based on the prior dealings of the parties, constitutes a valid acceptance. Silence was sufficient conduct to manifest acceptance or assent to a contract under such circumstances. Judgment for Hobbs (P) is affirmed.

EDITOR'S ANALYSIS: It is the overt manifestation of intent to contract rather than a party's subjective intent which controls. *O'Donnell v. Clinton*, 145 Mass. 461. While silence cannot create or impose a duty on strangers by the unilateral delivery of goods, a prior courts of dealings, plus retention of the goods, may create a manifestation of assent. If the prior relationship would not create a presumption of assent, it may be disregarded by the courts. *Bushel v. Wheeler*, 15 G.B. 442.

NOTES:

MORONE v. MORONE
Wife (P) v. Husband (D)
N.Y. Ct. App., 50 N.Y.2d 481, 429 N.Y.S.2d 592, 413 N.E.2d 1154
(1980).

NATURE OF CASE: Action to recover under an implied-in-law contract.

FACT SUMMARY: Mrs. Morone (P) asserted that a contract as to earnings and assets should be implied in law from the living-together relationship with Mr. Morone (D).

CONCISE RULE OF LAW: In the absence of contrary legislation, the court may decline to recognize the relationship of an unmarried couple living together as giving rise to an implied-in-law contract regarding their earnings and assets or the personal services which each may render.

FACTS: Mrs. Morone (P) and Mr. Morone (D) began living together without benefit of marriage in 1952. They had two children and held themselves out to the community as husband and wife. Eventually, Mrs. Morone (P) filed suit seeking to recover under the theory that an implied-in-law contract as to earnings and assets had arisen from the relationship. She also claimed that an oral agreement had been expressly entered into in 1952, whereby Mr. Morone (D) promised to support, maintain, and provide for her while she was to provide domestic services. The Special Term dismissed the complaint and the appellate division affirmed.

ISSUE: Does the relationship of an unmarried couple living together give rise to an implied-in-law contract regarding their earnings and assets or the personal services each renders?

HOLDING AND DECISION: (Meyer, J.) No. This court declines to follow the California courts and their decision in the *Marvin* case and will not recognize the relationship of couples living together as giving rise to an implied-in-law contract regarding their earnings and assets or the personal services each may render. Such would be inconsistent with the legislative policy enunciated in 1933 when common-law marriages were abolished in New York. Further-more, it is not reasonable to infer an agreement to pay for the services rendered when the relationship of the parties makes it natural that the services were rendered gratuitously. The notion of an implied contract between an unmarried couple living together is, thus, contrary to New York decisional law and legislative policy. However, any express agreement between unmarried persons living together is as enforceable as though they were not living together provided that illicit sexual relations were not part of the consideration of the contract. Thus, the courts below should have allowed Mrs. Morone (P) to proceed on her express contract claim. Affirmed as modified.

EDITOR'S ANALYSIS: Many of the jurisdictions which refuse to recognize an implied-in-law contract under such circumstances point to the substantially greater risk of fraud which arises when courts attempt to attach contractual significance to conduct within what is, by its nature, an essentially private and generally noncontractual relationship.

QUICKNOTES

CONDITION - Requirement; potential future occurrence upon which the existence of a legal obligation is dependent.

QUASI-CONTRACT - An implied contract created by law to prevent unjust enrichment.

NOTES:

MITCHILL v. LATH
Property buyer (P) v. Property seller (D)
N.Y. Ct. App., 247 N.Y. 377, 160 N.E. 646 (1928).

NATURE OF CASE: Appeal from order enforcing agreement for sale of land.

FACT SUMMARY: Mitchill (P) bought some property from Lath (D) pursuant to a full and complete written sales contract. She seeks to compel Lath (D) to perform on his parol agreement to remove an ice house on neighboring property.

CONCISE RULE OF LAW: An oral agreement is permitted to vary from a written contract only if it is collateral in form, does not contradict express or implied conditions of the written contract, and consists of terms which the parties could not reasonably have been expected to include in the written contract.

FACTS: Lath (D) made an oral agreement with Mitchill (D) that in consideration of Mitchill's (P) purchase of his property, he would remove an ice house that he maintained on neighboring property. Relying on Lath's (D) promise, Mitchill (P) made a written contract to buy the property. After she received possession of the property, however, Lath (D) refused to remove the ice house. Mitchill (P) sued to enforce the oral agreement. The lower courts ruled in her favor, and Lath (D) appealed, citing the Parole Evidence Rule.

ISSUE: Will an oral agreement which is not collateral, which contradicts express or implied conditions of a written contract, or which consists of terms which the parties could reasonably have been expected to embody in the original writing be permitted to vary from a written contract?

HOLDING AND DECISION: (Andrews, J.) No. An oral agreement is permitted to vary from a written contract only if it is collateral in form, does not contradict express or implied conditions of the written contract, and consists of terms which the parties could not reasonably have been expected to include in the original writing. In other words, the oral agreement must not be so clearly connected with the principal transaction as to be part and parcel of it. The agreement in this case does not satisfy this third requirement. The agreement regarding the ice house is so closely related to the subject of the sales contract that one would expect to find it there. Reversed and remanded.

DISSENT: (Lehman, J.) I agree with the general rule formulated by the majority, but disagree with its application to these facts. I feel that all of the elements necessary to permit an oral agreement to vary from a written one are present in this case.

EDITOR'S ANALYSIS: U.C.C. § 2-202 provides, "Terms with respect to which the writings of the parties agree or which are set forth in a writing intended by the parties as a final expression of their agreement may not be contradicted by evidence of any prior agreement or of a contemporaneous oral agreement but may be explained or supplemented by course of dealing or usage of trade, or by course of performance, and by evidence of consistent additional terms unless the court finds the writing to have been intended as a complete and exclusive statement of the terms of the agreement." The section, according to the official commentator, conclusively rejects any assumption that, because a writing is final in some respects, it is to be interpreted as including all matters agreed upon by the parties.

QUICKNOTES

COLLATERAL AGREEMENT - An agreement that is made prior to or contemporaneous with a written agreement, which is admissible in evidence as long as it is consistent with the written document.

EXPRESS CONDITION - A condition that is expressly stated in the terms of a written instrument.

IMPLIED CONDITION - A condition that is not expressly stated in the terms of an agreement, but which is inferred from the parties' conduct or the type of dealings involved.

NOTES:

HATLEY v. STAFFORD
Farmland lessee (P) v. Lessor (D)
Or. Sup. Ct., 284 Or. 523, 588 P.2d 603 (1978).

NATURE OF CASE: Appeal from award of damages for trespass.

FACT SUMMARY: Hatley (P) claimed that Stafford's (D) right to reclaim leased property was limited by an oral agreement.

CONCISE RULE OF LAW: For an oral term to be inconsistent with a writing, thereby barring its admission as evidence under the parol evidence rule, it must be contradictory to an express provision contained in the writing.

FACTS: Hatley (P) leased a tract of farmland from Stafford (D). The lease was negotiated by the parties themselves, without advice of counsel, and contained a provision whereby Stafford (D) would be permitted to "buy-out" Hatley's (P) right of possession for a maximum of $70 per acre for the purpose of developing a mobile home park. Otherwise, the lease was to run for one year. About six months into the lease, Stafford (D) took possession of the leased property. Hatley (P) contested the action, contending that the parties had orally agreed that the buy-out provision would only apply for a period of 30 to 60 days following the execution of the lease. He then brought suit for trespass, alleging damages in that the wheat crop which was destroyed by Stafford's (D) actions was worth $400 per acre. The trial court permitted introduction of the oral statement into evidence over Stafford's (D) objection and the jury rendered a verdict for Hatley (P). Stafford (D) appealed.

ISSUE: May an oral term which does not expressly contradict a provision contained in a written agreement be admitted into evidence?

HOLDING AND DECISION: (Howell, J.) Yes. The decision as to whether an agreement is only partially integrated (thereby allowing the introduction of additional parol evidence) is one of law, and is therefore made by the court, not the jury. As such, the court may allow the introduction of an oral term where that term is not inconsistent with a written term and where it is not a term that the instant parties would naturally have included in the original agreement. "Inconsistency" has been interpreted narrowly by the courts. For an oral term to be inconsistent with a writing, thereby barring its admission as evidence under the parol evidence rule, it must contradict an express written provision. In the instant case, the writing contained nothing with respect to the duration of the buy-out provision. Moreover, under the circumstances of the case, and especially in light of the unsophisticated level of dealings between the parties, the court could reasonably have found that the term was not one which the parties would naturally have included in the written agreement. Affirmed.

DISSENT: (Lent, J.) The majority's decision "interpreting" the parol evidence rule results in it being rendered virtually meaningless. The asserted oral condition was clearly inconsistent.

EDITOR'S ANALYSIS: The Restatement of Contracts (Second) §§ 209 and 213 address themselves to the subject of integrated agreements. Section 209 states that a writing is integrated when it constitutes the agreement between the parties in final and complete form. The question of integration is to be preliminarily determined by the court. Under § 213, parol evidence may not be admitted to the extent that it is inconsistent with a subsequent integrated agreement.

QUICKNOTES

PAROLE EVIDENCE RULE - Doctrine precluding parties to an agreement from introducing evidence of prior or contemporaneous agreements in order to repudiate or alter the terms of a written contract.

FOUR CORNERS - The express terms of a written document.

PARTIAL INTEGRATION - The incomplete process by which parties to a contract have adopted separate writings as the full and final expression of their agreement.

NOTES:

LONG ISLAND TRUST CO. v. INTERNATIONAL INSTITUTE FOR PACKAGING EDUCATION, LTD.

Bank (P) v. Borrower (D)

N.Y. Ct. App., 38 N.Y.2d 493, 381 N.Y.S.2d 445, 344 N.E.2d 377 (1976).

NATURE OF CASE: Action on promissory note.

FACT SUMMARY: Horowitz (D) and Rochman (D) claimed that their agreement to guarantee a note issued by the bank (P) was subject to an oral condition.

CONCISE RULE OF LAW: An oral condition to a written agreement may be proven so long as it in no way contradicts the express terms of the writing.

FACTS: The bank's (P) 90-day loan of $25,000 to the International Institute (D) was guaranteed by Horowitz (D), Rochman (D), and three others. Rochman (D) contended that the guarantee by himself and the others was made subject to certain conditions agreed to orally by the bank (P). One of those conditions was that no renewal of the note would be made unless all five of the guarantors endorsed it. When the bank agreed to renew the loan for 30 days and to loan an additional $10,000, Rochman (D) and Horowitz (D) endorsed the renewal, allegedly pursuant to the understanding that the other three guarantors would follow suit. However, only two of the others endorsed the note. Nevertheless, the bank (P) renewed it. When the loan was not repaid, the bank (P) brought suit against the International Institute (D) and the four guarantors who had signed the renewal. The trial court granted the bank (P) summary judgment on the ground that the oral conditions were inadmissible as evidence, and the Appellate Division affirmed. Rochman (D) and Horowitz (D) appealed.

ISSUE: May an oral condition to a written agreement be proven where the condition does not contradict the written terms?

HOLDING AND DECISION: (Jasen, J.) Yes. The parol evidence rule generally bars the admission into evidence of oral testimony which is contradictory to the express terms of a writing. However, an oral condition which addresses itself to a subject on which the writing is silent is not contradictory to that writing. As such, the oral condition to the writing may be proven. Under the laws of commercial paper, Horowitz (D) and Rochman (D) would not be liable for their guaranty promise if the oral condition requiring five signatures on a loan renewal is proven. Accordingly, summary judgment in favor of the bank (P) was incorrectly granted. Reversed and remanded.

DISSENT: (Breitel, J.) The oral testimony offered in this case falls squarely within the intended prohibitions of the parol evidence rule. By ruling otherwise, the majority opens the floodgates for those who wish to avoid the obligation of their written promises.

EDITOR'S ANALYSIS: The basis for the rule as it is generally understood is stated in *Pacific Gas & Electric Co. v. Thomas Drayage and Co.*, 69 Cal. 2d 33 (1968): "The test of admissibility of extrinsic evidence to explain the meaning of a written instrument is not whether it appears to the court to be plain and unambiguous on its face, but whether the offered evidence is relevant to prove a meaning to which the language of the instrument is reasonably susceptible." Experience has shown, however, that the rule is much more easily stated than applied.

QUICKNOTES

PAROLE EVIDENCE RULE - Doctrine precluding parties to an agreement from introducing evidence of prior or contemporaneous agreements in order to repudiate or alter the terms of a written contract.

CONDITION - Requirement; potential future occurrence upon which the existence of a legal obligation is dependent.

FOUR CORNERS - The express terms of a written document.

NOTES:

LIPSIT v. LEONARD
Employee (P) v. Employer (D)
64 N.J. 276, 315 A.2d 25 (1974).

NATURE OF CASE: Appeal from dismissal of actions for breach of contract and fraud.

FACT SUMMARY: Lipsit (P) sought damages for the alleged breach of an oral employment contract when he failed to receive a satisfactory offer of an equities interest in Leonard's (D) business, as promised.

CONCISE RULE OF LAW: An action in fraud may be based on a promise, even when the promise itself cannot be enforced under the law of contracts.

FACTS: Lipsit (P) was employed by Leonard (D) for a period of 7½ years. The employment was based on a series of annual letter agreements. Lipsit (P) claimed that the letters were accompanied by oral promises to the effect that Lipsit (P) would be given an equity interest in Leonard's (D) business. He claimed that the promise was the primary inducement in his leaving his former position to work for Leonard (D). The letter agreements did not mention the equity interest save for a vague statement in 1964 that some kind of ownership or profit-sharing plan might be developed that year. The development did not occur and further discussion ceased for several years, at which time Leonard (D) made an offer which Lipsit (P) found unacceptable. Lipsit (P) was terminated soon thereafter. He then brought suit for both breach of contract and fraud based on the alleged oral promises. The trial court, citing the parol evidence rule, disallowed the statements as evidence and dismissed both causes of action. The appellate division affirmed. Lipsit (P) appealed.

ISSUE: May a promise which cannot be enforced in contract provide the basis of an action in fraud?

HOLDING AND DECISION: (Per curiam) Yes. The lower courts were clearly correct in holding that the parol evidence rule bars the admission of the alleged oral statements in contradiction to the terms of the written agreement. Thus the breach of contract action must be dismissed. However, the fraud action should not be. This is because the parol evidence rule does not apply to charges based on an oral fraudulent promise. Fraud, in a case such as this, is a cause of action separate and distinct from the existence of a contract. It should be noted, however, that damages for an action for fraud in the inducement are limited to actual pecuniary loss or out-of-pocket expenses. It appears that Lipsit (P) may have difficulty in proving such damages. However he should be allowed to try if he so desires. Reversed in part and remanded.

EDITOR'S ANALYSIS: The fact that a transaction may give rise to both a contract and tort claim was discussed in *Hargrave v. Oki Nursery*, 636 F.2d 897 (2nd Gir. 1980). "Where the conduct alleged breaches a legal duty which exists independent of contractual relations between the parties, a plaintiff may sue in tort [as well as in contract]." Furthermore, the court noted "the plaintiff may recover in tort [in such cases] whether or not he has a valid claim for breach of contract."

QUICKNOTES

FRAUD IN THE INDUCEMENT - Occurs when a testator is induced to execute a testamentary instrument as a result of the misrepresentation of certain facts existing at the time of its creation that may have effected the manner in which the testator disposed of his property.

PAROL EVIDENCE RULE - Doctrine precluding parties to an agreement from introducing evidence of prior or contemporaneous agreements in order to repudiate or alter the terms of a written contract.

NOTES:

LaFAZIA v. HOWE
Delicatessan seller (P) v. Buyers (D)
R.I. Sup. Ct., 575 A.2d 182 (1990).

NATURE OF CASE: Appeal from summary judgment awarding damages for breach of promissory note.

FACT SUMMARY: After the Howes (D) failed to pay a promissory note they had given to LaFazia (P) as part of the purchase price for his delicatessen, they argued that, regardless of a disclaimer clause in the sales contract, the contract should be rescinded because they relied on material misrepresentations made by LaFazia (P) during negotiations.

CONCISE RULE OF LAW: A party who has executed a contract containing a merger clause and a provision disclaiming all prior representations may not successfully claim reliance on such representations.

FACTS: Mr. and Mrs. Howe (D) entered into a contract with LaFazia (P) to purchase a delicatessen for $60,000 down and a $30,000 promissory note. Despite initial misgivings about the profitability of the enterprise, the Howes (D) went ahead with the purchase after LaFazia (P) assured them that the business brought in over $450,000 a year. Clause 9 of the Memorandum of Sale stated that the Howes (D) were to rely on their own judgment and not on any representations of LaFazia (P) regarding the profits of the business. Clause 10 stated that no warranties had been made by LaFazia (P) and that the assets were to be sold "as is." When the deli failed to turn a profit, the Howes (D) sold the business with $10,000 on the promissory note still outstanding. LaFazia (P) sued for breach of the promissory note and the Howes (D) counterclaimed, arguing that LaFazia (P) made specific misrepresentations about the business in order to induce them to enter into the contract. LaFazia (P) moved for summary judgment on the claim and counterclaim, which the trial court granted. On appeal, the Howes (D) argued that the contract should be rescinded and that summary judgment was inappropriate because whether or not there was an intention to induce was an issue of material fact.

ISSUE: May a party who has executed a contract containing a merger clause and a provision disclaiming all prior representations successfully claim reliance on such representations?

HOLDING AND DECISION: (Fay, J.) No. A party who has executed a contract containing a merger clause and a provision disclaiming all prior representations may not successfully claim reliance on such representations. Here, the merger and nonreliance clauses contained in the sales contract precluded the Howes (D) from asserting that LaFazia (P) made material misrepresentations regarding the condition of the business. The provision in this case was a specific disclaimer, stating that the

Howes (D) were to rely on their own judgment regarding the very matter about which the Howes (D) later claimed to have been defrauded—the profitability of the business. The merger and disclaimer clauses were not procured by fraud but instead were read and understood by the Howes (D), who were represented by counsel at closing. Therefore, the Howes' (D) alleged reliance on LaFazia's (P) oral representations was not justifiable. To hold otherwise would make it impossible for two businessmen to ever agree that a buyer was not buying in reliance on the representations of a seller. Affirmed.

EDITOR'S ANALYSIS: Under the so-called Danaan rule invoked in this case, a general merger clause does not bar parol evidence of misrepresentation, but a specific merger clause disclaiming specific representations is deemed to bar such evidence. This is the minority rule, and it has met with unanimous disapproval among law review commentators. Under the majority rule, on the other hand, parol evidence is admissible to demonstrate that the agreement is void or voidable or to prove an action for deceit. In other words, fraud vitiates everything it touches. The tension between the two rules arises out of the need for parties to be able to argue that a purchaser is relying solely on his own inspection and the belief that no one should be able to contractually insulate himself from fraud.

QUICKNOTES

PAROL EVIDENCE RULE - Doctrine precluding parties to an agreement from introducing evidence of prior or contemporaneous agreements in order to repudiate or alter the terms of a written contract.

MATERIAL FACT - A fact without the existence of which a contract would not have been entered.

NOTES:

HOFFMAN v. CHAPMAN
Buyers of lot (D) v. Sellers (P)
Md. Ct. App., 182 Md. 208, 34 A.2d 438 (1943).

NATURE OF CASE: Appeal from reformation of a deed.

FACT SUMMARY: The Hoffmans (D) purchased part of a lot from the Chapmans (P) who accidentally deeded the entire lot.

CONCISE RULE OF LAW: If there is clear, convincing and strong evidence of a mutual mistake, the courts will reform an instrument to reflect the true intent of the parties.

FACTS: The Chapmans (P) owned a large lot containing several dwellings. The Chapmans (P) sold a portion of the tract, containing a bungalow, to the Hoffmans (D) who knew they were only purchasing a part of the lot. Through an error, the deed conveyed the entire lot. When the mistake was discovered, the Hoffmans (D) refused to convey the portion of the lot not covered by the original sale to the Chapmans (P). The court reformed the deed. The Hoffmans (D) alleged that the deed description rendered the contract so vague as to evidence that no meeting of the minds as to what was being sold occurred and the transaction was therefore void. The parol evidence rule was also raised as barring the admission of evidence to contradict the deed.

ISSUE: May a contract be reformed where there is strong, unequivocal and convincing evidence of a mutual mistake?

HOLDING AND DECISION: (Delaplaine, J.) Yes. Equity will reform an instrument where there is clear, convincing and strong proof of a mutual mistake. Here, there was the sales contract and a plot clearly showing the portion of the lot which the parties intended to be conveyed. The scribner who made the mistake worked as an agent for both parties. Under such circumstances, equity would be remiss in not conforming the deed to the intentions of the parties. Under such circumstances the parol evidence rule will not bar the introduction of such evidence. The plot and the sales contract clearly describe the property to be conveyed and the contract is not void for vagueness. The negligence herein was minor and resulted in no detriment to the Hoffmans (D), nor were they in any way misled by it. Affirmed.

EDITOR'S ANALYSIS: A mistake of law in the making of an agreement or the violation of a positive legal duty of care will normally prevent reformation absent additional factors. *Benesh v. Travelers' Ins. Co.*, 14 N.D. 39 and *Boyle v. Maryland State Faif*, 150 Md. 333. A ministerial mistake in drafting, even when by an attorney, may be reformed by equity to reflect the real intent of the parties. *Archer v. McClure*, 166 N.C. 140.

QUICKNOTES

MUTUAL MISTAKE - A mistake by both parties to a contract, who are in agreement as to what the contract terms should be, but the agreement as written fails to reflect that common intent; such contracts are voidable or subject to reformation.

PAROL EVIDENCE RULE - Doctrine precluding parties to an agreement from introducing evidence of prior or contemporaneous agreements in order to repudiate or alter the terms of a written contract.

REFORMATION OF CONTRACT - An equitable remedy whereby the written terms of an agreement are altered in order to reflect the true intent of the parties; reformation requires a demonstration by clear and convincing evidence of mutual mistake by the parties to the contract.

NOTES:

PACIFIC GAS & ELECTRIC CO. v. G. W. THOMAS DRAYAGE & RIGGING CO.

Utility company (P) v. Steam turbine repairer (D)
Ca. Sup. Ct., 69 Cal. 2d 33, 442 P.2d 641 (1968).

NATURE OF CASE: Action for damages for breach of a contract.

FACT SUMMARY: Thomas (D) contracted to repair Pacific's (P) steam turbine and to perform work at its own risk and expense and to indemnify Pacific (P) against all loss and damage. Thomas (D) also agreed not to procure less than $50,000 insurance to cover liability for injury to property. But when the turbine rotor was damaged, Pacific (P) claimed it was covered under that policy, while Thomas (D) said it was only to cover injury to third persons.

CONCISE RULE OF LAW: The test of admissibility of extrinsic evidence to explain the meaning of a written instrument is not whether it appears to the court to be plain and unambiguous on its face but whether the offered evidence is relevant to prove a meaning to which the language of the instrument is reasonably susceptible.

FACTS: Thomas (D) contracted to replace the upper metal cover on Pacific's (P) steam turbine and agreed to perform all work "at [its] own risk and expense" and to "indemnify" Pacific (P) against all loss, damage, expense, and liability resulting from injury to property arising out of or in any way connected with performance of the contract. Thomas (D) agreed to obtain not less than $50,000 insurance to cover liability for injury to property. Pacific (P) was to be an additional named insured, but the policy was to contain a cross-liability clause extending the coverage of Pacific's (P) property. During the work, the cover fell, damaging the exposed rotor in the amount of $25,144.51. Thomas (D) during trial offered to prove that its conduct and, under similar contracts entered into by Pacific (P), the indemnity clause were meant to cover injury to third person's property only, not to Pacific's (P).

ISSUE: Was Thomas' (D) offered evidence relevant to proving a meaning to which the language of the instrument was susceptible?

HOLDING AND DECISION: (Traynor, J.) Yes. While the trial court admitted that the contract was "the classic language for a third party indemnity provision," it held that the plain language of the contract would give a meaning covering Pacific's (P) damage. However, this admission by the court clearly shows the ambiguous nature of the agreement and the need for extrinsic evidence in order to clarify the intentions of the parties. Extrinsic evidence for the purpose of showing the intent of the parties could be excluded only when it is feasible to determine the meaning of the words from the instrument alone. Rational interpretation requires at least an initial consideration of all credible evidence to prove the intention of the parties.

EDITOR'S ANALYSIS: This case strongly disapproves of the "plain meaning rule," which states that if a writing appears clear and unambiguous on its face, the meaning must be determined from "the four corners" of the writing without considering any extrinsic evidence at all. The trial court applied this rule. However, the rule, while generally accepted but widely condemned, would exclude evidence of trade usage, prior dealings of the parties, and even circumstances surrounding the creation of the agreement. U.C.C. § 2-202 expressly throws out the plain meaning rule. Instead, it allows use of evidence of a course of performance or dealing to explain the writing "unless carefully negated." Here, C. J. Traynor greatly expanded the admission of extrinsic evidence to show intent. When he says it should not be admitted only when it is feasible "to determine the meaning the parties gave to the words from the instrument alone," he is saying in all practicality that extrinsic evidence to show intent should be admissible in just about any case, that rarely will the instrument be so exact as to clearly show intent.

QUICKNOTES

PAROLE EVIDENCE RULE - Doctrine precluding parties to an agreement from introducing evidence of prior or contemporaneous agreements in order to repudiate or alter the terms of a written contract.

FOUR CORNERS - The express terms of a written document.

EXTRINSIC EVIDENCE - Evidence that is not contained within the text of a document or contract but which is derived from the parties' statements or the circumstances under which the agreement was made.

NOTES:

MUNDY v. LUMBERMAN'S MUT. CAS. CO.
Insurance company (D) v. Silverware owner (P)
783 F.2d 21 (1st Cir. 1986).

NATURE OF CASE: Appeal from summary judgment denying damages for breach of contract.

FACT SUMMARY: After Lumberman's Mutual Casualty Co. (D) limited recovery on loss of silverware to $1,000, the Mundys (P) sued for unlimited coverage, arguing that they had not received adequate notice of the new policy.

CONCISE RULE OF LAW: An insured is bound by the terms of a renewal insurance policy as long as he receives the policy.

FACTS: When Lumberman's (D) renewed the Mundys' (P) insurance policy, it sent them the policy and a summary of the policy, both written in straightforward English using readable print. Both the policy and the summary contained Lumberman's (D) new $1,000 limit on recovery for loss of silverware. After their silverware was stolen, the Mundys (P) sued for the full value of their silverware, in excess of the $1,000 limit, arguing that the limitation had been buried in the policy's fine print. The district court, concluding that Lumberman's (D) notice was adequate, granted its motion for summary judgment. The Mundys (P) appealed.

ISSUE: Is an insured bound by the terms of a renewal insurance policy as long as he receives a copy of it?

HOLDING AND DECISION: (Breyer, J.) Yes. An insured is bound by the terms of a renewal insurance policy as long as he receives a copy of it. In this case, even a casual reading of the material mailed to the Mundys (P) would have given them adequate notice of the policy change. Far from being buried in fine print, the renewal policy plainly stated the $1,000 limitation under a boldface headline reading "Special Limits of Liability" and then reiterated it in the summary of changes accompanying the policy. Affirmed.

EDITOR'S ANALYSIS: The holding in *Mundy* is derived from the common law "duty to read" rule, which is commonly applied when interpreting fine-print terms in form contracts. According to this rule, unless a party can show that facts and circumstances prevented him from actually reading a contract, he is bound by it. A party who signs an instrument manifests assent to it and may not later complain that he did not read it or understand its contents. The basic justification for the rule is that no one could rely on a signed document if the other party could avoid the transaction by saying he had not read it. The same principle applies even if the contract has not been signed, as in *Mundy*, if the mere acceptance of a copy of the contract implies assent to its terms.

QUICKNOTES

ACCEPTANCE - Assent to the specified terms of an offer, resulting in the formation of a binding agreement.

MUTUAL ASSENT - A requirement of a valid contract that the parties possess a mutuality of assent as manifested by the terms of the agreement and not by a hidden intent.

NOTES:

HENNINGSEN v. BLOOMFIELD MOTORS, INC.

Driver (P) v. Automobile dealership (D)

N.J. Sup. Ct., 32 N.J. 358, 161 A.2d 69 (1960).

NATURE OF CASE: Action for breach of warranty.

FACT SUMMARY: Chrysler (D) limited damages to replacement for mechanical defects.

CONCISE RULE OF LAW: Where there is a gross disparity of bargaining power, a disclaimer of an implied warranty of merchantability and of the obligations arising therefrom is invalid as contrary to public policy.

FACTS: Mrs. Henningsen (P) was severely injured when a new Plymouth, purchased ten days before from Bloomfield Motors (D), crashed due to a mechanical defect. Henningsen (P) brought suit against both Bloomfield (D) and Chrysler (D) for damages arising from their breach of an implied warranty of merchantability. Chrysler (D) defended on the basis of a fine print clause on the reverse side of the sales contract which disclaimed all express or implied warranties and limited liability to repair of parts delivered to the factory. The court found the disclaimer ineffective and rendered judgment for Henningsen (P).

ISSUE: Where there is a gross disparity of bargaining power, may the manufacturer disclaim all warranties?

HOLDING AND DECISION: (Francis, J.) No. All of the major automobile manufacturers use a standardized contract containing the same disclaimer clause. The consumer is placed in a "take it or leave it" position. If he wants a new car, he must accept the conditions. No bargaining is present. The automobile companies have combined to utilize their superior bargaining power to remove all choice from the consumer. The dealers may not even modify the agreement. Most consumers lack the ability or opportunity to determine whether the automobile is in good working order. They must rely on the manufacturer/dealer who has disclaimed all liability beyond repair. The disclaimer itself is in fine print on the reverse side of the contract. It is not even labelled as a disclaimer or limited warranty. It does not specifically state that it excludes claims for personal injury. The buyer is not told to read it and it is not explained. We find that under all of the facts herein, that public policy requires that attempted disclaimers, based on unequal bargaining power, which attempt to waive the implied warranty of merchantability and the liabilities/obligations arising therefrom are invalid. Affirmed.

EDITOR'S ANALYSIS: Where parties are of equal bargaining power, a waiver of all warranties, including the implied warranty of merchantability, is deemed valid. Where a party has a reasoned choice, he may waive such warranties and his contractual obligations will be sustained. Exculpatory clauses such as the one in Henningsen have also been invalidated in consumer financing transactions, limitations required by common carriers, warehouse receipts, etc.

QUICKNOTES

UNCONSCIONABILITY - Rule of law whereby a court may excuse performance of a contract, or of a particular contract term, if it determines that such term(s) are unduly oppressive or unfair to one party to the contract.

WARRANTY - An assurance by one party that another may rely on a certain representation of fact.

IMPLIED WARRANTY OF MERCHANTABILITY - An implied promise made by a merchant in a contract for the sale of goods that such goods are suitable for the purpose for which they are purchased.

NOTES:

RICHARDS v. RICHARDS
Wife (P) v. Husband (D)
Wis. Sup. Ct., 181 Wis.2d 1007, 513 N.W.2d 118 (1994).

NATURE OF CASE: Review of exculpatory contract case dismissed with prejudice and affirmed on appeal.

FACT SUMMARY: When Jerilyn Richards (P) was injured while riding in her husband's (D) truck after signing a form contract releasing the truck's owner (D) from all liability for accidents to passengers, she argued that the form release was void as against public policy.

CONCISE RULE OF LAW: An exculpatory contract will be deemed void when the public policy of imposing liability on persons whose conduct creates an unreasonable risk of harm outweighs the public policy of freedom of contract.

FACTS: Jerilyn Richards (P) signed a "Passenger Authorization" form so she could accompany her husband Leo (D) when he worked as an over-the-road truck driver. Jerilyn Richards (P) was injured while riding as a passenger in a truck operated by Leo (D) and owned by Monkem Co. (D), her husband's (D) employer. Monkem Co. (D) claimed that the form was an exculpatory contract relieving Monkem Co. (D) and all of its affiliates from any and all liability for harm to the person signing the form. Jerilyn Richards (P) claimed that the form contravened public policy and was unenforceable. The lower court's enforcement of the exculpatory contract was affirmed on appeal, and Jerilyn Richards (P) appealed.

ISSUE: Will an exculpatory contract be deemed void when the public policy of imposing liability on persons whose conduct creates an unreasonable risk of harm outweighs the public policy of freedom of contract?

HOLDING AND DECISION: (Abrahamson, J.) Yes. An exculpatory contract will be deemed void when the public policy of imposing liability on persons whose conduct creates an unreasonable risk of harm outweighs the public policy of freedom of contract. First of all, in this case the title of the form was misleading since it would not be reasonably clear to the signer that a form entitled "Passenger Authorization" is in reality the passenger's agreement to release Monkem Co. (D) (and others) from liability. Secondly, the release is extremely broad and all-inclusive. The very breadth of the release underlines its one-sidedness; it is unreasonably favorable to Monkem Co. (D), which drafted it. Thirdly, the standard fine-print form was not negotiated or discussed by the parties before signing, and there was an inequality of bargaining power since Monkem Co. (D) wrote the agreement and also derived some benefit from it. The combination of these three factors leads to the conclusion that the contract is void and unenforceable as against public policy. Reversed.

EDITOR'S ANALYSIS: Form contracts are frequently associated with inequality of bargaining power. The general contract law assent doctrine seems violated by such form contracts. Speed and expediency may, however, serve to make them necessary in certain circumstances.

QUICKNOTES
FREEDOM OF CONTRACT - The constitutional right to enter into contractual relationships and freely determine the parameters of party obligations without undue legal interference.

NOTES:

BROEMMER v. ABORTION SERVICES OF PHOENIX

Abortion patient (P) v. Clinic (D)

Ariz. Sup. Ct., 173 Ariz. 148, 840 P.2d 1013 (1992).

NATURE OF CASE: Appeal from summary judgment denying damages for medical malpractice.

FACT SUMMARY: When Broemmer (P) filed a malpractice complaint against Abortion Services of Phoenix (D), Abortion Services (D) argued that Broemmer (P) had given up her right to a jury trial when she signed a standardized arbitration agreement prior to treatment.

CONCISE RULE OF LAW: An adhesion contract will be enforced unless it is unconscionable or beyond the reasonable expectations of the parties.

FACTS: When Broemmer (P), a 21-year-old, unmarried high school graduate, arrived for her appointment at Abortion Services of Phoenix (D), she was told to complete three forms, one of which was an agreement to arbitrate any dispute resulting from the fees and/or services of Abortion Services (D). The arbitration agreement included a provision requiring that any arbitrator appointed be a licensed obstetrician/gynecologist. The clinic staff did not attempt to explain the agreement to Broemmer (P) nor indicate that she was free to refuse to sign. Broemmer (P) filled out and signed the forms. When a doctor at Abortion Services (D) performed the abortion the following day, he punctured her uterus, requiring her to seek medical treatment. Broemmer (P) filed a malpractice complaint. Abortion Services (D) moved to dismiss on the ground that arbitration was required, and the trial court granted summary judgment. The court of appeal held that, although the agreement to arbitrate was an adhesion contract, it was enforceable because it did not fall outside Broemmer's (P) reasonable expectations and was not unconscionable. Broemmer (P) appealed.

ISSUE: Will an adhesion contract be enforced unless it is unconscionable or beyond the reasonable expectations of the parties?

HOLDING AND DECISION: (Moeller, J.) Yes. An adhesion contract will be enforced unless it is unconscionable or beyond the reasonable expectations of the parties. An adhesion contract is a standardized form offered on a "take it or leave it" basis which the consumer must accept without bargaining if she wants to obtain the desired product or service. The arbitration agreement signed by Broemmer (P) was an adhesion contract because it was prepared by Abortion Services (D), presented to Broemmer (P) as a condition of treatment on a "take it or leave it" basis, and its terms were nonnegotiable. Whether or not it was also enforceable depends on whether it was beyond Broemmer's (P) reasonable expectations. In this case, it was not reasonable to expect a high

school graduate to agree to arbitrate her medical malpractice claim, thus waiving her right to a jury trial, as a consequence of filling out three forms given her highly emotional state and her inexperience in commercial matters. Furthermore, it would be unreasonable to enforce the critical provision requiring that the arbitrator be a obstetrician/gynecologist when it was not a negotiated term and Abortion Services (D) failed to explain it or call attention to it. Because the arbitration agreement fell outside of Broemmer's (P) reasonable expectations and is, therefore, unenforceable, it is unnecessary to determine whether the contract is also unconscionable. Reversed and remanded.

DISSENT: (Martone, J.) The majority's decision reflects a preference for litigation over arbitration which is not in accord with current public policy considerations. There is nothing in this case that warrants a finding that an agreement to arbitrate a malpractice claim was not within the reasonable expectations of the parties. On the contrary, Broemmer (P), an adult, had an opportunity to read the document, which was legible and in bold letters, containing an agreement that was not bizarre, oppressive, or contrary to prior negotiations.

EDITOR'S ANALYSIS: *Broemmer* creates an exception to the traditional duty to read rule where the terms of the contract are unfair under the circumstances. In cases like *Broemmer*, the manifestation of assent that is ordinarily implied by a signature is insufficient because the assent is not reasoned or knowing. Consent requires an understanding of the provision in question (which Broemmer (P) admitted she did not have) as well as a reasonable opportunity to accept or decline the provision. Even if these two criteria are present, courts will still refuse to enforce a clause that is unconscionable or contrary to public policy.

QUICKNOTES

UNCONSCIONABILITY - Rule of law whereby a court may excuse performance of a contract, or of a particular contract term, if it determines that such term(s) are unduly oppressive or unfair to one party to the contract.

MUTUAL ASSENT - A requirement of a valid contract that the parties possess a mutuality of assent as manifested by the terms of the agreement and not by a hidden intent.

ACCEPTANCE - Assent to the specified terms of an offer, resulting in the formation of a binding agreement.

ADHESION CONTRACT - A contract, usually in standardized form, that is prepared by one party and offered to another, whose terms are so disproportionately in favor of the drafting party that courts tend to question the equality of bargaining power in reaching the agreement.

CHAPTER 4
POLICING THE BARGAIN

QUICK REFERENCE RULES OF LAW

1. **Competency to Contract.** Absent misrepresentation or tortious conduct, a minor who disaffirms a contract for the purchase of a nonnecessity may recover his purchase price without liability for damage, depreciation, or other diminution in value. (Halbman v. Lemke)

2. **Competency to Contract.** When a party's will has been overborne, so that in effect his actions are not his own, a charge of undue influence may be sustained. (Odorizzi v. Bloomfield School Dist.)

3. **Revisions of Contractual Duty.** A contract modification is voidable on the ground of duress when the party claiming duress establishes that its agreement to the modification was obtained by means of a wrongful threat from the other party which precluded the first party's exercise of free will. (Austin Instrument, Inc.v. Loral Corp.)

4. **Revisions of Contractual Duty.** A promise to pay a man for doing that which he is already under contract to do is without consideration. (Alaska Packers' Association v. Domenico)

5. **Revisions of Contractual Duty.** Where unforeseen circumstances make the performance of a contract unduly burdensome, and the parties agree in view of the changed conditions to an adjustment in price, a new contract supported by consideration is formed. (Brian Constr. & Dev. Co. v. Brighenti)

6. **Revisions of Contractual Duty.** Unless a contract is for the sale of goods, it is undisputed that the contract can be modified orally although it provides it can be modified only in writing. (Universal Builders, Inc. v. Moon Motor Lodge, Inc.)

7. **Revisions of Contractual Duty.** Mere refusal to pay a debt/contract is not duress. (Hackley v. Headley)

8. **Revisions of Contractual Duty.** A creditor cannot escape the discharging effect of a draft sent in satisfaction of a debt by adding words of non-acceptance. (Marton Remodeling v. Jensen)

9. **Revisions of Contractual Duty.** Agents, employees, and public officials acting within the scope of their employment or official duties cannot claim a reward offered to the general public for the performance of some specified act even though, as a general rule, it may be claimed by any person who performs such act. (Denney v. Reppert)

10. **Mistake, Misrepresentation, Warranty, and Nondisclosure.** An agreement may be rescinded if the consideration paid by one of the parties is so disproportionate to the value which he receives as to suggest constructive fraud. (Jackson v. Seymour)

11. **Mistake, Misrepresentation, Warranty, and Nondisclosure.** When there is a mutual mistake going to the very substance of what is being sold, no contract exists. (Sherwood v. Walker)

12. **Mistake, Misrepresentation, Warranty, and Nondisclosure.** A prompt rescission due to an honest clerical error in a bid for a building contract may relieve a party from an unfair and unintended bargain. (Elsinore Union Elementary School Dist. v. Kastorff)

13. **Mistake, Misrepresentation, Warranty, and Nondisclosure.** A representation that expresses the seller's opinion does not constitute an express warranty. (Tribe v. Peterson)

14. **Mistake, Misrepresentation, Warranty, and Nondisclosure.** In North Carolina, the doctrine of mutual mistake regarding a physical condition of real property is not a ground for the rescission of the sale of such property. (Hinson v. Jefferson)

15. **Mistake, Misrepresentation, Warranty, and Nondisclosure.** Innocent misrepresentations that reasonably induce reliance amount to an express warranty of habitability which, if breached, entitles the injured party to damages limited to the diminished value of the building. (Johnson v. Healy)

16. **Mistake, Misrepresentation, Warranty, and Nondisclosure.** When a home seller discloses only a portion of the information he has but leads the buyer to believe he has made a full disclosure, he will be liable if the buyer acts in reliance on that partial disclosure. (Cushman v. Kirby)

17. **Changed Circumstances Justifying Nonperformance.** In contracts in which the performance depends on the continued existence of a given person or thing, a condition is implied that the impossibility of performance arising from the perishing of the person or thing shall excuse the performance. (Taylor v. Caldwell)

18. **Changed Circumstances Justifying Nonperformance.** When a party by his own contract absolutely engages to do an act, performance is not excused by inevitable accident or other unforeseen contingency not within his control. (Tompkins v. Dudley)

19. **Changed Circumstances Justifying Nonperformance.** When destruction of the subject building renders performance impossible and such a possibility was not contemplated by either party, the owner of the subject building is liable for the amount of work done which had become so far identified with it as that but for the destruction it would have inured to him as contemplated by the contract. (Carroll v. Bowersock)

20. **Changed Circumstances Justifying Nonperformance.** A standard force majeure clause in a lease will not relieve a lessee of forfeiture for failure to comply with a condition mandating liability insurance. (Kel Kim Corp. v. Central Markets, Inc.)

21. **Changed Circumstances Justifying Nonperformance.** An act of God which damages or destroys goods to be sold under contract is justification for nonperformance of the contract only where the goods are specifically identified as the contract's subject matter. (Bunge Corp. v. Recker)

22. **Changed Circumstances Justifying Nonperformance.** While performance may be rendered impossible if it can only be accomplished with extreme and unreasonable difficulty, expense, injury, or loss, a mere increase in cost alone is not a sufficient excuse for nonperformance. (American Trading & Prod. Corp. v. Shell Int'l Marine, Ltd.)

23. **Changed Circumstances Justifying Nonperformance.** Where the object of one of the parties is the basis upon which both parties contract, the duties of performance are constructively conditioned upon the attainment of that object. (Krell v. Henry)

24. **Changed Circumstances Justifying Nonperformance.** The defense of commercial frustration requires that to excuse his nonpayment of rent a lessee must prove (1) that the risk of the frustrating event was not reasonably foreseeable, and (2) that the purpose for which the property was leased was totally or nearly totally destroyed. (Lloyd v. Murphy)

25. **Changed Circumstances Justifying Nonperformance.** A defendant may rely on frustration of purpose as a defense to a breach of contract claim if the risk of the occurrence of the frustrating event is not allocated by the contract to the defendant. (Chase Precast Corp. v. John J. Paonessa Co.)

26. Unconscionable Inequality. Courts of equity will not decree a specific performance where the contract is founded in fraud, imposition, mistake, undue advantage, or gross misapprehension—or where it is not certain, equitable, reasonable, mutual, on sufficient consideration, and consistent with public policy. (Woollums v. Horsley)

27. Unconscionable Inequality. Courts may avoid enforcement of a bargain that is shown to be unconscionable by reason of gross inadequacy of consideration. (Waters v. Min Ltd.)

28. Unconscionable Inequality. In order to find a contract clause "unconscionable" requires some showing of an absence of meaningful choice on the part of one of the parties together with contract terms which are unreasonably favorable to the other party. (Brower v. Gateway 2000, Inc)

29. Unconscionable Inequality. A clause permitting a buyer to unilaterally cancel an order is invalid if unreasonable and the buyer is in a substantially superior bargaining position. (Gianni Sport Ltd. v. Gantos Inc.)

HALBMAN v. LEMKE
Car purchaser (P) v. Seller (D)
Wis. Sup. Ct., 99 Wis. 2d 241, 298 N.W.2d 562 (1980).

NATURE OF CASE: Appeal from judgment in action to disaffirm contract.

FACT SUMMARY: Lemke (D) sought restitution for damage caused to a car by Halbman (P), a minor, before he disaffirmed the purchase.

CONCISE RULE OF LAW: Absent misrepresentation or tortious conduct, a minor who disaffirms a contract for the purchase of a nonnecessity may recover his purchase price without liability for damage, depreciation, or other diminution in value.

FACTS: Lemke (D) sold a car to Halbman (P), a minor, for the price of $1,250. After $1,100 of the purchase price had been paid, the car developed trouble. Halbman (P) took the car to a garage and had it repaired at a cost of $637.40. Halbman (P) did not pay the repair bill. Several months later, Halbman (P) informed Lemke (D) that he was disaffirming the contract and requested the return of his $1,100. Lemke (D) refused. Subsequently, the garage executed a lien for the repair bill and sold the car's engine and transmission. The car was later vandalized, rendering it unsalvageable. Halbman (P) brought suit, seeking the return of his $1,100. Lemke (D) countersued for the $150 due on the purchase price. The trial court found the contract to be disaffirmed and entered judgment for Halbman (P) in the sum of $1,100. Lemke (D) appealed, contending that Halbman (P) should have been required to make restitution for the damage caused to the car before disaffirmance.

ISSUE: Must a minor who disaffirms a contract for the purchase of an nonnecessary item make restitution for the diminution in value caused to that item?

HOLDING AND DECISION: (Callow, J.) No. The jurisdictions are split over the resolution of this issue. However, it appears that the better view is the one which provides that absent misrepresentation or tortious conduct, a minor who disaffirms a contract for the purchase of an nonnecessary item may recover his purchase price without liability for damage, depreciation, or other diminution in value. This view is more in keeping with the purpose behind the laws permitting a minor to disaffirm a contract, i.e. to protect him from improvident dealings with more experienced, and sometimes unethical, adults. To force Halbman (P) to compensate Lemke (D) for the damage inflicted upon his car, would be, in effect, to force him to undertake the responsibilities of his contract. Such a decision, if desired, should come from the legislature, and not the courts. Affirmed.

EDITOR'S ANALYSIS: Another justification usually given for the disaffirmance of a contract is the mental incompetency of one of the parties. At common law, this factor rendered the contract entirely void. However, most modern jurisdictions have modified the common law rule and now consider such contracts voidable at the insistence of the afflicted party only. Thus, in certain situations, a mentally incompetent person may be able to enforce a contract which he has made to his advantage.

QUICKNOTES

CONTRACT FOR NECESARRIES - A contract for things that are necessary to subsist or to maintain a manner of living, such as food, clothing and shelter.

CAPACITY TO CONTRACT - The legal and physical ability to enter into a contractual agreement, typically characterized by the ability to understand the consequences of one's actions.

VOIDABLE - A valid act that may later be avoided due to some defect, but that is binding until repudiated.

DISAFFIRMANCE - Words or actions evidencing an intent not to abide by the terms of a previous transaction.

NOTES:

ODORIZZI v. BLOOMFIELD SCHOOL DISTRICT

Teacher (P) v. School district (D)

Cal. Ct. App., 246 Cal. App. 2d 123 (1966).

NATURE OF CASE: Action to rescind resignation based on undue influence.

FACT SUMMARY: Odorizzi (P) was arrested on homosexual charges. Immediately after his release, the School District (D) convinced him to resign.

CONCISE RULE OF LAW: When a party's will has been overborne, so that in effect his actions are not his own, a charge of undue influence may be sustained.

FACTS: Odorizzi (P) was arrested for criminal homosexual activities. At the time he was under contract as a teacher for the School District (D). Immediately after he was released on bail the School District (D) convinced him to resign. Odorizzi (P) was subsequently acquitted of the charges, but was refused re-employment by the District (D). Odorizzi (P) brought suit to rescind his resignation. He charged duress, menace, fraud and undue influence. He claimed that the superintendent of the District (D) and the principal of his school came to his apartment immediately after his release. He had not slept in nearly 40 hours and was under severe emotional and physical stress. He was told that if he did not immediately resign, the District (D) would be forced to suspend him and then dismiss him, which would occasion embarrassing and humiliating publicity. However, if he resigned the matter would be kept quiet and his chance for future jobs would not be impaired. The trial court found nothing wrong with these actions, no confidential relationship existed, and that the District (D) would have been forced by law to suspend Odorizzi (P).

ISSUE: Where a party's physical and emotional condition is such that excessive persuasion leads to his own will being overborne, can he charge undue influence so as to rescind a resignation or contract?

HOLDING AND DECISION: (Fleming, J.) Yes. While none of Odorizzi's (P) allegations have any basis, he has made out a prima facie case of undue influence. In essence, the charge involves the use of excessive pressures to persuade one vulnerable to such pressures to decide a matter contrary to his own judgment. Extreme weakness or susceptibility is an important factor in establishing undue influence. It is normally found in cases of extreme youth or age or sickness. While it normally involves fiduciary or other confidential relationships, they are not necessary to the action. Here, extreme pressures were leveled against Odorizzi (P). He had just gone through an arrest, booking and interrogation procedure for a crime which, if well publicized, would

subject him to public humiliation. He was threatened with such publicity if he did not immediately resign. He was approached at his apartment, immediately after his release. He was not given the opportunity to think the matter over or to obtain outside advice. He was told that in any event he would be suspended and dismissed. These factors present a jury issue. If Odorizzi (P) can establish that he wouldn't have resigned but for these pressures and the jury finds that they were unreasonable and overbore his will, Odorizzi (P) could rescind his resignation. Judgment reversed and remanded for a new trial.

EDITOR'S ANALYSIS: Many types of contracts may be rescinded for undue influence. Mortmaine statutes are in effect in some states. These hold that bequests made to churches shortly before death and after a visit by religious leaders are void and unenforceable. Wills may be declared invalid where they were procured through undue influence. Contracts to sell land for far less than its value and transfers made in fear of civil or criminal prosecution are other examples.

QUICKNOTES

UNDUE INFLUENCE - Improper influence that deprives the individual freedom of choice or substitutes another's choice for the person's own choice.

RESCISSION - The canceling of an agreement and the return of the parties to their positions prior to the formation of the contract.

NOTES:

AUSTIN INSTRUMENT, INC. v. LORAL CORP.
Subcontractor (P) v. Radar set manufacturer (D)
N.Y. Ct. App., 29 N.Y.2d 124, 272 N.E.2d 533 (1971).

NATURE OF CASE: Action to recover damages for breach of contract.

FACT SUMMARY: Austin (P) threatened to withhold delivery of precision parts unless Loral (D) would raise the contract price.

CONCISE RULE OF LAW: A contract modification is voidable on the ground of duress when the party claiming duress establishes that its agreement to the modification was obtained by means of a wrongful threat from the other party which precluded the first party's exercise of free will.

FACTS: Loral (D) was under contract to produce radar sets for the government. The contract contained a liquidated damage clause for late delivery and a cancellation clause in case of default by Loral (D). Loral (D), who did a substantial portion of its business with the government, awarded Austin (P) a subcontract to supply some of the precision parts. Subsequently, Austin (P) threatened to cease delivery of the parts unless Loral (D) consented to substantial increases in the subcontract price. After contacting 10 manufacturers of precision gears and finding none who could produce the parts in time to meet its commitment to the government, Loral (D) acceded to Austin's (P) demand.

ISSUE: Is a contract modification acceded to by one party under circumstances amounting to economic duress enforceable against that party?

HOLDING AND DECISION: (Fuld, J.) No. A contract modification "is voidable on the ground of duress when it is established that the party making the claim was forced to agree to it by means of a wrongful threat precluding the exercise of his free will." Loral (D) has made out a classic case of economic duress in that: (1) Austin (P) threatened to withhold delivery of "needful goods" unless Loral (D) agreed, (2) Loral (D) could not obtain the goods from another source of supply, and (3) the ordinary remedy of an action for breach of the original subcontract would not be adequate [since so much was riding on Loral's (D) own general contract with the government]. Thus it is "manifest" that Austin's (P) threat deprived Loral (D) of his free will. "Loral (D) actually had no choice."

DISSENT: (Bergan, J.) Three dissenting judges felt that in applying the law of duress, the majority necessarily overturned crucial findings of fact by the lower courts.

EDITOR'S ANALYSIS: Although it has generally been held that a threat to breach a contract does not constitute economic duress, courts have recently begun to hold that various kinds of unethical business compulsion do constitute duress. The present case is an example of this trend. Note that even under the U.C.C. (which recognizes modification without consideration—§ 2-209) the requirement of good faith is ever present.

QUICKNOTES

ECONOMIC DURESS - Wrongful conduct that prevents the exercise of free will when entering into a business transaction by creating an apprehension of economic hardship.

CONTRACT MODIFICATION - A change to the terms of a contract without altering its general purpose.

CONSIDERATION - Value given by one party in exchange for performance, or a promise to perform, by another party.

NOTES:

ALASKA PACKERS' ASSOCIATION v. DOMENICO
Packing employer (D) v. Seamen (P)
117 F. 99 (9th Cir. 1902).

NATURE OF CASE: Libel action for breach of contract.

FACT SUMMARY: Seamen (P), who had agreed to ship from San Francisco to Alaska at a fixed pay, refused to continue working once they reached Alaska, and demanded a new contract with more compensation.

CONCISE RULE OF LAW: A promise to pay a man for doing that which he is already under contract to do is without consideration.

FACTS: A group of seamen (P) entered into a written contract with Alaska Packers' Association (D) to go from San Francisco to Alaska on the Packers' (D) ships, and to work as sailors and fishermen. Compensation was fixed at $60 for the season, and two cents for each salmon caught. Once they had reached port in Alaska, the seamen (P) refused to continue work and demanded that compensation be increased to $100. A superintendent for Packers' (D), unable to hire a new crew, drew up a new contract, substituted in the sum of $100. and signed it although he expressed doubt at the time that he had the authority to do so. The seamen (P) resumed work, but upon the ship's return to San Francisco, Packers' (D) refused to honor the new contract. The seamen (P) filed a libel action for breach of contract.

ISSUE: Is a promise to pay a man for performing a duty he is already under contract to perform, without consideration?

HOLDING AND DECISION: (Ross, J.) Yes. The performance of a pre-existing legal duty guaranteed by contract, is not sufficient consideration to support a promise. No astute reasoning can change the plain fact that the party who refuses to perform, and thereby coerces a promise from the other party to pay him an increased compensation for doing that which he is legally bound to do, takes an unjustifiable advantage of the necessities of the other party. The parties in the present case have not voluntarily rescinded or modified their contract. The Packers' (D) second contract with the seamen is unenforceable although the seamen completed their performance in reliance on it.

EDITOR'S ANALYSIS: A few cases have held that the promise to pay additional compensation is enforceable. Consideration is found in the promissee's giving up of his power to breach the first contract. In other words, by refusing to continue work, the promisee has invoked the option to pay money damages rather than to invest his labor in further performance. This view has been questioned on the ground that a promisee may have the power to breach a contract, but certainly not the legal right, and in any event, he should not be encouraged to do so.

QUICKNOTES

PRE-EXISTING DUTY - A common law doctrine that renders unenforceable a promise to perform a duty, which the promisor is already legally obligated to perform, for lack of consideration.

CONSIDERATION - Value given by one party in exchange for performance, or a promise to perform, by another party.

DETRIMENTAL RELIANCE - Action by one party, resulting in loss, that is based on the conduct or promises of another.

NOTES:

BRIAN CONST. AND DEV. CO. v. BRIGHENTI
Construction company (P) v. Foundation subcontractor (D)
176 Conn. 162, 405 A.2d 72 (1978).

NATURE OF CASE: Appeal in breach of construction contract action.

FACT SUMMARY: Brian (P) claimed that Brighenti (D) breached a subcontract to remove rubble from an excavation.

CONCISE RULE OF LAW: Where unforeseen circumstances make the performance of a contract unduly burdensome, and the parties agree in view of the changed conditions to an adjustment in price, a new contract supported by consideration is formed.

FACTS: Bennett contracted with the owner of property to construct a post office. He subsequently assigned the contract to Brian (P). Brian (P) subcontracted with Brighenti (D), who agreed to provide all the foundation work of the building. Included in the subcontract was the statement that Brighenti (D) agreed to do "everything requisite and necessary to finish the entire work properly." In return, he was to receive $104,326. Soon thereafter, Brighenti (D) discovered the remains of another building at the excavation site. This discovery was unanticipated by either party and would have required considerably more excavation work than originally thought. After Brighenti (D) refused to continue without additional compensation, Brian (P) agreed to payment of his extra cost plus 10%. Brighenti (D) returned to work for several days and then quit. Brian (P) was forced to complete the job himself, suffering large damages in the process. Brian (P) brought suit for breach of contract. The trial court found for Brighenti (D) on several grounds, including the fact that the "new" contract was not supported by consideration. Brian (P) appealed.

ISSUE: When the parties to a contract agree to increased compensation due to the existence of unforeseen circumstances, is a new, binding contract created?

HOLDING AND DECISION: (Loiselle, J.) Yes. It is an accepted principle that when a party agrees to perform an obligation which he is already obligated to perform, albeit for a different price, the second agreement does not constitute a valid contract. However, the doctrine of unforeseen circumstances provides an exception to the general rule. Under that doctrine, when unforeseen circumstances make the performance of a contract unduly burdensome, the parties may agree, in view of the changed conditions, to an adjustment in price. The new agreement thus created, constitutes a valid, binding contract. In the instant case, the record shows that the existence of the additional rubble at the excavation site was clearly unanticipated by the parties. Therefore,

Brian's (P) agreement to pay Brighenti (D) increased compensation for the work constituted a new, binding contract. Brighenti's (D) failure to carry out that contract was a material breach, for which Brian (P) is entitled to damages. Reversed.

EDITOR'S ANALYSIS: The concept of contractual modifications not needing consideration to be binding is a relatively recent one. U.C.C. § 2-209(1) seems to have extended the concept further than most in its flat statement that "[a]n agreement modifying a contract within this Article needs no consideration to be binding." Of course, certain conditions are set out and the comment to the section warns that "the extortion of a `modification' without legitimate commercial reason is ineffective as a violation of the duty of good faith." However, the section still represents a bold liberalization of this area.

QUICKNOTES

CONTRACT MODIFICATION - A change to the terms of a contract without altering its general purpose.

CONSIDERATION - Value given by one party in exchange for performance, or a promise to perform, by another party.

NOTES:

UNIVERSAL BUILDERS, INC. v. MOON MOTOR LODGE, INC.

Builder (P) v. Motel business (D)

Pa. Sup. Ct., 430 Pa. 550, 244 A.2d 10 (1968).

NATURE OF CASE: Action for damages for breach of a construction contract.

FACT SUMMARY: Universal (P) contracted in writing with Moon (D) to build a motel and restaurant. One condition was that all change orders had to be signed either by Moon (D) or the architect, but Moon's (D) agent requested many changes which Universal (P) made, which Berger promised would be paid. Moon (D) failed to pay for the extra work.

CONCISE RULE OF LAW: Unless a contract is for the sale of goods, it is undisputed that the contract can be modified orally although it provides it can be modified only in writing.

FACTS: Universal (P) contracted in writing with Moon (D) to build a motel and restaurant. The contract provided that all change orders had to be in writing and signed by Moon (D) or the architect. Despite this, Moon's (D) agent, Berger, who was keenly aware of project details and the contract provisions, requested extra work about which Universal (P) informed him that there would be extra cost. Berger promised the extra work would be paid for and he watched much of it being done. Moon (D) failed to pay a $127,760 balance due including extras.

ISSUE: Did Moon's (D) agent alter the written contract orally despite the provision for written alteration only?

HOLDING AND DECISION: (Eagen, J.) Yes. Unless a contract is for the sale of goods, it appears undisputed that the contract can be modified orally although there are provisions to the contrary. Or the extra work done under oral direction can be said to have been done under an oral agreement separate from the written contract and not containing the requirement of written authorization. Moon's (D) agent's direction for extra work often done while he was present makes it reasonable to infer that he was aware of the extra work to which he clearly did not protest, therefore impliedly promising to pay for the extras. The waiver of the provision requiring written authorization does not have to be express, if the agreement or permission is given while the performance of the condition is possible, and in reliance on the agreement or permission, while it is unrevoked, the promisee materially changes his position, Restatement (First) § 224. Therefore, when an owner requests a builder to do extra work, promises to pay for it, and watched it being done knowing it was not authorized in writing, he cannot refuse to pay on the ground there was no written change order.

EDITOR'S ANALYSIS: Here the court has moved away from the requirement of an express oral waiver being necessary to modify the (construction) contract which provides for only written modification to an implied oral waiver. Implication of the waiver will naturally depend on the circumstances of the case. Here, Moon (D), through its agent, knew that the work was being done at its request and did not object to it. Universal's (P) reliance on this implied Moon's (D) promise to pay for the work.

QUICKNOTES

CONTRACT MODIFICATION - A change to the terms of a contract without altering its general purpose.

CONSIDERATION - Value given by one party in exchange for performance, or a promise to perform, by another party.

DETRIMENTAL RELIANCE - Action by one party, resulting in loss, that is based on the conduct or promises of another.

NOTES:

HACKLEY v. HEADLEY
Employer (D) v. Log cutter (P)
Mich. Sup. Ct., 45 Mich. 569, 8 N.W. 511 (1881).

NATURE OF CASE: Action to recover amount contract.

FACT SUMMARY: Headley (P) was forced to accept less than the contract amount to avoid financial ruin.

CONCISE RULE OF LAW: Mere refusal to pay a debt/contract is not duress.

FACTS: Hackley (D) hired Headley (P) to cut logs for him. After the work was completed, Headley (P) presented his bill for $6,200. Hackley (D) disputed the amount and alleged that he only owed $4,260 and would give him $4,000. Because Headley (P) was in very bad financial shape he was forced to accept the lesser amount because he could not afford to wait for the money and press his claims. Headley (P) signed a release stating that the $4,000 represented payment in full. Headley (P) then brought suit for the balance alleging that the release had been obtained through economic duress. Hackley (D) appealed a judgment on the ground that Headley's (P) economic straits were not his fault and they, not he, were the cause of Headley's (P) being forced to accept a lesser amount.

ISSUE: Is the mere exercise of a legal right ever deemed duress?

HOLDING AND DECISION: (Cooley, J.) No. When a party merely exercises a right it may not be deemed duress. Hackley (D) had a legal right to dispute the amount of the value of the services. Hackley (D) was not responsible for Headley's (P) financial difficulties. But for them, Headley (P) could have pursued his remedies in the courts. Headley (P) freely chose to accept a lesser amount because of his personal financial difficulties. A transaction is only voidable for duress where one of the parties is forced to act in a manner inconsistent with his own free will. While Headley's (P) financial difficulties were the reason for accepting the lesser amount, they were not Hackley's (D) fault and cannot be deemed to be duress. Reversed.

EDITOR'S ANALYSIS: The appellate court remanded Headley. Ultimately, Headley's (P) release was deemed invalid on the ground that it was not supported by consideration. The concept of duress is, in some cases, difficult to distinguish from that of lack of consideration. Thus, courts frequently refuse to find duress present, but nevertheless void a transaction on the ground that the party who allegedly took advantage of the other's duress in fact gave no consideration. Courts, then, which are reluctant to find duress, conclude that an independent ground exists for voiding a transaction.

QUICKNOTES
DURESS - Unlawful threats or other coercive behavior by one person that causes another to commit acts that he would not otherwise do.

CONSIDERATION - Value given by one party in exchange for performance, or a promise to perform, by another party.

NOTES:

MARTON REMODELING v. JENSEN

Remodeler (P) v. Homeowner (D)

Utah Sup. Ct., 706 P.2d 607 (1985).

NATURE OF CASE: Appeal of award of damages for breach of contract.

FACT SUMMARY: Marton (P), engaged in a payment dispute with Jensen (D), added "not full payment" to a check Jensen (D) had sent as an accord and satisfaction, and cashed it.

CONCISE RULE OF LAW: A creditor cannot escape the discharging effect of a draft sent in satisfaction of a debt by adding words of non-acceptance.

FACTS: Marton (P) was engaged by Jensen (D) to remodel Jensen's (D) house, on a "time and materials" basis. Marton (P) submitted a bill of $6,538.12. Jensen (D) contended he had been overcharged and offered to pay $5,000. Marton (P) refused. Jensen (D) subsequently sent a draft for $5,000 bearing words to the effect that the draft represented an accord and satisfaction. Marton (P) cashed the check after writing "not full payment" on it. Marton (P) later brought an action to recover the unpaid balance. The trial court awarded Marton (P) $1,538.12, plus punitive damages and attorney fees. Both sides appealed.

ISSUE: Can a creditor escape the discharging effect of a draft sent in satisfaction of a debt by adding words of nonacceptance?

HOLDING AND DECISION: (Howe, J.) No. A creditor cannot escape the discharging effect of a draft sent in satisfaction of a debt by adding words of non-acceptance. The general rule is that when a claim is whole and unliquidated, the acceptance by the creditor of an amount offered in satisfaction of the debt cannot lose its settlement nature by the addition of a reservation by the creditor. The law favors settlement of disputes, and the law of accord and satisfaction would be eviscerated if the rule was otherwise. Here, Marton (P) did accept an amount offered in satisfaction, and that discharged the debt. Reversed.

EDITOR'S ANALYSIS: Technically speaking, in a situation such as this, a unilateral contract is formed. The debtor offers by tendering the draft, and the creditor accepts by endorsing it. As Marton (P) discovered to his regret, actions in this area of law speak louder than words.

QUICKNOTES

ACCORD AND SATISFACTION - A second agreement between parties to satisfy the outstanding debt in an original agreement for less than the amount owed, and the payment of that new amount in satisfaction of the original debt.

PUNITIVE DAMAGES - Damages exceeding the actual injury suffered for the purposes of punishment, deterrence and comfort to plaintiff.

NOTES:

DENNEY v. REPPERT
Employee of bank (P) v. Officer (D)
Ky. Ct. App., 432 S.W.2d 647 (1968).

NATURE OF CASE: Suit to determine who is entitled to a reward.

FACT SUMMARY: Denney (P), an employee of the First State Bank, contended he was entitled to a reward offered for the arrest and conviction of three men who robbed that bank. The trial court gave the reward to Reppert (D), an officer from another jurisdiction who assisted in the arrest.

CONCISE RULE OF LAW: Agents, employees, and public officials acting within the scope of their employment or official duties cannot claim a reward offered to the general public for the performance of some specified act even though, as a general rule, it may be claimed by any person who performs such act.

FACTS: The Kentucky Bankers Association sought to make good on its promise to give a reward of $500 for the arrest and conviction of each bank robber, when three men were arrested and convicted for robbing a member bank, First State Bank, of over $30,000. Murrell Denney (P) was one of several bank employees claiming the reward for his assistance in giving the police details of the crime, identifying the robbers, etc. Reppert (D) was one of the three officers of the law who made the arrest, he being the only one outside of his county of jurisdiction. Others who gave valuable information to the arresting officers never filed a reward claim via the procedure set forth in the offer; nonetheless, they also sought the reward. So, the Kentucky Bankers Association asked the circuit court to determine who should get the reward. All claimants were defendants in the action in which it was decided Reppert (D) was the one so entitled since all the others were either performing already existing duties as employees or public officials or did not comply with the filing terms and conditions of the reward offer. Denney (P) disputed that decision.

ISSUE: Is a bank employee entitled to a reward offered to the general public for performing acts within the scope of his employment?

HOLDING AND DECISION: (Myre, Spec. Commr.) No. Although the general rule is that a reward offered to the general public is payable to anyone performing the specified act, this is not the case for agents, employees, and public officials who are acting within the scope of their employment or official duties. Bank employees have a duty to protect and conserve the bank's moneys and to safeguard its interests. Thus, only Reppert (D), who was out of his jurisdiction and under no legal duty to make the arrest, is eligible for the reward.

EDITOR'S ANALYSIS: The reasoning here can be analogized to that in *Schaefer v. Brunswick Laundry, Inc.* As in that case, the person who performed was already under a legal obligation to do so. Therefore, there could be no consideration given for extra compensation by doing something which the promisor was already obliged to do. Lacking consideration, there is no contract and no right to payment to be enforced.

QUICKNOTES

PRE-EXISTING DUTY - A common law doctrine that renders unenforceable a promise to perform a duty, which the promisor is already legally obligated to perform, for lack of consideration.

UNILATERAL CONTRACT - An agreement pursuant to which a party agrees to act, or to forbear from acting, in exchange for performance on the part of the other party.

CONSIDERATION - Value given by one party in exchange for performance, or a promise to perform, by another party.

NOTES:

JACKSON v. SEYMOUR
Landowner (P) v. Brother (D)
Va. Sup. Ct. App., 193 Va. 735, 71 S.E.2d 181 (1952).

NATURE OF CASE: Accounting and rescission.

FACT SUMMARY: Seymour (D), Jackson's (P) brother, purchased her land for a comparatively small price. It was later discovered that there was valuable timber on the land.

CONCISE RULE OF LAW: An agreement may be rescinded if the consideration paid by one of the parties is so disproportionate to the value which he receives as to suggest constructive fraud.

FACTS: Lucy Jackson (P) owned a tract of land adjacent to property owned by her brother, Benjamin Seymour (D). Being in need of money, she (P) sold him (D) the property for $275. At the time of the sale, neither party realized that there was valuable timber on the land. Seymour (D) eventually learned of the timber, cut and marketed it, and realized a profit of more than $2,300. When Jackson (P) learned of her brother's (D) good fortune, she (P) tendered $275 and demanded the return of the property and the proceeds of the timber sale. Her brother (D) refused her demand, whereupon she (P) filed suit claiming that he (D) had been guilty of actual fraud in knowingly misrepresenting the value of the land at the time of purchase. By her action, she (P) sought rescission of the deed she (P) had executed in favor of her brother (D), and prayed for an accounting of all profits realized from the timber transaction. Jackson (P) later attempted to establish constructive fraud, and finally amended her complaint to allege a mutual mistake. The trial court eventually dismissed her complaint, and Jackson (P) appealed.

ISSUE: May an agreement be rescinded because of the inadequacy of the consideration paid by one of the parties thereto?

HOLDING AND DECISION: (Eggleston, J.) Yes. An agreement may be rescinded if the consideration paid by one of the parties is so disproportionate to the value which he receives as to suggest constructive fraud. Jackson (P) has not demonstrated that Seymour (D) committed actual fraud. However, the confidential relationship between the parties, the inadequacy of the price paid, Jackson's (P) financial distress at the time of the sale, Seymour's (D) rejection of his sister's (P) offer to repurchase the land at the original sale price, and Jackson's (P) habitual reliance upon Seymour's (D) business advice, are all factors from which constructive fraud may be inferred. Therefore, Jackson (P) is entitled to the relief requested by her complaint, and to such other relief as fairly restores each party to the status enjoyed prior to the sale of the land.

EDITOR'S ANALYSIS: This case represents an exception to the established rule that the courts will not evaluate the adequacy of the consideration paid by either of the parties to a transaction. Although it recognized the general rule, the *Jackson v. Seymour* court was impressed by the apparently unequal bargaining positions of the two parties and by the close and confidential relationship which they enjoyed with one another. In the absence of such mitigating circumstances, most states would have held that a party must suffer the consequences of a foolish transaction.

QUICKNOTES

RESCISSION - The canceling of an agreement and the return of the parties to their positions prior to the formation of the contract.

NOMINAL CONSIDERATION - Consideration that is so insignificant that it does not represent the actual value received from the agreement.

CONSTRUCTIVE FRAUD - A breach of duty or other circumstances where trust or confidence is unfairly disadvantaged, permitting a court to find that fraud exists even though there was no knowledge of fraud on the part of the breaching party.

NOTES:

SHERWOOD v. WALKER
Purchaser of cow (P) v. Seller (D)
Mich. Sup. Ct., 66 Mich. 568, 33 N.W. 919 (1887).

NATURE OF CASE: Action for replevin.

FACT SUMMARY: Walker (D) sold a cow as barren to Sherwood (P) and refused to turn it over when he learned it was with calf.

CONCISE RULE OF LAW: When there is a mutual mistake going to the very substance of what is being sold, no contract exists.

FACTS: Walker (D) agreed to sell a specific cow to Sherwood (P) for $80, both parties apparently believing it to be barren. If not barren, the cow was worth from $750-$1,000. Prior to delivering the cow, Walker (D) learned it was with calf. Walker (D) attempted to rescind the contract. Sherwood (P) brought a replevin action to obtain the cow alleging that title to it had already passed to him. The court found for Sherwood (P). Walker (D) appealed alleging that the contract was for the sale of a barren cow for meat, not a breeding cow.

ISSUE: Will a mutual mistake going to the very substance of the bargain invalidate a contract?

HOLDING AND DECISION: (Morse, J.) Yes. While this is a very close case, what the parties thought was being sold/purchased was a barren cow which could only be used for meat. In reality, the cow was fertile and with calf. Where the very substance of the bargain was based on a mutual mistake, equity may refuse enforcement of the contract. Mere errors as to quantity or quality will not invalidate the contract no matter how material. Here, the mistake went to what was really being purchased, a barren cow. In such cases, where there was a mutual mistake going to the very essence of what was being sold, no contract exists.

DISSENT: (Sherwood, J.) There was no mutual mistake. Sherwood (P) believed the cow to be fertile and it was. Merely because he chose not to believe in Walker's (D) opinion but dealt with the cow on Walker's (D) basis does not mean there was a mutual mistake. Both parties had equal knowledge and neither relied on the belief of the other. In any event, a mutual mistake of this nature should not invalidate the contract. A cow is a cow. Merely because the parties have mistaken one of the qualities/capabilities of the animal is not grounds for denying enforcement of the contract.

EDITOR'S ANALYSIS: In *Backus v. Maclaury*, 278 App. Div. (1951), Backus purchased a bull at auction for $5,000. Eighteen months later they discovered it was sterile. The court found that no test could determine sterility until a bull was twelve months old.

Where both parties know or should know that there is doubt as to certain matters, a mutual mistake as to them will not invalidate the contract. A different result might have been found if the buyer was not in the cattle business and was unaware of the potential problem.

QUICKNOTES
MUTUAL MISTAKE - A mistake by both parties to a contract, who are in agreement as to what the contract terms should be, but the agreement as written fails to reflect that common intent; such contracts are voidable or subject to reformation.

MATERIAL TERM - A contractual term that is an essential part of the agreement, to the extent that its omission from performance can be construed as a breach of the contract.

REPLEVIN - An action to recover personal property wrongfully taken.

NOTES:

ELSINORE UNION ELEMENTARY SCHOOL DISTRICT. v. KASTORFF

School district (P) v. Building contractor (D)
Calif. Sup. Ct., 54 Cal.2d 380, 353 P.2d 713 (1960).

NATURE OF CASE: Appeal of judgment awarding damages for refusal to execute a building contract.

FACT SUMMARY: When a written bid for a building contract contained a clerical error and was promptly rescinded by Kastorff (D), he claimed that the bargain was void.

CONCISE RULE OF LAW: A prompt rescission due to an honest clerical error in a bid for a building contract may relieve a party from an unfair and unintended bargain.

FACTS: Kastorff (D) was a building contractor who submitted a bid to make some additions to Elsinore Union Elementary School District's (P) school buildings. Kastorff (D) made a clerical error when computing the total amount of the bid which he submitted to Elsinore Union (P). Elsinore Union (P) voted to grant Kastorff (D) the contract. The next day Kastorff (D) discovered the mistake and called Elsinore Union (P) to inform them of the clerical error and to rescind his bid. Kastorff (D) also wrote Elsinore Union (P) informing them of the miscalculation. Elsinore Union (P) voted not to release Kastorff (D) and later mailed him a written contract. Kastorff (D) returned the contract unsigned and again asked to be released. Elsinore Union (P) then retained another contractor to do the work and filed suit against Kastorff (D). Elsinore Union (P) asked for damages equal to the difference between Kastorff's (D) bid and the actual cost of the work and for recovery on a bond posted by Kastorff's (D) surety. The trial court found that Elsinore Union (P) did not know of Kastorff's (D) withdrawal of his bid when it requested him to sign the contract and concluded that it was entitled to damages in the amount sued for. Kastorff (D) appealed.

ISSUE: May a prompt rescission due to an honest clerical error in a bid for a building contract relieve a party from an unfair and unintended bargain?

HOLDING AND DECISION: (Schauer, J.) Yes. A prompt rescission due to an honest clerical error in a bid for a building contract may relieve a party from an unfair and unintended bargain. There was evidence presented that Elsinore Union (P) knew of the mistake when they voted not to grant Kastorff's (D) request to withdraw his bid. The inadvertent clerical error does not rise to the level of a "neglect of legal duty" sufficient to preclude his being relieved from an inequitable bargain. Reversed.

EDITOR'S ANALYSIS: Courts will generally grant relief for unilateral clerical or mathematical mistakes. Only in cases of extreme negligence would a mistake of facts be actionable. There are times when a mistake may be inferred from the terms of the offer itself. Relief is granted if it is reasonable to assume that the offeree should have known of the mistake.

QUICKNOTES

UNILATERAL MISTAKE - Occurs when only one party to an agreement makes a mistake and is generally not a basis for relief by rescission or reformation.

RESCISSION - The canceling of an agreement and the return of the parties to their positions prior to the formation of the contract.

NOTES:

TRIBE v. PETERSON
Horse purchaser (P) v. Horse seller (D)
Wyo. Sup. Ct., 964 P.2d 1238 (1998).

NATURE OF CASE: Appeal of denial of recovery in a breach of warranty action.

FACT SUMMARY: Tribe (P) sued the Petersons (D) when the horse Tribe (P) purchased from the Petersons (D) bucked, causing Tribe (P) injury.

CONCISE RULE OF LAW: A representation that expresses the seller's opinion does not constitute an express warranty.

FACTS: Tribe (P) purchased a horse from the Petersons (D). Prior to making the purchase, Tribe (P) claimed that the Petersons (D) expressly guaranteed to Tribe (P) that the horse would not buck. The Petersons (D) asserted that the horse never bucked when they, or any of its previous owners, rode him. The testimony conflicts as to whether the Petersons (D) guaranteed that the horse would never buck in the future. A prior owner of the horse described the horse as being calm and gentle and stated that the horse did not buck and that anybody with riding experience could ride him. Prior to selling the horse, the Petersons (D) had the horse examined by a veterinarian who concluded that the horse was sound, gentle, kind and did what was asked of him. The veterinarian found the horse to be so calm that she did not use a sedative, which most horses need, when she examined him. The description of the horse in the sales brochure was that he was a "quiet ... and extra gentle gelding easy to catch, haul and shoe," and "overly kind which makes him a definite kids prospect." Tribe (P) purchased the horse on his belief that he had been guaranteed that this horse would never buck. Subsequent to the purchase, the horse bucked, injuring Tribe's (P) left wrist, and Tribe (P) sued the Petersons (D) for breach of warranty. Tribe (P) alleged that the Petersons (D) breached an express warranty that the horse would never buck and that they negligently and fraudulently misrepresented the horse's nature. A jury found in favor of the Petersons (D), the court denied Tribe's (P) motion for judgment as a matter of law, and Tribe (P) appealed.

ISSUE: Did the written description of the horse and the verbal representations by the Petersons (D) create an express warranty that the horse was a calm and gentle horse that would never buck?

HOLDING AND DECISION: (Taylor, J.) No. The written description of the horse and verbal representations by the Petersons (D) did not create an express warranty that the horse was a calm and gentle horse that would never buck but rather were opinions. An express warranty is created by an affirmation of fact made by the seller to the buyer which relates to the goods and becomes a part of the basis of the bargain. For an express warranty to exist, there must be an unequivocal statement concerning the thing sold which is relied on by the buyer and which is understood to be an assertion concerning the items sold and not an opinion. In this case, the jury's conclusion that the Petersons (D) are not liable to Tribe (P) for damages for breach of an express warranty could reasonably be reached on the evidence presented at trial. There was evidence to support a finding that the description of the horse in the sales brochure was the Petersons (D) opinion regarding the horse's disposition. The testimony of all the witnesses reveals that the horse was calm and gentle with everyone except for Tribe (P). Moreover, Mrs. Tribe (P) called Mrs. Peterson (D) shortly after the sale to comment on how well she was getting along with the horse; she stated that she loved him and was interested in buying more like him. The disposition of a horse may be affected by the rider, the equipment, the type of feed, or a new environment. Thus, even if the brochure constituted an express warranty, the warranty was not breached. Furthermore, the Petersons (D) denied that they guaranteed that the horse would never buck and the record supports the jury's finding that no express warranty was given as to the horse's future behavior. Lastly, there is overwhelming evidence that the information provided by the Petersons (D) did not misrepresent the horse's disposition. Affirmed.

EDITOR'S ANALYSIS: A practical concern that the court might have had was that if they allowed recovery in this case, there would be an increase in litigation by buyers of animals against sellers when the animals acted in ways contrary to what the buyer anticipated.

NOTES:

HINSON v. JEFFERSON
Land purchaser (P) v. Seller (D)
N.C. Sup. Ct., 287 N.C. 422, 215 S.E.2d 102 (1975).

NATURE OF CASE: Action to rescind sale of real property.

FACT SUMMARY: Hinson (P) sought to rescind her purchase of land due to the mutual mistake of the parties.

CONCISE RULE OF LAW: In North Carolina, the doctrine of mutual mistake regarding a physical condition of real property is not a ground for the rescission of the sale of such property.

FACTS: Hinson (P) purchased a parcel of land from Jefferson (D). The deed restricted use of the acquired property to residential purposes. Because the land was not served by a municipal sewage disposal system, the construction of a septic tank was necessary. However, as Hinson (P) became ready to begin construction, she was informed by a county health official that the proximity of her property to a local swamp would necessitate the expenditure of several hundred thousand dollars before she would be allowed to construct her septic tank. Hinson (P) immediately sought rescission of the contract from Jefferson (D), who had not previously known of the sewage problem. He refused, and Hinson (P) brought suit for rescission based on mutual mistake. The trial court denied relief and the court of appeals reversed. Jefferson (D) appealed.

ISSUE: Does North Carolina recognize the doctrine of mutually mistaken assumptions as a ground for rescission of a real property sale?

HOLDING AND DECISION: (Copeland, J.) No. The general rule in real property transactions has long been caveat emptor. As the rule has been eroded, however, several exceptions have arisen. One is the doctrine of mutual mistake. Under this doctrine, where both parties to a contract are mistaken as to a material fact, the contract may be rescinded. The instant case concerns not a mutual mistake of fact, however; Hinson (P) got the property she bargained for. Instead, it was a mistake of assumption; i.e., the assumption that both parties held that the subject property was suitable for construction of a residence. No North Carolina case has ever held the doctrine of mutually mistaken assumptions to constitute a ground for rescission of a sale of real property. This is because of the vast uncertainty surrounding the doctrine and the difficulty in practically implementing it. However, this does not mean that Hinson (P) has no remedy in the instant case. Another of the special exceptions to the caveat emptor doctrine is the recognition of implied warranties. This case appears to be a perfect example of a case in which a breach of implied warranty should be found. Because of deed restrictions, Hinson's (P) land was limited to residential construction. Accordingly, the vendor, Jefferson (D), will be held to have impliedly warranted that the land was suitable for

that purpose. Since it was not, rescission is proper. Affirmed, as modified.

EDITOR'S ANALYSIS: The court's decision that relief may be granted on warranty, rather than mistake, grounds is similar, in effect, to the provisions of U.C.C. § 2-313. Subsection(1)(b)of 2-313 provides that "any description of the goods which is made part of the basis of the bargain creates an express warranty that the goods shall conform to the description." Therefore, it could be assumed that a sales contract restricting the buyer of goods to a particular purpose will be held to create a warranty that the goods are suitable for that purpose.

QUICKNOTES

MUTUAL MISTAKE - A mistake by both parties to a contract, who are in agreement as to what the contract terms should be, but the agreement as written fails to reflect that common intent; such contracts are voidable or subject to reformation.

WARRANTY - An assurance by one party that another may rely on a certain representation of fact.

RESCISSION - The canceling of an agreement and the return of the parties to their positions prior to the formation of the contract.

NOTES:

JOHNSON v. HEALY
Purchaser of home (P) v. Builder/seller (D)
Conn. Sup. Ct., 176 Conn. 97, 405 A.2d 54 (1978).

NATURE OF CASE: Cross-appeals from award of damages for breach of warranty and denial of damages for negligence.

FACT SUMMARY: Johnson (P) bought a house from Healy (D), the builder, who had unknowingly constructed it on improper fill, resulting in substantial damage to the foundation and the sewer lines as the house settled.

CONCISE RULE OF LAW: Innocent misrepresentations that reasonably induce reliance amount to an express warranty of habitability which, if breached, entitles the injured party to damages limited to the diminished value of the building.

FACTS: While negotiating the sale of a house, Healy (D), the builder-vendor, stated to Johnson (P), the buyer, that the house was made of the best material and that there was nothing wrong with it. Unbeknownst to Healy (D), unsuitable fill had been placed on the lot some time before he purchased the property to build on. After Johnson (P) bought the house for $17,000, it began to settle due to the improper fill, causing foundation and sewer line problems, which cost him approximately $5,000 to repair. Johnson (P) estimated it would cost $27,000 to construct a new foundation and filed suit for misrepresentation and negligence. The trial court found in his favor on the claim of misrepresentation and awarded $5,000 for breach of warranties. However, it found in favor of Healy (D) on the claim of negligence, having concluded that Healy (D) had no actual knowledge of the soil defects on the lot. Both parties appealed.

ISSUE: Do innocent misrepresentations that reasonably induce reliance amount to an express warranty of habitability which, if breached, entitles the injured party to damages limited to the diminished value of the building?

HOLDING AND DECISION: (Peters, J.) Yes. Innocent misrepresentations that reasonably induce reliance amount to an express warranty of habitability which, if breached, entitles the injured party to damages limited to the diminished value of the building. Although the rule of caveat emptor—let the buyer beware—used to be the established rule regarding sale of real estate, courts now recognize claims for negligence and express and implied warranty, just as they have in sale-of-goods cases. In this case, Healy (D) had been engaged in the real estate business for about 30 years, and his indefinite statement that there was "nothing wrong" with the house could have convinced Johnson (P) that Healy (D) had sufficient factual information to justify his general opinion about the quality of the house. Because this statement could have reasonably induced reliance by Johnson (P), it amounted to an express warranty of workmanlike construction and

fitness for habitation. Therefore, Healy (D) may be held liable despite the absence of written warranties concerning the fitness or condition of the house. However, because neither Healy (D) nor the building inspector had actual or constructive notice of the lot's instability, Healy (D) could not be held liable for negligence. Damages for breach of warranty claims are to be measured by the difference in value between the property as it was represented and the property as it actually was. This will place Johnson (P) in the same position he would have enjoyed if the property had been as warranted, which is the general rule of contract law as applied to the sale of a new house. Since the reasonable cost of repairs is often a good approximation for damages that are difficult to prove, the lower court must distinguish between expenses for repairs incident to the breach and expenses for improvement, which it failed to do at trial. Judgment set aside and remanded on the issue of damages only.

EDITOR'S ANALYSIS: In general, liability for active misrepresentation is broader than liability for simple nondisclosure. Note that if Healy (D) had known about the improper fill but had made no representations of any kind about the house or about subsurface conditions, he would have been liable for damages only if the court concluded that he had a duty to disclose. According to the Restatement (Second) Torts § 551(2), a duty to disclose arises in situations involving facts that are concealed or are unlikely to be discovered because of the special relationship between the parties, the course of their dealings, or the nature of the fact itself. In this case, the determinative factor might be whether improper fill is the type of information that the buyer would be expected to discover by ordinary inspection and inquiry.

QUICKNOTES

MISREPRESENTATION - A statement or conduct by one party to another that constitutes a false representation of fact.

WARRANTY - An assurance by one party that another may rely on a certain representation of fact.

NOTES:

CUSHMAN v. KIRBY
Home purchasers (P) v. Seller (D)
Vt. Sup. Ct., 148 Vt. 571, 536 A.2d 550 (1987).

NATURE OF CASE: Appeal from denial of a directed verdict and from assessment of damages in suit for misrepresentation.

FACT SUMMARY: The Cushmans (P) purchased a house after being assured by Kirby (D), the seller, that the well water on the property was fine, only to discover that the water was in fact sulfurous and undrinkable.

CONCISE RULE OF LAW: When a home seller discloses only a portion of the information he has but leads the buyer to believe he has made a full disclosure, he will be liable if the buyer acts in reliance on that partial disclosure.

FACTS: The Cushmans (P) entered into negotiations with the Kirbys (D) for the purchase of a home. During a tour of the house, the Cushmans (P), having discovered a water treatment system in the basement, inquired as to the kind of water on the premises. Mrs. Kirby (D) assured them that the water was good but just a little hard and that the system in the basement would take care of it. Mr. Kirby (D) remained silent. The Kirbys (D) were both aware that the well water on the property contained enough sulfur to warrant special treatment, but neither mentioned anything about the presence of the sulfur to the Cushmans (P). After closing, the Cushmans (P) discovered that the water was in fact sulfur water, which, even if treated, would only be tolerably drinkable. Therefore, they chose to hook up to the city water supply at a cost of $5,000, plus annual water bills. They then brought an action against the Kirbys (D) for misrepresentation regarding the quality of the well water on the property, which resulted in a jury verdict in favor of the Cushmans (P) in the amount of $6,600. The Kirbys (D) appealed, claiming that, in the absence of any affirmative misrepresentations to the Cushmans (P) regarding water quality, the trial court erroneously denied their motions for directed verdicts and instructed the jury on the wrong standard for assessing damages.

ISSUE: When a home seller discloses only a portion of the information he has but leads the buyer to believe he has made a full disclosure, will he be liable if the buyer acts in reliance on that partial disclosure?

HOLDING AND DECISION: (Dooley, J.) Yes. When a home seller discloses only a portion of the information he has but leads the buyer to believe he has made a full disclosure, he will be liable if the buyer acts in reliance on that partial disclosure. In this case, although Mrs. Kirby's (D) statements about the well water were not actually false, they fell short of full disclosure about the presence of sulfur in the water, of which Mrs. Kirby (D) was well aware. Because the Cushmans (P) then relied on the truth of Mrs.

Kirby's (P) statements about the extent of the water problem when making their decision to buy the house, there was sufficient evidence to make out a case of actionable fraud, and it was not error to deny Mrs. Kirby's (D) motion for directed verdict. On the other hand, the claim for fraud against Mr. Kirby (D) was based exclusively on his silence while Mrs. Kirby (D) was making her statements about water quality. A different standard of conduct applies to him, namely that a home seller has a duty to disclose material defects about which he has knowledge at the time of sale. Since Mrs. Kirby's (D) statements amounted to an inadequate disclosure constituting a misrepresentation, Mr. Kirby (D) had an affirmative duty to speak, in light of his knowledge about the sulfur in the water. Since Mr. Kirby's (D) liability was a question clearly within the province of the jury, the trial court correctly denied his motion for a directed verdict also. Furthermore, the jury determined the appropriate damage award by compensating the Cushmans (P) for the loss they actually sustained, placing them in the same position that they would have been in had they not been defrauded. Affirmed.

EDITOR'S ANALYSIS: According to the Restatement (Second) of Contracts § 161, a nondisclosure may constitute a misrepresentation when the nondiscloser knows that the disclosure (1) is necessary to prevent a previous assertion from being a misrepresentation or from being fraudulent or material or (2) would correct a mistake of the other party as to a basic assumption on which that party is making the contract, if nondisclosure amounts to a failure to act in good faith and in accordance with reasonable standards of fair dealing.

QUICKNOTES

MISREPRESENTATION - A statement or conduct by one party to another that constitutes a false representation of fact.

MATERIAL TERM - A contractual term that is an essential part of the agreement, to the extent that its omission from performance can be construed as a breach of the contract.

DIRECTED VERDICT - A verdict ordered by the court in a jury trial.

NOTES:

TAYLOR v. CALDWELL
Event promoter (P) v. Hall (D)
King's Bench, 3 Best and S. 826 (1863).

NATURE OF CASE: Action for damages for breach of a contract for letting of premises.

FACT SUMMARY: Taylor (P) contracted to let Caldwell's (D) hall and gardens for four fetes and concerts, for four days, for 100 pounds per day. Taylor (P) expended money in preparation and for advertising, but Caldwell (D) could not perform when the hall burned down without his fault.

CONCISE RULE OF LAW: In contracts in which the performance depends on the continued existence of a given person or thing, a condition is implied that the impossibility of performance arising from the perishing of the person or thing shall excuse the performance.

FACTS: By written agreement Caldwell (D) agreed to let the Surrey Gardens and Musical Hall at Newington, Surrey for four days for giving four "Grand Concerts" and "Day and Night Fetes." Taylor (P) was to pay 100 pounds at the end of each day. Before any concerts were held, the hall was completely destroyed by fire without any fault of either of the parties. Taylor (P) alleged that the fire and destruction of the hall was a breach and that it resulted in his losing large sums in preparation and advertising for the concerts and fetes.

ISSUE: Was Caldwell (D) excused from performance by the accidental destruction of the hall and gardens which had made his performance impossible?

HOLDING AND DECISION: (Blackburn, J.) Yes. Caldwell (D) was excused from performance. First, the agreement was not a lease but a contract to "let." The entertainments that were planned could not be made without the existence of the hall. Ordinarily, when there is a positive contract to do something that is not unlawful, the contractor must perform or pay damages for not doing it even if an unforeseen accident makes performance unduly burdensome or even impossible. This is so when the contract is absolute and positive and not subject to either express or implied conditions, and that if it appears that the parties must have known from the beginning that the contract could not be fulfilled unless a particular, specified thing continued to exist and there is no express or implied warranty that the thing shall exist, the contract is not positive and absolute. It is subject to the implied condition that the parties shall be excused in case, before breach, performance becomes impossible from the perishing of the thing without fault of the contractor. This appears to be within the intention of the parties when they enter into a contract. The excuse from the contract's performance is implied in law because from the nature of the contract it is apparent it was made on the basis of the continued existence of the particular, specified thing.

EDITOR'S ANALYSIS: It was important for J. Blackburn not to find the agreement to be a lease, otherwise the decision would come within direct conflict of *Paradine v. Jane*, K. B., 1647, 82 Eng. Rep. 897, which held that a lease must be performed to the letter despite unforeseen hardship or good fortune. Next, performance is excused only if the destruction of the specified thing is without fault. Had Caldwell (D) been shown to be guilty of arson in the destruction of the hall, he would not have been excused. If there is impossibility of performance due to no one's fault, the one seeking to enforce performance takes the risk. It might be said that the court was actually apportioning the loss it the contract was, in effect, a joint venture with Taylor (P) paying Caldwell (D) 100 pounds out of each day's admission fees to the concerts (Caldwell (D) was supplying the band). The view of this case is found in U.C.C. § 2-613 where for total destruction of the specified thing, the contract is avoided, or if the specified thing is goods which have so deteriorated as to no longer conform, the contract can be avoided or the goods can be accepted with an allowance for their lesser value. Note that there is not a satisfactory distinction between a contract to let and a lease.

QUICKNOTES

IMPOSSIBILITY - A doctrine relieving the parties to a contract from liability for nonperformance of their duties thereunder, if the subject matter of the contract ceases to exist, a person essential to the performance of the contract is deceased, or the service or goods contracted for has become illegal.

WARRANTY - An assurance by one party that another may rely on a certain representation of fact.

CONDITION - Requirement; potential future occurrence upon which the existence of a legal obligation is dependent.

NOTES:

TOMPKINS v. DUDLEY
School district trustee (P) v. Guarantor (D)
N.Y. Ct. App, 25 N.Y. 272 (1862).

NATURE OF CASE: Appeal from denial of damages for breach of a building contract.

FACT SUMMARY: When a building under construction burned down prior to its completion, Dudley (D), who had guaranteed the building contractor's performance, was sued for damages.

CONCISE RULE OF LAW: When a party by his own contract absolutely engages to do an act, performance is not excused by inevitable accident or other unforeseen contingency not within his control.

FACTS: Tompkins (P), trustees of a school district, entered into an agreement with a builder for a new schoolhouse. Dudley (D) guaranteed the building contract on the part of the builder. The building was not finished on time and burned down several days before completion. Tompkins (P) sued to recover the money paid on account and for damages resulting from the non-performance of the contract. Dudley (D) claimed that he should not be held liable because the destruction of the building by fire and inevitable accident was not his fault. The trial court's verdict for Dudley (D) was affirmed, and Tompkins (P) appealed.

ISSUE: When a party by his own contract absolutely engages to do an act, is performance excused by inevitable accident or other unforeseen contingency not within his control?

HOLDING AND DECISION: (Davies, J.) No. When a party by his own contract absolutely engages to do an act, performance is not excused by inevitable accident or other unforeseen contingency not within his control. It is deemed to be his own fault and folly that he did not expressly provide against contingencies and he bears the risk of loss prior to completion. As guarantor, Dudley (D) is liable for damages due as a result of the builder's non-performance of his contract. Reversed.

EDITOR'S ANALYSIS: Modern practices in the construction industry have made such cases infrequent. Insurance usually covers the builder's losses from fire, theft, and other hazards. It is now standard practice to require the owner to purchase worksite property insurance, also known as a "builder's risk" policy.

QUICKNOTES

RISK OF LOSS - Liability for damage to or loss of property that is the subject matter of a contract for sale.

IMPRACTICABILITY - A doctrine relieving the parties to a contract from liability for nonperformance of their duties thereunder, if the subject matter of the contract ceases to exist.

IMPOSSIBILITY - A doctrine relieving the parties to a contract from liability for nonperformance of their duties thereunder, if the subject matter of the contract ceases to exist, a person essential to the performance of the contract is deceased, or the service or goods contracted for has become illegal.

NOTES:

CARROLL v. BOWERSOCK

Warehouse owner (D) v. Concrete installer (P)

Kan. Sup. Ct., 100 Kan. 270, 164 P. 143 (1917).

NATURE OF CASE: Suit to recover for work done under construction contract.

FACT SUMMARY: A fire destroyed Carroll's (D) warehouse, in which Bowersock (P) had performed some of the work necessary to construct a re-enforced concrete floor as specified in a contract between the two.

CONCISE RULE OF LAW: When destruction of the subject building renders performance impossible and such a possibility was not contemplated by either party, the owner of the subject building is liable for the amount of work done which had become so far identified with it as that but for the destruction it would have inured to him as contemplated by the contract.

FACTS: Bowersock (P) put in concrete footings, built wooden forms for concrete pillars to support the floor, and installed reinforcing rods in those column forms as part of his contract to put a re-enforced concrete floor in Carroll's (D) warehouse. Subsequently, a fire destroyed the warehouse, which was the fault of neither party. When Bowersock (P) succeeded in his suit to recover for his performance before the fire, Carroll (D) appealed.

ISSUE: Can a party recover for performance executed prior to the destruction of the building which is the subject of a repair contract when neither party contemplated such an event?

HOLDING AND DECISION: (Burch, J.) Yes. When further performance of a repair or refurbishing contract is rendered impossible by the destruction of the subject building through neither party's fault, the owner is liable to pay for any performance previously rendered if such would have inured to the owner's benefit. That which was contracted for cannot be obtained, and neither party can hold the other for something which was not contemplated. Thus, only the doctrine of unjust enrichment arises to fix the owners liability for the performance rendered prior to destruction. Since Carroll (D) should only pay for what benefits he might receive unjustly, liability is fixed by the amount of work which had become so far identified with the warehouse that it would have inured to him. Because the column and floor forms were temporary devices which would not have been part of the finished floor, they, unlike the cutting away of the old wooden floor and removing the necessary part of it, were not such benefits. Thus, the judgment requiring payment for all of this work is reversed.

DISSENT: (Johnston, J.) The upright rods set and tied together were a part of the building, and recovery for them should be allowed.

EDITOR'S ANALYSIS: Had the parties herein not assumed that particular warehouse would continue to exist, failure to completely construct the concrete floor would have barred any recovery by Bowersock (P). By such action, Bowersock (P) would have assumed an unconditional obligation to construct the floor and the risk of a destruction of the warehouse preventing such would have been his. This was the type of reasoning evidenced in *Tompkins v. Dudley.*

QUICKNOTES

IMPRACTICABILITY - A doctrine relieving the parties to a contract from liability for nonperformance of their duties thereunder, if the subject matter of the contract ceases to exist.

IMPOSSIBILITY - A doctrine relieving the parties to a contract from liability for nonperformance of their duties thereunder, if the subject matter of the contract ceases to exist, a person essential to the performance of the contract is deceased, or the service or goods contracted for has become illegal.

FRUSTRATION OF PURPOSE - A doctrine relieving the parties to a contract from liability for nonperformance of their duties thereunder when the purpose of the agreement ceases to exist due to circumstances not subject to either party's control.

QUASI-CONTRACT - An implied contract created by law to prevent unjust enrichment.

NOTES:

KEL KIM CORP. v. CENTRAL MARKETS, INC.
Skating rink lessee (P) v. Lessor (D)
N.Y. Ct. App., 70 N.Y. 2d 900, 519 N.E. 2d 295 (1987).

NATURE OF CASE: Appeal of summary judgment dismissing action seeking declaratory relief.

FACT SUMMARY: Kel Kim Corp. (P), unable to comply with a lease condition mandating insurance coverage due to a tight insurance market, contended that lease's force majeure clause excused performance of the condition.

CONCISE RULE OF LAW: A standard force majeure clause in a lease will not relieve a lessee of forfeiture for failure to comply with a condition mandating liability insurance.

FACTS: Central Markets, Inc. (D) leased certain property to Kim Corp. (P) to be used as a skating rink. One condition in the lease was that Kel Kim (P) carry liability insurance. The lease carried a standard force majeure clause. Due to the liability insurance crisis of the mid 1980's, Kel Kim (P) proved unable to secure liability coverage. When Central Markets (D) demanded compliance or forfeiture, Kel Kim (P) filed a declaratory relief action, contending that the force majeure clause excused its obligation to maintain insurance. The trial court granted summary judgment, dismissing the action and voiding the lease. The appellate division affirmed. Kel Kim (P) appealed.

ISSUE: Will a standard force majeure clause in a lease relieve a lessee of forfeiture for failure to comply with a condition mandating liability insurance?

HOLDING AND DECISION: (Per curiam) No. A standard force majeure clause in a lease will not relieve a lessee of forfeiture for failure to comply with a condition mandating liability insurance. Force majeure clauses, which are clauses excusing nonperformance due to circumstances beyond the control of the parties, are narrowly construed. It is the policy of the law that parties to a contract should decide for themselves how to allocate risks, and to give expansive readings to force majeure clauses would invite excessive judicial encroachment into an area best left to private decision-making. Generally speaking, unless the situation presented to a court is not specifically enumerated in the clause, the court will not imply it into the clause. Here, a failure to obtain insurance due to an insurance industry crisis is not specifically mentioned in the clause, so the clause will not be read to cover this situation. Affirmed.

EDITOR'S ANALYSIS: The clause contained a general catchall phrase, which excused nonperformance for "other similar causes beyond the control of such party." Kel Kim (P) argued that this phrase put the situation at hand within the clause. The court disagreed, stating that the phrase would be construed only to cover the same kind of eventualities as enumerated in the clause.

QUICKNOTES
FORCE MAJEURE CLAUSE - Clause pursuant to an oil and gas lease, relieving the lessee from liability for breach of the lease if the party's performance is impeded as the result of a natural cause that could not have been prevented.

EXPRESS CONDITION - A condition that is expressly stated in the terms of a written instrument.

NOTES:

BUNGE CORP. v. RECKER
Soy bean purchaser (P) v. Farmer (D)
519 F.2d 449 (8th Cir. 1975).

NATURE OF CASE: Appeal from award of damages in breach of contract action.

FACT SUMMARY: Recker (D) defended breach of contract charges on the ground that an act of God prevented his delivery of soy beans on the date specified because bad weather caused him to suffer heavy crop losses.

CONCISE RULE OF LAW: An act of God which damages or destroys goods to be sold under contract is justification for nonperformance of the contract only where the goods are specifically identified as the contract's subject matter.

FACTS: Recker (D), a farmer, contracted to sell 10,000 bushels of soy beans to Bunge (P) at a specified price. Delivery was to occur during January 1973, although Bunge (P) reserved the right to extend the time of delivery. Severe winter weather subsequently destroyed a large part of Recker's (D) crop. He informed Bunge (P) of this fact in mid-January. Bunge (P) responded by extending the date of delivery to March 31. When delivery was not made at that time, Bunge (P) brought suit for breach of contract. Recker (D) defended solely on the ground that he was prevented from performing by an act of God. The trial court found for Bunge (P), holding that Recker's (D) compliance with the contract was not limited to beans grown on his farm. The court further found that Bunge (P) acted in bad faith in that the sole reason for extending the delivery date was to increase damages. Accordingly, damages were granted in the amount of market price over contract price on January 31, rather than computing the higher damages as of March 31. Bunge (P) appealed the damages award.

ISSUE: Will an act of God which destroys goods to be sold under contract excuse nonperformance of the contract where the destroyed goods were not specifically identified as the contract's subject matter?

HOLDING AND DECISION: (Kilkenny, J.) No. The contract did not specify that the beans had to be grown on Recker's (D) land. Instead, it merely called for delivery of a certain quantity of the beans. Since the beans destroyed on Recker's (D) land were not specifically identified in the contract, Recker (D) may not assert the act of God defense as justification for nonperformance of the contract. The trial court was correct in that judgment. However, it was incorrect in finding that Bunge's (P) damages were limited due to its lack of good faith in extending the time of delivery. "Lack of good faith" is tantamount to an assertion of fraud. However, fraud was not raised as an affirmative defense by Recker (D) and Bunge (P) was therefore not put on notice that it would have to answer such charges. It must be given that opportunity on remand. Reversed and remanded.

EDITOR'S ANALYSIS: See Posner and Rosenfield, "Impossibility and Related Doctrines in Contract Law: An Economic Analysis," 6 J. Legal Studies 83 (1977), in which the authors argue that the basis for allocating risk in contract actions should be the respective abilities of the parties to bear the risk. The determination is made based on which party is in a better position to prevent the risk from being realized, and which party can insure against the loss at a lower cost. The analysis applies only in those situations in which the contract has not expressly allocated the risk between the parties.

QUICKNOTES
RISK OF LOSS - Liability for damage to or loss of property that is the subject matter of a contract for sale.

NOTES:

AMERICAN TRADING & PRODUCTION CORP. v. SHELL INTERNATIONAL MARINE, LTD.

Vessel charter (P) v. Offshore company (D)
453 F.2d 939 (2d Cir. 1972).

NATURE OF CASE: Suit for additional expenses under a charter contract.

FACT SUMMARY: Via a contract stating Texas as a departure point and Bombay, India as point of destination, Shell (D) chartered American Trading's (P) tank vessel for a voyage with a full cargo of lube oil. When the customary route was changed because of the closing of the Suez Canal, extra expenses were incurred.

CONCISE RULE OF LAW: While performance may be rendered impossible if it can only be accomplished with extreme and unreasonable difficulty, expense, injury, or loss, a mere increase in cost alone is not a sufficient excuse for nonperformance.

FACTS: Shell (D) signed a contract chartering a tank vessel, Washington Trader, from American Trading (P) on March 23, 1967. It provided the voyage would be from Texas to Bombay, India and would be for shipping a full cargo of lube oil at the prevailing rate under the American Tanker Rate Schedule (ATRS). This was $14.25 per long ton of cargo, plus 75%, and a charge of 85 cents per long ton for passage through the Suez Canal. Having departed on May 15, 1967 with a 16,183.32 long ton cargo, the Washington Trader was advised of possible diversion, due to a Suez Canal crises, on May 29. On May 30, the vessel arrived in Spanish Morocco, bunkered, and sailed on May 31st. On June 5, the ship's master was advised of possible trouble, and it was suggested he delay entering the Suez Canal pending clarification. When the Canal was then closed, Shell (D), on June 5, was contacted and diversion approval requested. In a June 6 response, Shell (D) said it was American Trading's (P) decision since the contract required delivery of the cargo without qualification as to route. That same day American Trading (P) advised Shell (D) the boat would proceed via the Cape of Good Hope, reserving all rights for extra compensation. This resulted in arriving 30 days too late and traveling 18,055 miles instead of 9,709. American Trading (P) sought to secure $131,978.44 in addition to the $417,327.36 Shell (D) had paid on May 26. When Shell (D) refused to pay the extra compensation, American Trading (P) sued. Although recognizing the parties may have expected the usual Suez route would be followed, the trial court found for Shell (D). American Trading (P) appealed.

ISSUE: Is a mere increase in the cost of performance a sufficient excuse for nonperformance?

HOLDING AND DECISION: (Mulligan, J.) No. While commercial impracticability because of extreme and unreasonable difficulty,

expense, injury, or loss will render performance impossible, a mere increase in cost alone is an insufficient excuse for nonperformance. There being no such extreme and unreasonable expense herein, the doctrine of commercial impracticability is not applicable. Furthermore, even after being alerted on May 29 of a possible diversion, the master sailed on the 31st of May and proceeded across the Mediterranean. Without such action, that cost could have been avoided. The parties may have expected the customary Suez route would be the probable route, but such was not agreed to be the exclusive route; the shipping industry recognizes the Cape route as an acceptable alternative. Thus, destruction of one means did not render the contract legally impossible to perform and discharge the unperformed delivery obligation. So, there is no basis for a quantum meruit analysis and the judgment is affirmed.

EDITOR'S ANALYSIS: Discharge via impracticability is recognized in U.C.C. § 2-615 and Restatement Section 454. In effect, the doctrine of impracticability offers relief from performance upon a finding of what amounts to subjective impossibility of high degree. As such, some courts are reluctant to accept anything short of impossibility, preferring to enforce modifications of the original contract or finding a mutual mistake of fact.

QUICKNOTES

IMPOSSIBILITY - A doctrine relieving the parties to a contract from liability for nonperformance of their duties thereunder, if the subject matter of the contract ceases to exist, a person essential to the performance of the contract is deceased, or the service or goods contracted for has become illegal.

IMPRACTICABILITY - A doctrine relieving the parties to a contract from liability for nonperformance of their duties thereunder, if the subject matter of the contract ceases to exist.

MUTUAL MISTAKE - A mistake by both parties to a contract, who are in agreement as to what the contract terms should be, but the agreement as written fails to reflect that common intent; such contracts are voidable or subject to reformation.

NOTES:

KRELL v. HENRY

Apartment owner (P) v. Coronation viewer (D)
Ct. App., 2 K.B. 740 (England) (1903).

NATURE OF CASE: Action for damages for breach of a contract for a license for use.

FACT SUMMARY: Henry (D) paid a deposit of £25 to Krell (P) for the use of his apartment in Pall Mall, London, for the purpose of a viewing sight for King Edward VII's coronation procession. The King became ill causing a delay of the coronation upon which Henry (D) refused to pay a £50 balance for which Krell (P) sued.

CONCISE RULE OF LAW: Where the object of one of the parties is the basis upon which both parties contract, the duties of performance are constructively conditioned upon the attainment of that object.

FACTS: In two letters of June 20, 1902, Henry (D) contracted through Krell's (P) agent, Bisgood, to use Krell's (P) flat in Pall Mall, London, to view the coronation procession of King Edward VII which had been advertised to pass along Pall Mall. The contract made no mention of this purpose. The period of use of the flat was the daytime only of June 26 and 27, 1902 for £75, £25 paid in deposit with the £50 remainder due on June 24, 1902. Henry (D) became aware of the availability of Krell's (P) flat as an announcement to that effect had been made which was reiterated by Krell's (P) housekeeper who showed Henry (D) the rooms. When the King became very ill, the coronation was delayed and Henry (D) refused to pay the £50 balance, for which Krell (P) brought suit.

ISSUE: Was the defeat of the basis upon which Henry (D) contracted a defeat of the contract?

HOLDING AND DECISION: (Williams, J.) Yes. It can be inferred from the surrounding circumstances that the rooms were taken for the purpose of viewing the processions and that was the foundation of the contract. It was not a lease of the rooms—they could not be used at night—but a license for use for a particular purpose. With the defeat of the purpose of the contract, the performance is excused.

EDITOR'S ANALYSIS: This case is an extension of *Taylor v. Caldwell* and, as in that case, it was necessary to remove the roadblock of a lease in order to avoid a conflict with *Paradine v. Jane.* The rule explained here is "frustration of purpose" or "commercial frustration." It has not been made clear whether this doctrine rests upon the failure of consideration or the allocation of the risks. While there is a frustration, performance is not impossible. No constructive condition of performance has failed as Krell (P) made no promise that the condition would occur. Rather, a constructive condition based upon the attainment of the purpose or object has arisen. Note that the frustration should be total or nearly total though that is a matter of degree.

QUICKNOTES

IMPOSSIBILITY - A doctrine relieving the parties to a contract from liability for nonperformance of their duties thereunder, if the subject matter of the contract ceases to exist, a person essential to the performance of the contract is deceased, or the service or goods contracted for has become illegal.

FRUSTRATION OF PURPOSE - A doctrine relieving the parties to a contract from liability for nonperformance of their duties thereunder when the purpose of the agreement ceases to exist due to circumstances not subject to either party's control.

CONDITION - Requirement; potential future occurrence upon which the existence of a legal obligation is dependent.

CONSIDERATION - Value given by one party in exchange for performance, or a promise to perform, by another party.

NOTES:

114

LLOYD v. MURPHY
Leasor of premises (P) v. Lessee (D)
Cal. Sup. Ct., 25 Cal.2d 48, 153 P.2d 47 (1944).

NATURE OF CASE: Action for declaratory relief to determine rights under a lease.

FACT SUMMARY: Murphy (D), Lloyd's (P) lessee, was restricted in the use of the demised premises to the sale of gasoline and new cars, but with the outbreak of World War II, the federal government ordered the sale of new cars discontinued.

CONCISE RULE OF LAW: The defense of commercial frustration requires that to excuse his nonpayment of rent a lessee must prove (1) that the risk of the frustrating event was not reasonably foreseeable, and (2) that the purpose for which the property was leased was totally or nearly totally destroyed.

FACTS: Lloyd (P) leased certain premises to Murphy (D) for five years beginning September 1941, for the sole purpose of selling new cars and gasoline. In January 1942, after the outbreak of World War II, the federal government ordered the sale of new cars discontinued. Within a month, the order was modified to allow the sale of new cars to those in the military and to those with preferential ratings. Lloyd (P) modified the restriction and allowed Murphy (D) to use the premises for any legitimate commercial purpose or to sublet. Despite this, Murphy (D) vacated the premises shortly thereafter, and Lloyd (P) reentered the premises. Lloyd (P) then brought this action for declaratory relief to determine his rights under the lease, and for judgment for unpaid rent. The trial court held that war conditions did not terminate Murphy's (D) obligations, that Lloyd's (P) modification was effective, and that Lloyd (P) should recover the unpaid rent. Murphy (D) appealed, arguing that his obligations were commercially frustrated.

ISSUE: Does the defense of commercial frustration require that to excuse his nonpayment of rent a lessee must prove (1) that the risk of the frustrating event was not reasonably foreseeable, and (2) that the purpose for which the property was leased was totally, or nearly totally, destroyed?

HOLDING AND DECISION: (Traynor, J.) Yes. The defense of commercial frustration requires that to excuse his nonpayment of rent, a lessee must prove (1) that the risk of the frustrating event was not reasonably foreseeable, and (2) that the purpose for which the property was leased was totally, or nearly totally, destroyed. The defense has been limited to cases of extreme hardship so that businesspersons can continue to rely with certainty on their contracts. First, if an event was foreseeable, there should have been provision for it in the contract, and the absence of such a provision gives rise to an inference that the risk was assumed. Thus, governmental acts that make performance unprofitable or more difficult or expensive do not excuse the duty to perform. Here, when the lease was executed, the automotive industry was in the process of conversion to supply military needs, and automobile sales were soaring because the public anticipated the restriction of production and sales. The risk of war and restrictions on the auto industry were not so remote as to be unforeseeable. Second, the purpose of the lease was not totally, or nearly totally, destroyed, but only restricted. Lloyd (P) waived the restrictions. The property had use value which was demonstrated by its being rerented shortly thereafter. Affirmed.

EDITOR'S ANALYSIS: English cases have not applied the frustration doctrine to leases on the ground that an estate is conveyed to the lessee which carries with it all risks. The question is simply who should bear the risk of destruction of the purpose of the transaction. With less than near total destruction, the consequences of applying the doctrine of frustration to a leasehold would be undesirable. Confusion would result from different decisions of the definition of "substantial" frustration, and litigation would probably be increased as lessees repudiated their leases when they found their businesses less profitable because of regulations accompanying a national emergency.

QUICKNOTES
FRUSTRATION OF PURPOSE - A doctrine relieving the parties to a contract from liability for nonperformance of their duties thereunder when the purpose of the agreement ceases to exist due to circumstances not subject to either party's control.

RISK OF LOSS - Liability for damage to or loss of property that is the subject matter of a contract for sale.

NOTES:

CHASE PRECAST CORP. v. JOHN J. PAONESSA CO.

Concrete median supplier (P) v. Construction contractor (D)

Mass. Sup. Jud. Ct., 409 Mass. 371, 566 N.E.2d 603 (1991).

NATURE OF CASE: Appeal from denial of damages for breach of contract.

FACT SUMMARY: When a highway reconstruction project was halted due to citizen protests, John J. Paonessa Co. (D), the contractor, canceled the contract with its supplier, Chase Precast Corp. (P), after Chase (P) had already produced one-half of the concrete median barriers required by the project.

CONCISE RULE OF LAW: A defendant may rely on frustration of purpose as a defense to a breach of contract claim if the risk of the occurrence of the frustrating event is not allocated by the contract to the defendant.

FACTS: In 1982, Massachusetts entered into two contracts with Paonessa (D) to replace a highway grass median strip with precast concrete barriers. Paonessa (D) subsequently contracted with Chase (P) to supply the concrete median barriers. After Chase (P) had produced about one-half of the barriers, angry residents brought a halt to the project. On June 7, 1983, Paonessa (D) notified Chase (P) by letter to stop producing the barriers, which Chase (P) did as soon as it received the letter on June 8. Paonessa (D) paid Chase (P) for all the barriers it had produced at the contract price. Chase (P) then brought an action against Paonessa (D) to recover its anticipated profit on the barriers called for in the contract but not produced. The trial court ruled in favor of Paonessa (D) based on impossibility of performance. The appeals court affirmed but noted that the doctrine of frustration of purpose was a more accurate description of the basis of the trial judge's decision than the doctrine of impossibility. Chase (P) appealed.

ISSUE: May a defendant rely on frustration of purpose as a defense to a breach of contract claim if the risk of the occurrence of the frustrating event is not allocated by the contract to the defendant?

HOLDING AND DECISION: (Lynch, J.) Yes. A defendant may rely on frustration of purpose as a defense to a breach of contract claim if the risk of the occurrence of the frustrating event is not allocated by the contract to the defendant. Frustration of purpose is defined by the Restatement (Second) of Contracts § 265 (1981) as follows: "Where, after a contract is made, a party's principal purpose is substantially frustrated without his fault by the occurrence of an event the nonoccurrence of which was a basic assumption on which the contract was made, his remaining duties to render performance are discharged, unless the language or the circumstances indicate the contrary." Since Paonessa (D) was in no way responsible for the state's elimination of the median

barriers from the project, whether it can rely on the defense of frustration turns on whether elimination of the barriers was a reasonably foreseeable risk allocated by the contracts to Paonessa (D). Because Chase (P) had supplied barriers to the state before, it was aware of the state's power to eliminate items from its contracts, paying only the contract unit price for items actually accepted. Chase (P) was also aware that lost profits were not an element of damage, giving further credence to the state's power to decrease quantities. But even if the parties were aware generally of the state's power to eliminate contract items, they did not contemplate the cancellation of a major portion of the project of such a widely used item as concrete median barriers and did not allocate the risk of such cancellation. Affirmed.

EDITOR'S ANALYSIS: Note the difference between impossibility and frustration as defenses to a breach of contract. The supplier of goods or services who finds himself unable to perform will use the impossibility defense. The buyer of the goods and services will typically use the defense of frustration. This is because it is always possible for the buyer to fulfill his promise to pay, even if he is no longer in need of the service or product and will essentially gain nothing for his money. To further add to the confusion, the Restatement (Second) of Contracts employs the same four criteria for both frustration and impossibility.

QUICKNOTES

FRUSTRATION OF PURPOSE - A doctrine relieving the parties to a contract from liability for nonperformance of their duties thereunder when the purpose of the agreement ceases to exist due to circumstances not subject to either party's control.

RISK OF LOSS - Liability for damage to or loss of property that is the subject matter of a contract for sale.

IMPOSSIBILITY - A doctrine relieving the parties to a contract from liability for nonperformance of their duties thereunder, if the subject matter of the contract ceases to exist, a person essential to the performance of the contract is deceased, or the service or goods contracted for has become illegal.

NOTES:

WOOLLUMS v. HORSLEY

Businessman (P) v. Uneducated recluse (D)

Ky. Ct. App., 93 Ky. 582, 20 S.W. 781 (1892).

NATURE OF CASE: For specific performance of a sale of oil, gas, and mineral rights.

FACT SUMMARY: Horsley (P), a knowledgeable businessman, succeeded in getting Woollums (D), an uneducated and sick recluse, to enter into a sales contract for the gas, mineral, and oil rights to his land for forty cents an acre (when the value of such was about $15 an acre). When Woollums (D) refused to convey a deed thereto, Horsley (P) sought specific performance.

CONCISE RULE OF LAW: Courts of equity will not decree a specific performance where the contract is founded in fraud, imposition, mistake, undue advantage, or gross misapprehension—or where it is not certain, equitable, reasonable, mutual, on sufficient consideration, and consistent with public policy.

FACTS: In August, 1887, an agent for Horsley (P) entered into a contract with Woollums (D)—an old, diseased, and uneducated recluse—for the sale of his mineral, gas, and oil rights for 40 cents an acre. Horsley (P) was an experienced businessman who was familiar with the land in that area and was buying such rights in thousands of acres. In April, 1889, Woollums' (D) land was worth $15 an acre, the value of the land being almost totally the mineral wealth. Horsley (P), furthermore, was advised a railroad might be coming through in the future. When Woollums (D) refused to convey a deed, Horsley (P) sought specific performance, saying his failure to pay the purchase money was due to the fact Woollums (D) refused to survey the land to ascertain the quantity subject to the per-acre sales price. Woollums' (D) main defense was that the contract was obtained through undue advantage and under such circumstances as would preclude equitable relief. Woollums (D) appealed a judgment for Horsley (P).

ISSUE: Can specific performance be denied because of the inequitable circumstances under which an otherwise legal contract was obtained?

HOLDING AND DECISION: (Holt, J.) Yes. Equitable relief being within the court's discretion, specific performance can be refused when the underlying contract evidences a hard or unconscionable bargain. Ethics are considered when equitable remedies are sought. The lack of mutual knowledge of the circumstances and the inadequate purchase price point to the conclusion that Woollums (D) was misled and acted under gross misapprehension. The contract being inequitable, unreasonable, and grounded upon insufficient consideration, the specific performance should have been denied.

EDITOR'S ANALYSIS: This case well illustrates the equitable principle that he who comes into equity must come with clean hands. Any inequitable, unethical, or immoral conduct on the plaintiff's part in the transaction at hand renders applicable the "unclean hands" doctrine. Thus, equitable relief may be barred even though the contract is technically legal and would support recovery at law.

QUICKNOTES

SPECIFIC PERFORMANCE - An equitable remedy whereby the court requires the parties to perform their obligations pursuant to a contract.

EQUITABLE REMEDY - A remedy that is based upon principles of fairness as opposed to rules of law.

CONSIDERATION - Value given by one party in exchange for performance, or a promise to perform, by another party.

MALUM PROHIBITUM - An action that is not inherently wrong, but which is prohibited by law.

NOTES:

WATERS v. MIN LTD.
Annuity purchase (P) v. Unconscionable buyer (D)
Mass. Sup. Jud. Ct., 412 Mass. 64, 587 N.E.2d 231 (1992).

NATURE OF CASE: Review of judgment ordering rescission of contract and dismissal of counterclaim for specific enforcement.

FACT SUMMARY: For $50,000, Waters (P) was persuaded to sell an annuity worth $189,000, a contract that she subsequently claimed was unconscionable.

CONCISE RULE OF LAW: Courts may avoid enforcement of a bargain that is shown to be unconscionable by reason of gross inadequacy of consideration.

FACTS: Waters (P) had purchased an annuity contract with the proceeds of an accident settlement. She later became romantically involved with Beauchemin, an ex-con who introduced her to drugs and suggested that she sell the annuity to Min (D). Min (D) drafted the contract documents with the assistance of legal counsel, but Waters (P) represented herself. In return for the annuity, which had a cash value of $189,000 and a long-term value of $694,000, Min (D) agreed to forgive a debt that Beauchemin owed them and to pay Waters (P) $50,000. Waters (P) later brought suit to rescind the contract on the ground of unconscionability. Min (D) counterclaimed and sought specific performance of the contract. The trial court found the contract to be unconscionable and dismissed the counterclaim. Min (D) appealed.

ISSUE: May a court avoid enforcement of a bargain that is shown to be unconscionable by reason of gross inadequacy of consideration?

HOLDING AND DECISION: (Lynch, J.) Yes. Courts may avoid enforcement of a bargain that is shown to be unconscionable by reason of gross inadequacy of consideration. Gross disparity in the values exchanged is an important factor to be considered in determining whether a contract is unconscionable. In this case, Beauchemin introduced Waters (P) to drugs, exhausted her credit card, unduly influenced her, suggested that she sell her annuity, initiated the contract negotiations, and personally benefitted from them. Moreover, the cash value of the annuity policy was four times greater than the price to be paid by Min (D). The disparity of interests in this case is so gross that no court can resist the inference that it was improperly obtained and is unconscionable. Affirmed.

EDITOR'S ANALYSIS: The common law and Uniform Commercial Code approaches to unconscionability have been expanded in modern statutes. This case could probably have been brought equally well as fraud. In general, a party seeking damages for fraud is entitled to recover such damages as will compensate her for the loss or injury actually sustained and will place her in the

same position that she would have occupied had she not been defrauded.

QUICKNOTES

UNCONSCIONABILITY - Rule of law whereby a court may excuse performance of a contract, or of a particular contract term, if it determines that such term(s) are unduly oppressive or unfair to one party to the contract.

CONSIDERATION - Value given by one party in exchange for performance, or a promise to perform, by another party.

RESCISSION - The canceling of an agreement and the return of the parties to their positions prior to the formation of the contract.

NOTES:

BROWER v. GATEWAY 2000, INC.

Consumers (P) v. Computer manufacturer (D)

N.Y. Sup. Ct. App. Div., 246 A.D.2d 246 (1998).

NATURE OF CASE: Class action challenging validity of a contract.

FACT SUMMARY: Purchasers (P) of Gateway (D) computers brought a class action suit to determine the validity of a standards terms and conditions agreement containing an arbitration clause.

CONCISE RULE OF LAW: In order to find a contract clause "unconscionable" requires some showing of an absence of meaningful choice on the part of one of the parties together with contract terms which are unreasonably favorable to the other party.

FACTS: Consumers (P) bought computers from Gateway (D) through a direct-sales system, by mail or phone order. Gateway (D) included with the materials purchased a standard agreement, which notified the buyer that if it kept the product for 30 days it was bound to the terms and conditions of the agreement. The agreement provided for final arbitration in the case of any dispute. Plaintiffs commenced this action for compensatory and punitive damages alleging deceptive sales practices. Gateway (D) moved to dismiss based on the arbitration clause. Plaintiffs claimed the arbitration clause was invalid under UCC 2-207, unconscionable under UCC 2-302, and an unenforceable adhesion contract. The IAS court dismissed the complaint based on the arbitration clause and plaintiffs appealed.

ISSUE: To find a contract clause "unconscionable," does it require some showing of an absence of meaningful choice on the part of one of the parties together with contract terms which are unreasonably favorable to the other party?

HOLDING AND DECISION: (Milonas, J.) Yes. To find a contract clause "unconscionable" requires some showing of an absence of meaningful choice on the part of one of the parties together with contract terms which are unreasonably favorable to the other party. First, the IAS court properly rejected plaintiffs' claim that the arbitration clause was invalid under UCC 2-207. Plaintiffs claimed that the arbitration clause constituted a material alternation of their preexisting oral agreement, since it was not bargained for or accepted. Under that section, a material alteration constitutes a proposal for addition to the contract that becomes a part of the contract only upon plaintiffs' express acceptance. However, the clause was not an alteration of the parties' agreement but a provision of the sole contract existing between them. The contract was formed when the merchandise was retained past 30 days. Thus, the contract was outside the scope of UCC 2-207. Second, the plaintiffs claimed that the arbitration clause constituted an unenforceable contract of adhesion in that it involved no meaningful choice or negotiation on the part of the consumer. This argument, too, was properly rejected by the IAS court. While the parties did not possess equal bargaining power, that factor alone does not make a contract one of adhesion. As that court noted, if the consumer is in a position to return the goods and purchase them from a competitor, the consumer is not in a "take it or leave it" position. Here the consumer has 30 days to determine whether the goods and the terms of the agreement were satisfactory and had an unqualified right to return the merchandise. Last, the plaintiffs argued that the contract was unenforceable under UCC 2-302 on the basis that the arbitration clause was unconscionable due to the unduly burdensome procedure and cost for the individual consumer. The IAS court found that while this class-action suit may be less costly, that does not alter the binding effect of the valid arbitration clause in the agreement. Under New York law, unconscionability requires a showing that a contract is both "procedurally" and "substantively" unconscionable when made. This requires some showing of an "absence of meaningful choice on the part of one of the parties together with contract terms which are unreasonably favorable to the other party." With respect to the procedural element, the court looks to the formation process, considering such factors as the setting of the transaction, the experience and education of the inferior party, whether the seller used high pressure tactics, and any disparities in bargaining power between the parties. None of these factors support the plaintiffs' claim. The purchasers had 30 days to thoroughly examine the equipment and read the contract. Furthermore, the arbitration clause was not hidden within a long, complex document. The substantive element requires an examination of whether the terms of the agreement were fair. The possible inconvenience of the arbitration site, Chicago, alone does not rise to the level of unconscionability. This court does find, however, that the excessive cost factor entailed in arbitration is unreasonable and serves to deter an individual from invoking the process. While generally a court must find both procedural and substantive unconscionability to declare an agreement invalid, the substantive element alone may suffice. Remanded.

EDITOR'S ANALYSIS: The case here was remanded for the purpose of determining whether Gateway's (D) substitution of the American Arbitration Association (AAA) for the International Chamber of Commerce (ICC) as an arbitrator would also be unconscionable.

GIANNI SPORT LTD. v. GANTOS, INC.
Apparel seller (P) v. Purchaser
Mich. Ct. App., 151 Mich. App. 598, 391 N.W.2d 760 (1986).

NATURE OF CASE: Appeal of award of damages for breach of contracts.

FACT SUMMARY: Gantos, Inc. (D) contracted to purchase certain women's apparel from Gianni Sport, Ltd. (P), reserving the right to cancel at any time.

CONCISE RULE OF LAW: A clause permitting a buyer to unilaterally cancel an order is invalid if unreasonable and the buyer is in a substantially superior bargaining position.

FACTS: Gantos, Inc. (D) contracted to purchase certain women's apparel from Gianni Sport, Ltd. (P). The contract permitted Gantos (D) to cancel the purchase order as to any non-delivered goods at any time. The purchase order comprised about 22% of Gianni's (P) sales that year; Gantos (D) was a much larger concern. Gantos (D) notified Gianni (P) that it was canceling the order. The terms were renegotiated, and Gantos (D) obtained the goods at half the original price. Gianni (P) brought suit for the original purchase price. The trial court held the clause unconscionable, and rendered judgment for Gianni (P). Evidence had shown that small sellers like Gianni (P) had similar clauses imposed on them by larger purchasers like Gantos (D) as a matter of course.

ISSUE: Will a clause permitting a buyer to unilaterally cancel an order be invalid if unreasonable and the buyer is in a substantially superior bargaining position?

HOLDING AND DECISION: (Per curiam) Yes. A clause permitting a buyer to unilaterally cancel an order is invalid if unreasonable and the buyer is in a substantially superior bargaining position. A provision in a contract will be void as unconscionable if the parties are of sufficiently disparate bargaining power and the term is substantively unreasonable. A court will void such a clause only if it results in oppression and unfair surprise, not if it merely drives a hard bargain on the weaker party. Here, Gantos, Inc. (D) was much larger and more powerful than Giann (P). The provision left Gianni (P) in the position of having to virtually give his product away. The trial court determined that this constituted oppression, and this court does not find that determination clearly erroneous. Affirmed.

EDITOR'S ANALYSIS: U.C.C. § 2-302, which governs unconscionability, only applies to sales contracts. Courts have developed doctrines of more general application in an effort to prevent unconscionable contracts. One of the most universal rules is the imposition of a duty of good faith on parties to a contract. This duty is recognized in the vast majority of jurisdictions.

QUICKNOTES

UNCONSCIONABILITY - Rule of law whereby a court may excuse performance of a contract, or of a particular contract term, if it determines that such term(s) are unduly oppressive or unfair to one party to the contract.

NOTES:

CHAPTER 5
THE MATURING AND BREACH OF CONTRACT DUTIES

QUICK REFERENCE RULES OF LAW

1. **The Effects of Express Conditions.** Where it is doubtful whether words create a promise or an express condition, they are usually interpreted as creating a promise, thereby avoiding a forfeiture. (Howard v. Federal Crop Ins. Corp)

2. **The Effects of Express Conditions.** If a party to a contract can avoid his duties under the contract on the happening of a certain event, that party has the burden of proof as to the happening of that event. (Gray v. Gardner)

3. **The Effects of Express Conditions.** An appellate court is not bound by a lower court's interpretation or construction of a contract when such is based solely upon the terms of the written instrument without the aid of extrinsic evidence and where there is no conflict in the evidence or the determination was made upon incompetent evidence. (Parsons v. Bristol Dev. Co.)

4. **The Effects of Express Conditions.** Evidence to the intention of the parties may show that a promise to pay "as received" means that "receipt" was a condition precedent to the promisor's duty to pay. (Mascioni v. I.B. Miller, Inc.)

5. **The Effects of Express Conditions.** An injured plaintiff who does not notify her insurer for several months after learning of a claim does not act with reasonable promptness and thereby violates the policy's requirement of immediate notice. (Royal-Globe Ins. Co. v. Craven)

6. **The Effects of Express Conditions.** An insurer's acts or conduct inducing the insured not to bring suit estops the insurer from asserting a contractual condition relating to a time limitation for filing suit thereunder. The limitation becomes effective again, having been suspended, at such time the insurer gives notice to the insured that the reason for withholding suit is no longer effective. (Gilbert v. Globe & Rutgers Fire Ins. Co.)

7. **The Effects of Express Conditions.** When no objection is made to overdue payments not made in accordance with the strict terms of the contract and the same are accepted, an order of business is established inconsistent with rigid insistence upon a forfeiture or penalty clause. (Porter v. Harrington)

8. **The Effects of Express Conditions.** A condition in a contract may be waived, but no waiver is implied by mere acceptance of the proffered performance. (Clark v. West)

9. **The Effects of Express Conditions.** An express condition precedent to give notice before filing suit under a contract must be fulfilled before suit is filed. (Inman v. Clyde Hall Drilling Co.)

10. **The Effects of Express Conditions.** An insured who belatedly gives notice of an insurance claim may nonetheless recover on the insurance contract by rebutting the presumption that the delay prejudiced the insurer. (Aetna Cas. & Sur. Co. v. Murphy)

11. **Conditions of Satisfaction** A condition may be excused in the event of impracticability if the occurrence of the condition is not a material part of the agreed exchange and forfeiture would otherwise result. (Grenier v. Compratt Constr. Co.)

12. **Conditions of Satisfaction.** Where a party has substantially performed, unreasonable withholding of an architect's certificate constitutes a waiver of the condition requiring it. (Nolan v. Whitney)

13. **Conditions of Satisfaction.** When "satisfaction" contracts involve taste, fancy, etc., a jury may only inquire as to whether the party is honestly dissatisfied, not as to whether the dissatisfaction is reasonable. (Fursmidt v. Hotel Abbey Holding Corp.)

14. **Constructive Conditions: The Order of Performance.** Where there is a bilateral contract, suit may be brought by a party without his pleading that he performed his side of the bargain. (Nichols v. Raynbred)

15. **Constructive Conditions: The Order of Performance.** Breach of a covenant by one party to a contract relieves the other party's obligation to perform another covenant which is dependent thereon, the performance of the first covenant being an implied condition precedent to the duty to perform the second covenant. (Kingston v. Preston)

16. **Constructive Conditions: The Order of Performance.** Where a contract contains mutual promises to pay (or perform some other act), one of which may or is to be performed before the other, the latter promise is an independent obligation the nonperformance of which merely gives rise to a cause of action and does not defeat the right of the party making it to recover for a breach of the other promise. (Price v. Van Lint)

17. **Constructive Conditions: The Order of Performance.** In a bilateral contract based on promises that must be exchanged in a certain order, performance of the first is a constructive condition precedent to the other's duty to perform. (Conley v. Pitney Bowes)

18. **Constructive Conditions: The Order of Performance.** If the vendor of real estate is unable to perform his part of an executory contract when such performance is due, a formal tender or demand by the vendee is not required for maintenance of an action by him to recover the money paid on the contract or damages. (Ziehen v. Smith)

19. **Constructive Conditions: The Order of Performance.** While a vendor of real estate with incurable title defects is automatically in default, a vendor with curable title must be put in default by the vendee's tender of performance and demand for a good title deed. (Cohen v. Kranz)

20. **Constructive Conditions: The Order of Performance.** Failure to insist upon strict performance of an independent covenant can preclude a party from suit based on that designation when the lapse of time thus engendered has altered the nature of the covenants. (Beecher v. Conradt)

21. **Constructive Conditions: The Order of Performance.** In the event of a buyer's breach, a court may award the seller the amount of the purchase price in lieu of specific performance. (Osborne v. Bullins)

22. **Constructive Conditions: The Order of Performance.** Where a contract is made to perform work and no agreement is made as to payment, the work must be substantially performed before payment can be demanded. (Stewart v. Newbury)

23. **Constructive Conditions: The Order of Performance.** The occurrence of a condition precedent creates the duty of counter performance. (Tipton v. Feitner)

24. **Protecting the Exchange on Breach.** A party is not bound to honor a contract after the specified date of performance. (Oshinsky v. Lorraine Mfg. Co.)

25. **Protecting the Exchange on Breach.** Under the U.C.C. a seller has the right to correct defective performance within a reasonable time provided notice of intent is given. (Bartus v. Riccardi)

26. Protecting the Exchange on Breach. Acceptance of goods occurs when the buyer, after a reasonable opportunity to inspect the goods, signifies to the seller that he will take them in spite of their nonconformity or fails to make an effective rejection. (Plateq Corp. of North Haven v. Machlett Labs., Inc.)

27. Protecting the Exchange on Breach. There can be no recovery on a contract as distinguished from quantum meruit unless there is substantial performance which is defined as where the performance meets the essential purpose of the contract. (Plante v. Jacobs)

28. Protecting the Exchange on Breach. A court may refuse to order rescission where only a breach of contract has occurred rather than an utter failure of consideration or a repudiation by the party in breach. (Worcester Heritage Society, Inc. v. Trussell)

29. Protecting the Exchange on Breach. An anticipatory repudiation of a contract is a definite and unequivocal manifestation of an intention on the part of the repudiator that he will not render the promised performance when the time fixed for it in the contract arrives. (Wholesale Sand & Gravel, Inc. v. Decker)

30. Protecting the Exchange on Breach. The failure of a contractor's (or subcontractor's) performance to constitute "substantial" performance may justify the owner in refusing to make a progress payment. (K & G Constr. Co. v. Harris)

31. Protecting the Exchange on Breach. The reasonable belief that the other party to a contract will be unable to perform does not relieve one of his own duty to perform his contractual obligations. (Hathaway v. Sabin)

32. Protecting the Exchange on Breach. The right of a party to a contract to demand adequate assurances of performance by the other party is predicated on reasonable grounds for insecurity regarding such performance. (Cherwell-Ralli, Inc. v. Rytman Grain Co.)

33. Protecting the Exchange on Breach. In a unilateral contract for the payment in installments after default of one or more, no repudiation can amount to an anticipatory breach of the rest of the installments not yet due. (Greguhn v. Mutual of Omaha Ins. Co.)

34. Protecting the Exchange on Breach. Where there is a substantial defect with respect to the nature, character, or situation, and in regard of which he is not put on inquiry, specific performance will not be decreed as against him. (Reigart v. Fisher)

HOWARD v. FEDERAL CROP INSURANCE CORP.
Tobacco farmer (P) v. Insurer (D)
540 F.2d 695 (4th Cir. 1976).

NATURE OF CASE: Appeal from denial of proceeds of an insurance policy.

FACT SUMMARY: Federal Crop Insurance Corp. (FCIC) (D) claimed that Howard's (P) violation of a condition precedent negated its obligation to pay.

CONCISE RULE OF LAW: Where it is doubtful whether words create a promise or an express condition, they are usually interpreted as creating a promise, thereby avoiding a forfeiture.

FACTS: Howard (P) suffered losses to his tobacco crop due to alleged rain damage. He notified FCIC (D), with whom he had an insurance policy, of the loss. However, before an FCIC (D) agent was able to come out and inspect the land, Howard (P) plowed under the tobacco field, including the damaged stalks, in order to plant a cover crop of rye, which he claimed was necessary for preservation of the soil. The plowing under of the damaged crop was in violation of a provision in the FCIC (D) insurance policy. Claiming that the provision constituted a condition precedent to its obligation to pay, FCIC (D) refused to settle the claim. Howard (P) brought suit to recover on the policy, but the trial court found for FCIC (D). Howard (P) appealed, arguing that the subject provision constituted a promise, rather than a condition precedent.

ISSUE: Where it is doubtful whether words constitute a promise or express condition, should they be interpreted as constituting a promise?

HOLDING AND DECISION: (Widener, J.) Yes. It is a well established maxim that the law abhors a forfeiture. Therefore, a provision which does not clearly constitute a condition precedent should be interpreted as creating a mere promise. In such a manner, the imposition of a forfeiture is avoided. In the instant case, the offending clause did not specify that Howard's (D) agreement not to destroy evidence of an asserted claim constituted a condition precedent to FCIC'S (D) obligation to pay. Thus, a condition precedent will generally not be found. Accordingly, summary judgment in FCIC's (D) favor was improperly granted. Reversed and remanded.

EDITOR'S ANALYSIS: The distinction between a condition and a mere promise, on which the Howard decision primarily rests, was described by one court as follows. "A condition is distinguished from a promise in that it creates no right or duty in and of itself but is merely a limiting or modifying factor . . . If the condition is not fulfilled, the right to enforce the contract does not come into existence." See *Lach v. Cahill*, 138 Conn. 418, 85 A. 2d 481 (1951).

QUICKNOTES

EXPRESS CONDITION - A condition that is expressly stated in the terms of a written instrument.

CONDITION PRECEDENT - The happening of an uncertain occurrence, which is necessary before a particular right or interest may be obtained or an action performed.

PROMISE - The expression of an intention to act, or to forbear from acting, granting a right to the promisee to expect and enforce its performance.

NOTES:

GRAY v. GARDNER
Seller (P) v. Purchase of whale oil (D)
Mass. Sup. Jud. Ct., 17 Mass. 188 (1821).

NATURE OF CASE: Action for breach of contract.

FACT SUMMARY: Gardner (D) promised to pay an extra 25 cents a gallon for whale oil if a certain amount of oil came into port by October 1st.

CONCISE RULE OF LAW: If a party to a contract can avoid his duties under the contract on the happening of a certain event, that party has the burden of proof as to the happening of that event.

FACTS: Gardner (D) entered into a contract with Gray (P) for the purchase of whale oil. The price was to be 85 cents per gallon if no more oil was received in Nantucket and New Bedford than had been received there the previous year. If more oil was received there from whaling ships, then the price for the oil was only to be 60 cents. At midnight on the last day of the period a whaling ship entered Nantucket harbor. It had not docked prior to the expiration of the period specified in the contract. Gardner (D) argued that its oil should be included in the total and that with the addition of this oil he should only have to pay 60 cents per gallon. The trial court ruled that the agreement called for the docking of the vessel and Gardner (D) had the burden of the proof to show that the vessel had arrived on the last day of the period since he was seeking to escape contractual obligations. Gardner (D) claimed that this was a condition precedent and that Gray (P) must establish that the condition did not occur before he could enforce the promise.

ISSUE: Does the party attempting to escape contractual liability have the burden of proving that a condition has or has not occurred?

HOLDING AND DECISION: (Parker, J.) Yes. The court held that since Gardner (D) was going to be able to avoid some of his duties under the contract if more whale oil came into port this year than in the previous year, he had the burden of proof to show the happening of that event. Gardner (D) was bound by his promise to pay 85 cents a gallon for the whale oil unless a subsequent condition occurred and that promise remained in force until he could show the happening of the condition. It was necessary for Gardner (D) to show that the vessel in question had come to anchor or had been moored and since he could only show that the vessel was coming towards the port on October 1st, he didn't sustain his burden of proof. Therefore, the court found for Gray (P).

EDITOR'S ANALYSIS: It is usually unnecessary, in terms of substantive law, to distinguish between condition precedents and condition subsequents. However, from a procedural point of view, the distinction has great significance. As this famous case illustrates, the party to whom a duty is owed, as a rule, must prove the occurrence of a condition precedent which has discharged his obligation of counter-performance. On the other hand, the party who owes the duty usually has the burden of showing that he has been released from his obligation by the occurrence of a condition subsequent.

QUICKNOTES

CONDITION SUBSEQUENT - Potential future occurrence that extinguishes a party's obligation to perform pursuant to the contract.

CONDITION PRECEDENT - The happening of an uncertain occurrence, which is necessary before a particular right or interest may be obtained or an action performed.

NOTES:

PARSONS v. BRISTOL DEVELOPMENT CO.
Architect (P) v. Builder (D)
Cal. Sup. Ct., 62 Cal. 2d 861, 402 P.2d 839 (1965).

NATURE OF CASE: Suit to recover for services performed and to foreclose a mechanic's lien.

FACT SUMMARY: Parsons (P) contracted with Bristol Development (D) to design and supervise construction of an office building. The contract provided that payment for the second phase (construction) was conditioned on obtaining an eco-nomically feasible financing arrangement. When such was obtained by Bristol Development (D) on the condition that it show clear title to the land, Parsons (P) completed a major portion of this work before a problem with adverse title laid waste to the loan arrangement.

CONCISE RULE OF LAW: An appellate court is not bound by a lower court's interpretation or construction of a contract when such is based solely upon the terms of the written instrument without the aid of extrinsic evidence and where there is no conflict in the evidence or the determination was made upon incompetent evidence.

FACTS: The contract whereunder Parsons (P) was hired to design and supervise construction of an office building for Bristol Development (D) provided that the ability to obtain a loan which made the project economically feasible in Bristol's (D) determination was condition precedent to any duty or obligation for Bristol (D) to commence, continue, or complete the construction phase or pay Parsons (P) therefore. It also stated that notification to proceed with the construction phase would result in an obligation to pay an estimated 25% of Parsons' (P) fee, and that Bristol (D) would be obliged to pay the remaining 75% only from construction loan funds. After obtaining the necessary loan offer, Bristol (D) told Parsons (P) to proceed with construction on March 14, 1961 and paid him 25% of the fee for all work. However, the loan was conditioned upon a showing of clear title to the land, and on May 23, 1961, James Freeman filed an action against Bristol (D) claiming adverse title. Thus, on August 15, 1961, Parsons (P) was notified by Bristol (D) to stop work. Claiming he had performed 95% of the construction phase work, Parsons (P) sued Bristol (D) and Freeman to recover for his services and to foreclose a mechanic's lien. The trial court, finding Bristol's (D) obligation to pay any more was conditioned upon the existence of construction loan funds, entered a judgment for Bristol (D). Having appealed this decision, Parsons (P) contended the appellate court had the obligation to interpret the contract anew and claimed that a savings clause, designed to secure partial payment if the project was abandoned or suspended, was not covered by the aforementioned clause relating payment to the existence of construction loan funds.

ISSUE: Does the lower court's construction of a contract, based solely upon the terms of the written instrument without the aid of evidence, and where there is no conflict in the evidence or a determination has been made upon incompetent evidence, preclude the appellate court from interpreting it anew?

HOLDING AND DECISION: (Traynor, J.) No. An appellate court is not bound by a lower court's construction of a contract once it determines such was erroneous. This is the case when there is no conflict in the evidence or when a determination was made upon incompetent evidence and the construction was based solely upon the terms of the written instrument without the aid of evidence. There was no conflict in the extrinsic evidence in this case; an independent determination of the meaning of the contract is proper. Accordingly, we find that the trial court properly determined that payments beyond an estimated 25% of Parsons' (P) fee for the construction phase were to be made only from construction loan funds. Therefore, the judgment is affirmed.

EDITOR'S ANALYSIS: When there is no conflict in the evidence, the appellate court is in as good a position to interpret a contract, based solely upon its written terms without the aid of evidence, as is a trial court. Therefore, the reason for accepting the lower court's judgment, if it is in any way reasonable, disappears. It is only when the credibility of extrinsic evidence is involved that the ability of construction at the trial level becomes superior to that of the appellate courts. In that instance, then, the appellate court rightly defers to any reasonable determination at the lower level.

QUICKNOTES

CONDITION PRECEDENT - The happening of an uncertain occurrence, which is necessary before a particular right or interest may be obtained or an action performed.

EXTRINSIC EVIDENCE - Evidence that is not contained within the text of a document or contract but which is derived from the parties' statements or the circumstances under which the agreement was made.

NOTES:

MASCIONI v. I.B. MILLER, INC.

Concrete wall subcontractor (P) v. General contractor (D)

N.Y. Ct. App., 261 N.Y. 1, 184 N.E. 473 (1933).

NATURE OF CASE: Action to recover damages for breach of contract.

FACT SUMMARY: Miller (B) promised to pay his subcontractor, Mascioni (P), but payment was qualified as follows: "Payments to be made as received from the Owner."

CONCISE RULE OF LAW: Evidence to the intention of the parties may show that a promise to pay "as received" means that "receipt" was a condition precedent to the promisor's duty to pay.

FACTS: Mascioni (P) subcontracted to erect concrete walls as specified in a contract between Miller (B), the general contractor, and the owner. Miller's (D) promise to pay Mascioni (P) contained the qualification: "Payments to be made as received from the Owner." Mascioni (P) sought to recover payment for his work even though Miller (D) had received no payments from the owner.

ISSUE: In a promise to pay money "as received," does the promisor assume an absolute obligation to pay (i.e. the qualification is only for the sake of convenience)?

HOLDING AND DECISION: (Lehman, J.) No. A promise to pay money "as received from the Owner" may imply that the promisor's receipt of money from the owner is a condition precedent to his obligation to perform. Upon the happening of the event, i.e., receipt of payment, the obligation to complete performance arises. Whether the defendant's express promise to pay is construed as a promise to pay "if" payment is made by the owner or "when" such payment is made, "the result must be the same; since if the event does not befall, or a time coincident with the happening of the event does not arrive, in neither case may performance be exacted." Even if the language in the present case is ambiguous, the trier of fact made the determination in favor of Miller (D), and that determination is not erroneous as a matter of law.

EDITOR'S ANALYSIS: The court here was fairly conclusory on the issue of the qualification as a "condition precedent." The court essentially found that the qualification was indeed ambiguous and thereafter deferred to the trier of fact, who had heard parol evidence of the actual intention of the parties. The underlying issue (as the court points out) is, in practical terms: Who assumed the risk of non-payment by the owner? This frequent, but still troublesome, question can usually be answered only by the introduction at trial of such extrinsic evidence as custom, usage of trade, or additional oral agreements.

QUICKNOTES

CONDITION PRECEDENT - The happening of an uncertain occurrence, which is necessary before a particular right or interest may be obtained or an action performed.

NOTES:

ROYAL-GLOBE INS. CO. v. CRAVEN
Insurance company (P) v. Insured (D)
Mass. Sup. Ct., 411 Mass. 629, 585 N.E.2d 315 (1992).

NATURE OF CASE: Appeal from summary judgment denying release from obligation to enter arbitration.

FACT SUMMARY: Because Craven (D) waited four months before notifying Royal-Globe Ins. Co. (P) of her involvement in a hit-and-run accident, Royal-Globe (P) sought a declaration that it had no obligation to submit to arbitration after denying her claim because Craven (D) did not comply with her contractual obligation to give timely notice of her claim.

CONCISE RULE OF LAW: An injured plaintiff who does not notify her insurer for several months after learning of a claim does not act with reasonable promptness and thereby violates the policy's requirement of immediate notice.

FACTS: On September 19, 1979, Craven (D) was injured in a hit-and-run automobile accident. She was taken to the hospital by ambulance, where she remained in intensive care for several days. She was released from the hospital 23 days after the accident. She returned to work approximately three months after the accident. On January 23, 1980, four months after the accident, Craven (D) gave formal notice of her claim to Royal-Globe (P). Royal-Globe's (P) policy required that the insured notify it within 24 hours if the insured has been involved in a hit-and-run accident, or, in any event, the insured must notify the company promptly of the accident or loss. Royal-Globe (P) paid various claims belonging to Craven (D) but denied her claim for recovery under her uninsured motorist policy. When Craven (D) filed for arbitration of that claim, Royal-Globe (P) filed suit, seeking a declaration that it had no obligation to submit to arbitration. Royal-Globe (P) argued that it was not liable under the uninsured motorist policy because Craven (D) did not comply with her contractual obligation to give timely notice of her claim. Craven (D) contended that Royal-Globe (P) was estopped from raising her failure of notice as a basis to deny liability. On cross-motions for summary judgment, the trial court entered a summary judgment for Craven (D), denied Royal-Globe's (P) motion for summary judgment, and ordered that the matter proceed to arbitration. Royal-Globe (P) appealed.

ISSUE: Does an injured plaintiff who does not notify her insurer for several months after learning of a claim fail to act with reasonable promptness, thereby violating the policy's requirement of immediate notice?

HOLDING AND DECISION: (Abrams, J.) Yes. An injured plaintiff who does not notify her insurer for several months after learning of a claim fails to act with reasonable promptness, thereby violating the policy's requirement of immediate notice. A 24-hour notice requirement may be excused because of disability. In this case, for example, because Craven (D) was in the intensive care unit during the first 24 hours after the accident, she could not be expected to notify Royal-Globe (P) of her claim. Although disability tolls the running of the 24-hour period, it does not dispense with it altogether. Therefore, once the disability is removed, the requirement of prompt notice—but not necessarily within 24 hours—is reimposed. "Prompt" is defined as performed readily or immediately, without hesitation or delay. Craven's (D) notice more than four months after the accident was not prompt. Furthermore, Royal-Globe's (P) investigation and denial of Craven's (D) claim does not estop it from denying liability because of her late notice. To claim estoppel, Craven (D) would have to show that she had been induced by Royal-Globe's (P) conduct to forgo steps to prevent a default under the policy; Craven (D) cannot make this showing because the default had already occurred by the time Royal-Globe (P) denied the policy. Therefore, Royal-Globe (P) is not estopped from denying liability on the basis of Craven's (D) delayed notice. Reversed.

EDITOR'S ANALYSIS: The prompt notice requirement litigated in Royal-Globe is an example of an express condition precedent. A condition precedent is an act or event, other than a lapse of time, which must occur before a duty to perform a promised performance arises. If the condition does not occur and is not excused, then the other party is no longer required to perform. If the condition is met, then the other party is obliged to keep its promise; failure to do so constitutes a breach.

QUICKNOTES
EXPRESS CONDITION - A condition that is expressly stated in the terms of a written instrument.

CONDITION PRECEDENT - The happening of an uncertain occurrence, which is necessary before a particular right or interest may be obtained or an action performed.

EXCUSE OF CONDITION - The removal of a condition as a bar to performance or nonperformance of an obligation, either by waiver or occurrence of that condition.

NOTES:

GILBERT v. GLOBE & RUTGERS FIRE INS. CO.

Beach cottage owner (P) v. Insurance company (D)

Or. Sup. Ct., 91 Or. 59, 174 P. 1161, rehearing denied 178 P. 358 (1919).

NATURE OF CASE: Action to recover under fire insurance policy.

FACT SUMMARY: Gilbert's (P) beach cottage burned on October 2, 1912. Relying on promises of payment made by Globe & Rutgers Fire Ins. Co. (D), Gilbert (P) failed to file suit until June 29, 1916, even though the policy provided no suit would be sustainable unless filed within twelve months from the date of the fire.

CONCISE RULE OF LAW: An insurer's acts or conduct inducing the insured not to bring suit estops the insurer from asserting a contractual condition relating to a time limitation for filing suit thereunder. The limitation becomes effective again, having been suspended, at such time the insurer gives notice to the insured that the reason for withholding suit is no longer effective.

FACTS: Gilbert (P) insured his beach cottage against fire with Globe & Rutgers Fire Ins. Co. (D). When an October 2, 1912 fire totally destroyed the cottage, an adjuster for Globe & Rutgers (D) accompanied Gilbert to the site and assessed the loss at $1,531. Subsequently, Astoria Box and Lumber Co. brought suit against Gilbert (P), and the court issued a writ of garnishment compelling Globe & Rutgers (D) to pay the Lumber Co. the sum due Gilbert (P) for the loss under the $1,200 policy. Absent some letters Gilbert (P) sent to Globe & Rutgers (D) demanding payment, no further action was taken until this suit commenced by Gilbert (P) on June 29, 1916. The policy had a clause making sustainable only those suits commenced within 12 months following the fire. Gilbert (P) alleged that Globe & Rutgers (D) made promises to pay as soon as the garnishment proceedings were disposed of, not refusing to pay until more than a year had elapsed after the date of the fire. The trial court's judgment for Gilbert (P) in the full amount of the policy was appealed and reversed by the Circuit Court. The decision by the Circuit Court was based on the fact that Gilbert (P) knew from a conversation with the adjuster on October 2, 1913, his claim would be contested and he still delayed suit until June 29, 1916—not a reasonable time after notification. The present petition for a rehearing contests that rationale.

ISSUE: Does an insurer's action or conduct inducing an insured not to sue within the contractually mandated time limit constitute an estoppel which is lifted once the insurer notifies the insured the reason for refraining from suit no longer is operative?

HOLDING AND DECISION: (Johns, J.) Yes. Unlike waiver of a condition, actions which merely estop an insured from asserting a contractually mandated time limit for filing suit result in a mere

suspension of the time limit and not a complete elimination of the provision. Thus, once the inducement to refrain from suit in an insurance case is removed by notice to the insured the payment will be contested, the condition as to timely suit arises again. However, since Gilbert (P) did not commence his action within 12 months of such notice the judgment is correct and the rehearing is denied.

EDITOR'S ANALYSIS: The case suggests that a condition limiting time for suit on the contract can be revived after the law operates to preclude a party from alleging the same because of his own act or conduct. However, a waiver, seen as a voluntary relinquishment of a known right, results in the extinction of the condition absent consent of the other party. Thus, had Globe & Rutgers' (D) actions been considered a waiver, this suit could have been maintained and Gilbert (P) would have recovered.

QUICKNOTES

EXPRESS CONDITION - A condition that is expressly stated in the terms of a written instrument.

NOTES:

PORTER v. HARRINGTON
Seller of land (D) v. Purchaser
Mass. Sup. Jud. Ct., 262 Mass. 203, 159 N.E. 530 (1928).

NATURE OF CASE: Suit for specific performance of an agreement to convey land.

FACT SUMMARY: The contract under which Harrington was to buy two lots from Porter (D) made timely payment of the essence. It provided that after a 31-day payment default or failure to perform any other contractual condition, Porter (D) could, without notice, exercise an option to terminate the contract and keep all money paid as liquidated damages. Furthermore, it set forth that waiver of a breach of any term or condition would not be a waiver of any subsequent breach of that same or any other condition.

CONCISE RULE OF LAW: When no objection is made to overdue payments not made in accordance with the strict terms of the contract and the same are accepted, an order of business is established inconsistent with rigid insistence upon a forfeiture or penalty clause.

FACTS: The court which heard Harrington's (P) suit to require Porter (D) to convey land made the findings of fact that follow. In 1919, Porter (D) entered into a written contract to sell two lots to Harrington (P) for a $60 initial payment and $10 monthly payments of the balance. The first lot was conveyed in February, 1922, when paid for. Owing $578.54 on January 1, 1923, Harrington (P) made no payments that year. In 1924 he paid $60 in installments and the taxes. In 1925 Harrington (P) paid $60 in installments. A $40 payment was made on March 25, 1926, but a $30 payment tendered on November 9, 1926, was refused, Porter (D) informing Harrington (P) that he had exercised his option to close the account on August 1, 1926. The contract made prompt performance and time of the essence; provided that a default continuing for 31 days or failure to promptly perform any other condition gave Porter (D) the option to cancel the contract without notice, keeping all monies paid as liquidated damages; and stipulated waiver of a breach of any term was not a waiver of any other or subsequent breach of the same or any other term. From a decree in Harrington's (P) favor, Porter (D) appealed.

ISSUE: Is strict enforcement of a penalty or forfeiture clause precluded by failure to object to a course of dealings whereby overdue payments not made in accordance with the strict terms of the contract are accepted?

HOLDING AND DECISION: (Rugg, J.) Yes. Although parties have a right to make a stated time for performance the essence of a contract, a course of conduct whereby overdue payments are accepted amounts to a waiver of rights under the forfeiture or penalty clauses. The actions which lulled Harrington (P) into a justifiable assumption that, regardless of the contracts, he would be given indulgence in making his payments are not without consequence and were harsh, oppressive, and vindictive. To permit forfeiture absent any notice or warning would, in view of this conduct, be unconscionable.

EDITOR'S ANALYSIS: A continuous routine of accepting delinquent payments results in a waiver of strict compliance as to future payments, which makes, the cases hold, preliminary notice and demand a necessary prerequisite to the declaring of a forfeiture thereafter. Perhaps one method of dealing with this problem would be to send to the obligor a statement each time a non-timely payment is accepted that acceptance of such is not a waiver of any contractual provision and that the contract will be strictly enforced in the future regardless of the acceptance of the late payment.

QUICKNOTES

CONDITION - Requirement; potential future occurrence upon which the existence of a legal obligation is dependent.

EXCUSE OF CONDITION - The removal of a condition as a bar to performance or nonperformance of an obligation, either by waiver or occurrence of that condition.

SPECIFIC PERFORMANCE - An equitable remedy whereby the court requires the parties to perform their obligations pursuant to a contract.

PENALTY CLAUSE - A contractual clause providing for the payment of a fixed amount upon one party's default; generally not enforced by courts since the amount listed is often not an accurate measure of the damages suffered.

TIME IS OF THE ESSENCE - Contract provision specifying that the time period in which performance is rendered constitutes an essential term of the agreement.

NOTES:

CLARK v. WEST
Legal treatise publisher (D) v. Writer (P)
N.Y. Ct. App., 193 N.Y. 349, 86 N.E. 1. (1908).

NATURE OF CASE: Action for breach of contract and an accounting.

FACT SUMMARY: West (D) paid Clark (P) only $2 per page for writing a legal treatise and Clark (P) demanded the $6 per page he had been promised if he quit drinking, alleging that West (D) had not objected when he (P) continued to drink.

CONCISE RULE OF LAW: A condition in a contract may be waived, but no waiver is implied by mere acceptance of the proffered performance.

FACTS: West (D) entered into a contract with Clark (P) whereby Clark (P) was to write a multi-volume treatise on corporations for West (D). The contract price was $6 per page if Clark (D) totally abstained from liquor during the contract, or $2 per page if he drank. West (D) became aware that Clark (P) was drinking moderately during the term of the contract, but made no objection. West (D) accepted Clark's (P) work and paid him $2 per page. Clark (P) sued for the difference claiming that he was owed $6 per page. West (D) demurred: and both the trial court and the court of appeals sustained the demurrer. Clark (P) appealed, claiming that West (D) had waived the abstinence requirement and that the waiver was effective since abstinence was a mere condition precedent to West's (D) obligation to pay $6 per page.

ISSUE: May a condition precedent to performance be waived?

HOLDING AND DECISION: (Werner, J.) Yes. A condition to a contract may be waived, but mere acceptance of performance does not constitute a waiver. While it is West's (D) contention that Clark's (P) abstinence was the consideration for the payment of $6 rather than $2, a careful analysis of the contract shows that it was the writing of the treatise, rather than abstinence, which was the bargained-for consideration. Since abstinence was not the consideration for the contract, it was a condition which could be waived without a new agreement based upon a good consideration. No formal agreement or additional consideration is required to waive a condition precedent to performance. West (D) received and accepted the bargained-for consideration, i.e., the treatise. If the condition was waived, then West (D) is liable for the $6 contract price, but mere silence and acceptance of performance will not be deemed a waiver of the condition. However, since Clark (P) alleges an express waiver of the condition, he should be allowed to prove this at trial. The demurrer is therefore overruled and the case remanded for trial.

EDITOR'S ANALYSIS: Frequently, as in *Clark*, it is difficult to determine whether one is dealing with a promise or a condition. Modification of a promise typically requires a new consideration, while the waiver of a condition does not. A condition may be described as qualifying a contractual duty by providing either that performance is not called for unless a stated event occurs or fails to occur, or that performance may be suspended or terminated if a stated event occurs or fails to occur. Stated more simply, the condition is outside of and modifies the promised performance called for under the contract.

QUICKNOTES

CONDITION PRECEDENT - The happening of an uncertain occurrence, which is necessary before a particular right or interest may be obtained or an action performed.

CONSIDERATION - Value given by one party in exchange for performance, or a promise to perform, by another party.

ACCEPTANCE - Assent to the specified terms of an offer, resulting in the formation of a binding agreement.

NOTES:

INMAN v. CLYDE HALL DRILLING COMPANY

Employee (P) v. Employer (D)

Alaska Sup. Ct., 369 P.2d 498 (1962).

NATURE OF CASE: Action for damages for breach of an employment contract.

FACT SUMMARY: Clyde Hall Drilling Company (D) employed Inman (P) under a contract which provided that a 30-day written notice of claim had to be given to the company as an express condition precedent to a remedy.

CONCISE RULE OF LAW: An express condition precedent to give notice before filing suit under a contract must be fulfilled before suit is filed.

FACTS: Inman (P) worked for Clyde Hall Drilling Company (D) under a contract that provided for a 30-day written notice of claim to be given to the company as an express condition precedent to a remedy and barred any action on the contract unless such notice was given. Inman (P) sued Clyde Hall Drilling Company (D) for breach of contract but failed to give the requisite notice. Inman (P) alleged that the notice provision was void as against public policy, that the filing of the suit served as adequate notice within the 30-day period, and that the company had repudiated the contract by anticipatory breach, which gave him an excuse from performing the condition. Clyde Hall (D) moved for summary judgment.

ISSUE: Where there is an express condition precedent to filing suit in a contract, does such have to be fulfilled before suit is filed?

HOLDING AND DECISION: (Dimond, J.) Yes. It is the function of the judiciary to allow parties to contract as freely as the law will allow and the court will maintain and enforce contracts absent a showing that the court is used as an instrument of inequity or the contract is unconscionable. In this case, there is nothing to suggest that the contract was unconscionable or unfair. Inman (P) showed knowledge of its terms—particularly the notice provision. To hold that filing a complaint was effective notice under the provision would be to ignore the express provision of the contract. There was no anticipatory breach by Clyde Hall (D) which would have entitled Inman (P) to conclude the contract had been repudiated. Also, there is no showing that Clyde Hall (D) prevented Inman (P) in some way from performing the condition precedent. Summary judgment affirmed.

EDITOR'S ANALYSIS: It is rare for a court to excuse a condition simply because of hardship to the promisee or lack of a substantial interest which the promisor seeks to promote. Here, there was no showing of the actual purpose of the notice provision nor prejudice to Clyde Hall (D) by not having notice, yet the court not only upheld the provision but barred an action on the contract because of Inman's (P) failure to abide by it. This case represents the general trend of courts to uphold express conditions precedent where

there is no fraud, bad faith, illegality, or other inequitable circumstances brought on by the promisor.

QUICKNOTES

EXPRESS CONDITION - A condition that is expressly stated in the terms of a written instrument.

CONDITION PRECEDENT - The happening of an uncertain occurrence, which is necessary before a particular right or interest may be obtained or an action performed.

EXCUSE OF CONDITIION - The removal of a condition as a bar to performance or nonperformance of an obligation, either by waiver or occurrence of that condition.

NOTES:

AETNA CASUALTY & SURETY CO. v. MURPHY
Insurance company (P) v. Lease terminator (D)
Conn. Sup. Ct., 206 Conn. 409, 538 A.2d 219.

NATURE OF CASE: Appeal from summary judgment denying payment of insurance proceeds.

FACT SUMMARY: Murphy (D) delayed over two years in notifying his insurance company of a claim against him.

CONCISE RULE OF LAW: An insured who belatedly gives notice of an insurance claim may nonetheless recover on the insurance contract by rebutting the presumption that the delay prejudiced the insurer.

FACTS: When Murphy (D) terminated a lease with Aetna's (P) insured, he damaged the premises, which gave rise to a claim for those damages. Although Murphy (D) was served with the complaint on November 21, 1983, he did not notify his insurance company of the claim until January 10, 1986. Murphy's (D) insurer, Chubb, became a third party defendant by Murphy's (D) impleading. Murphy's (D) insurance contract provided: "In the event of an occurrence, written notice . . . shall be given by or for the insured to the company . . . as soon as practible." Murphy (D) delayed over two years in notifying Chubb of the claim against him. Chubb claimed that Murphy (D) had inexcusably and unreasonably delayed in complying with the notice provision in the insurance contract and obtained summary judgment. This appeal followed.

ISSUE: Can an insured who belatedly gives notice of an insurance claim nonetheless recover on the insurance contract by rebutting the presumption that the delay prejudiced the insurer?

HOLDING AND DECISION: (Peters, J.) Yes. An insured who belatedly gives notice of an insurance claim may nonetheless recover on the insurance contract by rebutting the presumption that the delay prejudiced the insurer. Three considerations are key to deciding this case. First is that the contract is one of adhesion. Because the contract is drawn up by the insurer, the insured, who merely "adheres" to it, has little choice as to its terms. Clearly, Murphy (D), like any other insured, had no opportunity to bargain as to the consequences of delayed notice of a claim. Second, is that the insured's noncompliance with the notice provision will cause a forfeiture. Because he will lose his insurance coverage despite dutiful payment of insurance premiums, Murphy's (D) failure to comply with the notice provision operates as a forfeiture. Third, the insurer's legitimate purpose of assuring itself a fair opportunity to investigate accidents and claims can be protected by demanding strict compliance with regard to the notice requirement in the contract. A proper balance between the interests of the insurer and the insured requires a factual inquiry into whether, in the circumstances of a case, the insurer has been prejudiced by its insured's delay in providing notice of a claim. Here, Chubb (D) was not automatically discharged of its contract duties because of Murphy's (D) delay; however, summary judgment was warranted because Murphy's (D) affidavit opposing summary judgment contained no factual basis for a claim that Chubb (D) had not been materially prejudiced by the delay. Affirmed.

EDITOR'S ANALYSIS: There exists a split of authority on the issue of whether an insured can attempt to rebut the presumption of prejudice to the insurer. Some states allow the insured to prove lack of prejudice, while other jurisdictions continue to enforce delayed notice provisions literally. This all translates into a question of materiality. Generally, express conditions in a contract must be strictly performed, while constructive, or implied-in-fact conditions can be satisfied by substantial performance. Either type of condition must meet the requirement that it is material to allow a party relief from the other party's noncompliance.

QUICKNOTES

ADHESION CONTRACT - A contract, usually in standardized form, that is prepared by one party and offered to another, whose terms are so disproportionately in favor of the drafting party that courts tend to question the equality of bargaining power in reaching the agreement.

EXPRESS CONDITION - A condition that is expressly stated in the terms of a written instrument.

CONSTRUCTIVE CONDITION - A condition that is not expressly stated in or implied by the terms of an agreement, but is imposed by law.

REBUTTABLE PRESUMPTION - A rule of law, inferred from the existence of a particular set of facts, that is conclusive in the absence of contrary evidence.

NOTES:

GRENIER v. COMPRATT CONSTR. CO.
Road builders (P) v. Construction Company (D)
Conn. Sup. Ct., 189 Conn. 144, 454 A.2d 1289 (1983).

NATURE OF CASE: Appeal from award of damages for breach of contract.

FACT SUMMARY: Compratt Constr. Co. (D) conditioned its obligation to pay the Greniers (P) for construction work on receipt of a letter of certification from the city engineer, who refused to write the letter.

CONCISE RULE OF LAW: A condition may be excused in the event of impracticability if the occurrence of the condition is not a material part of the agreed exchange and forfeiture would otherwise result.

FACTS: As part of a settlement agreement arising out of a previous contract dispute, Frank (P), John (P), and Eugene Grenier (P) agreed to construct a number of subdivision roads in exchange for a payment of $25,500. "Completion" of the roads was defined under the agreement as (1) work necessary to obtain a certificate of occupancy on any subdivision lot and (2) provision of a letter to Compratt Constr. Co. (D) from the city engineer by June 30, 1978, certifying that such certificates were obtainable. However, after the roads were completed, the Greniers (P) discovered that the city engineer did not typically write such letters. The city attorney, however, was willing to write a letter authorizing the building inspector to issue certificates of occupancy and did so on July 10, 1978. The certificates were subsequently issued. When Compratt (D) refused to pay the Greniers (P) for their work, they filed suit. Compratt (D) counterclaimed to enforce the liquidated damages clause in the contract. The trial court found that the Greniers (P) had failed to complete the roads on June 30 but concluded that the July 10 letter from the city attorney constituted compliance with the contract as of that date, and, therefore, the Greniers (P) were entitled to the $25,500 contract price. The court also awarded Compratt (D) liquidated damages of $2,500 for the delay of one-and-a-half weeks. Compratt (D) appealed, arguing that the city engineer's failure to give a written certification precluded recovery by the Greniers (P).

ISSUE: May a condition be excused in the event of impracticability if the occurrence of the condition is not a material part of the agreed exchange and forfeiture would otherwise result?

HOLDING AND DECISION: (Peters, J.) Yes. A condition may be excused in the event of impracticability if the occurrence of the condition is not a material part of the agreed exchange and forfeiture would otherwise result. Contracting parties are free to impose conditions upon contractual liability. Building contracts often provide that a third party such as an architect or engineer shall decide when one of the contracting parties has fulfilled the requirements of the contract. If, however, the work has been properly done, but certification is unavailable because of the death or insanity of the engineer, the condition will be excused. Similarly, if the engineer refuses to certify the work, and his decision is arbitrary or in bad faith, the condition will be excused. In this case, the city engineer, although physically able to produce the certificate desired by the Greniers (P), refused to do so. The city engineer's refusal to exercise any written judgment at all is tantamount to an engineer's failing to give the parties what they bargain for by refusing, in bad faith, to certify work. Since Compratt's (D) major concern was that the roads be acceptable so that certificates of occupancy could be obtained, rather than the letter itself, the failure to produce the engineer's letter was not a material part of the agreed exchange in the contract. Therefore the parties' inability to procure the city engineer's letter entirely excused the Greniers (P) from their duty to produce it. The Greniers (P) may therefore recover the contract price, not because they have substantially performed but because there has been full performance, the limiting condition having been excused. The $25,500, however, may be offset by an amount calculated under the liquidated damages clause to reflect the delay by the Greniers (P) in obtaining an alternative certification from the city attorney. Affirmed.

EDITOR'S ANALYSIS: In general, a condition which is only collateral to the main contract and serves to severely penalize one party while enriching the other will not be enforced. On the other hand, if the condition does not involve a forfeiture or amount to a penalty, and the possibility of the condition's nonoccurrence was foreseeable at the time the contract was entered into, then most courts will allow the condition to be operative.

QUICKNOTES
IMPRACTICABILITY - A doctrine relieving the parties to a contract from liability for nonperformance of their duties thereunder, if the subject matter of the contract ceases to exist.

CONDITION - Requirement; potential future occurrence upon which the existence of a legal obligation is dependent.

EXCUSE OF CONDITION - The removal of a condition as a bar to performance or nonperformance of an obligation, either by waiver or occurrence of that condition.

NOLAN v. WHITNEY
Mason (P) v. Homeowner (D)
N.Y. Ct. App., 88 N.Y. 648 (1882).

NATURE OF CASE: Action to recover balance of contract payments due.

FACT SUMMARY: Although Nolan (P) had substantially performed his contractual duties, he was unable to obtain an architect's certificate required to obtain the final contract payment.

CONCISE RULE OF LAW: Where a party has substantially performed, unreasonable withholding of an architect's certificate constitutes a waiver of the condition requiring it.

FACTS: Nolan (P) agreed to do all masonry work on a house owned by Whitney (D). Payments were to be made periodically, the final payment to be withheld until an architect's certificate was obtained from Morrill. Nolan's (P) masonry work had some trivial defects and Morrill refused to issue the certificate. Nolan (P) brought suit to recover the amount due. Whitney (D) alleged that obtaining the certificate was a condition precedent to recovery. The referee found that the defects were trivial and the withholding of the certificate was unreasonable. A $200 deduction for the defects was allowed from the final payment.

ISSUE: Where a party has substantially performed, may a third party, whose approval is a condition precedent to payment, withhold approval because the work has not literally complied with every contract requirement?

HOLDING AND DECISION: (Earl, J.) No. The law does not require that performance must literally comply with every term of the contract. Minor changes/defects of a trivial nature are excused under the doctrine of substantial performance. Where a third party's approval of the performance is a condition precedent to payment, the approval may not be unreasonably withheld, i.e. the party must act reasonably and in good faith. If the third party has acted unreasonably, the court will find that the condition has been waived. This is the case herein and the referee's award is affirmed.

EDITOR'S ANALYSIS: Note that in cases involving fancy, taste, etc., the rule is different. Only good faith dissatisfaction is required to be shown. The reasonableness of the disapproval is immaterial. Where no work/benefit has been furnished the defendant, many courts hold that if the dissatisfaction was honest and in good faith, the reasonableness of it is immaterial. The plaintiff has only lost anticipated profits and this was a risk he assumed in the contract since goods can be resold elsewhere. *Van Iderstine Co. v. Barret Leather Co.*, 242 N.Y. 425 (1926).

QUICKNOTES

SUBSTANTIAL PERFORMANCE - Performance of all the essential obligations pursuant to an agreement.

CONDITION PRECEDENT - The happening of an uncertain occurrence, which is necessary before a particular right or interest may be obtained or an action performed.

LOST PROFITS - The potential value of income earned or goods which are the subject of the contract; may be used in calculating damages where the contract has been breached.

NOTES:

FURSMIDT v. HOTEL ABBEY HOLDING CORP.
Valet (P) v. Hotel company (D)
N.Y. Sup. Ct., App. Div., 10 A.D.2d 447, 200 N.Y.S.2d 456 (1960).

NATURE OF CASE: Action in damages for breach of contract.

FACT SUMMARY: Fursmidt (P) and his son (P) agreed to perform valet services to the satisfaction of Hotel Abbey Holding Corp. (D).

CONCISE RULE OF LAW: When "satisfaction" contracts involve taste, fancy, etc., a jury may only inquire as to whether the party is honestly dissatisfied, not as to whether the dissatisfaction is reasonable.

FACTS: Fursmidt (P) and his son (P) had been long-time valets for Hotel Abbey (D). Fursmidt (P) entered into a new three-year contract with the Hotel agreeing that it should be the sole judge of the "sufficiency and propriety of the services." The Hotel closely controlled and supervised all of Fursmidt's (P) activities. The Hotel (D) subsequently dismissed Fursmidt (P) approximately six months later. Fursmidt (P) brought suit for damages for breach of contract. The jury was instructed that it was to find whether the Hotel's (D) dissatisfaction was honest and whether it was reasonable. Hotel (D) appealed the judgment rendered against it alleging that under the contract, if it was honestly dissatisfied it was immaterial whether it acted reasonably or not.

ISSUE: When a "satisfaction" contract involves taste, fancy, etc., is the reasonableness of honest dissatisfaction relevant?

HOLDING AND DECISION: (Rabin, J.) No. When a "satisfaction" contract involves performance to the taste, fancy, sensibilities, etc., of another, the only question which a jury may consider is whether the party is honestly dissatisfied. It is immaterial whether honest dissatisfaction with the services is reasonable or not. That power was vested solely in the party by the contract. He alone can make the decision so long as he acted honestly. Proof of how the employee performed is admissible as going to the honesty of the dissatisfaction. The case must be remanded for a retrial of the issue. Reversed.

EDITOR'S ANALYSIS: In cases involving satisfaction with items having mechanical utility, operative fitness, or marketability, a somewhat different standard is applied by most jurisdictions. Dissatisfaction must be honest and reasonable based on all of the factors present. *Hummel v. Stern*, 21 App. Div. 544. It has also been applied to repairs to equipment. *Duplex Safety Boiler Co. v. Garder*, 101 N.Y. 387. Whether or not work is unsatisfactory may be determined by objective factors, whereas in a "taste" situation it is personal to the buyer/client, customer, etc.

QUICKNOTES

MATERIAL TERM - A contractual term that is an essential part of the agreement, to the extent that its omission from performance can be construed as a breach of the contract.

CONDITION - Requirement; potential future occurrence upon which the existence of a legal obligation is dependent.

NOTES:

NICHOLS v. RAYNBRED
Lender of cow (P) v. Borrower (D)
King's Bench, Hobart 88 (1615).

NATURE OF CASE: Assumpsit for damages for breach of contract.

FACT SUMMARY: Nichols (P) promised to deliver to Raynbred's (D) use a cow for which Raynbred (D) promised to give Nichols (P) 50 shillings.

CONCISE RULE OF LAW: Where there is a bilateral contract, suit may be brought by a party without his pleading that he performed his side of the bargain.

FACTS: Nichols (P) promised to deliver to Raynbred's (D) use a cow. In return, Raynbred (D) promised to give Nichols (D) 50 shillings. Without ever pleading that he delivered the cow to Raynbred (D), Nichols (P) brought an action in assumpsit for the money. Nichols (P) had judgment, and Raynbred (D) appealed.

ISSUE: Where there is a bilateral contract, may suit be brought by a party without his pleading that he performed his side of the bargain?

HOLDING AND DECISION: Yes. Where there is a bilateral contract, suit may be brought by a party without his pleading that he performed his side of the bargain. The promises must have been given at the same instant or otherwise they would have been without consideration. Affirmed.

EDITOR'S ANALYSIS: The case appears in order to illustrate the history of constructive conditions. Simply put, at one time there were no constructive conditions. It need not have been implied that Nichols (P) delivered the cow before he could sue for the price for its use. Similarly, Raynbred (D) could have brought suit for the use of the cow without alleging that he paid the money for it. Needless to say, this is no longer accepted law.

QUICKNOTES

BILATERAL CONTRACT - An agreement pursuant to which each party promises to undertake an obligation, or to forbear from acting, at some time in the future.

CONSTRUCTIVE CONDITION - A condition that is not expressly stated in or implied by the terms of an agreement, but is imposed by law.

NOTES:

KINGSTON v. PRESTON
Business purchaser (P) v. Buyer (D)
Kings Bench, 2 Doug. 689 (1773).

NATURE OF CASE: Action to recover damages for breach of contract.

FACT SUMMARY: Preston (D) agreed to sell his business to Kingston (P) and Kingston (P) agreed to, but did not, give security for the payments.

CONCISE RULE OF LAW: Breach of a covenant by one party to a contract relieves the other party's obligation to perform another covenant which is dependent thereon, the performance of the first covenant being an implied condition precedent to the duty to perform the second covenant.

FACTS: Preston (D) agreed (among other things) to sell his business to Kingston (P). Kingston (P) agreed (among other things) to give sufficient security for his payments. Kingston's (P) personal worth was negligible. Kingston (P) failed to provide sufficient security and thereafter Preston (D) refused to sell.

ISSUE: When one party agrees to sell and a second party agrees to give sufficient security for his payments, are those covenants mutual and independent so that it is no excuse for non-performance by the first party for him to allege breach of covenant by the second party?

HOLDING AND DECISION: (Lord Mansfield) No. When one party covenants to sell and a second party covenants in return to give sufficient security for his payments, those covenants are dependent. Therefore, Kingston (P) must show that he has provided or is ready and willing to provide sufficient security as a condition precedent to Preston's duty to sell. The dependence or independence of covenants is to be determined from the intention of the parties which in turn will normally be determined by the "order of time in which the intent of the transaction requires their performance." Here the security was to be given "at and before the sealing and delivery of the deeds" conveying the business. Thus, according to the "temporal sequence" test, Preston's (D) duty to convey his business was dependent on Kingston's (P) giving of sufficient security. Furthermore, "it would be the greatest injustice if the plaintiff [Kingston (P)] should prevail." The giving of sufficient security was the essence of this agreement and "therefore, must necessarily be a condition precedent."

EDITOR'S ANALYSIS: Although Lord Mansfield in this famous decision focused on the time sequence of the contract provisions (e.g., a provision to be performed after another provision is dependent on that other provision) he was very likely reacting primarily to the personal poverty of Kingston (P) and the "injustice" that would be done by making Preston (D) go through with his performance and then sue poor Kingston (P) for damages. [Kingston (P), presumably, might run the business into the ground very quickly, leaving Preston's (D) court victory a purely theoretical one.] Note that Lord Mansfield, in determining the time sequence (which he felt was so important), apparently looked not only to the contract itself but also to what he thought must have been the reasonable intentions of the parties.

QUICKNOTES

CONSTRUCTIVE CONDITION - A condition that is not expressly stated in or implied by the terms of an agreement, but is imposed by law.

COVENANT - A written promise to do, or to refrain from doing, a particular activity.

CONDITION PRECEDENT - The happening of an uncertain occurrence, which is necessary before a particular right or interest may be obtained or an action performed.

NOTES:

PRICE v. VAN LINT
Borrower (P) v. Lender (D)
N.M. Sup. Ct., 46 N.M. 58, 120 P.2d 611 (1941).

NATURE OF CASE: Suit for damages.

FACT SUMMARY: Van Lint (D) was unable to secure money for a loan he contracted to make to Price (P), in return for a mortgage on the property Price (P) purchased.

CONCISE RULE OF LAW: Where a contract contains mutual promises to pay (or perform some other act), one of which may or is to be performed before the other, the latter promise is an independent obligation the nonperformance of which merely gives rise to a cause of action and does not defeat the right of the party making it to recover for a breach of the other promise.

FACTS: Van Lint (D) agreed to loan Price (P) $1,500 by February 1, 1940. The money was to be used to build a house on land Price (P) had purchased from Van Lint's (D) employer. Van Lint (D) was to receive a mortgage to secure the loan. The title to the property was to come from the Netherlands and both parties realized that it might not arrive by February 1, 1940. Price (P) entered into a contract to have the house built on the land, but Van Lint (D) found that he could not raise the $1,500. This caused a 2½ month delay in the construction of Price's (P) house. Price (P) brought suit for damages from the breach of contract. Van Lint (D) defended alleging that Price (P) could not have tendered a mortgage on February 1, 1940 since he did not receive a deed to the property until March 1940. Since Price (P) could not perform, Van Lint's (D) counter-performance was excused. The court found that the promises were independent and Price (P) was granted a judgment.

ISSUE: Are mutual contractual promises independent obligations if the time for performance of one may or is to arrive before the time for performance of the other?

HOLDING AND DECISION: (Sadler, J.) Yes. When the time for performance of one of the mutual contractual promises may or is to arrive before the time for the performance of the other, the obligations are independent. Thus, nonperformance of one does not preclude recovery for breach of the other. Rather, it gives rise to a cause of action in the promisee. Both parties knew of the probable delay of the deed and that it could well be past February 1, 1940 when it arrived. Thus, Price's (P) obligation to give a mortgage was independent of Van Lint's (D) obligation to deposit the loan money on February 1, 1940. So, Price's (P) action is not barred and Van Lint (D) is left with his cause of action. The trial court was correct in allowing Price (P) to assert his right to sue for breach.

EDITOR'S ANALYSIS: If the contract is bilateral, the inference is that performance of the first obligation is an implied-in-law condition precedent to the duty of the other party to perform later. A time for counter-performance may not be specified in the contract. Normally, the courts will find that custom in the trade of reasonable practices controls in such situations. For example, if no progress payments are provided for in a construction or supply contract, the court might find that no payment is due until performance is completed.

QUICKNOTES

CONSTRUCTIVE CONDITION - A condition that is not expressly stated in or implied by the terms of an agreement, but is imposed by law.

BILATERAL CONTRACT - An agreement pursuant to which each party promises to undertake an obligation, or to forbear from acting, at some time in the future.

CONDITION PRECEDENT - The happening of an uncertain occurrence, which is necessary before a particular right or interest may be obtained or an action performed.

DEPENDENT OBLIGATIONS - An obligation between contracting parties whose performance is dependent upon the initial performance of another promise, and therefore need not occur until the first obligation has been fulfilled.

NOTES:

CONLEY v. PITNEY BOWES
Employee (P) v. Employer (D)
34 F.3d 714 (8th Cir. 1994).

NATURE OF CASE: Appeal from summary judgment denying damages for personal injury.

FACT SUMMARY: When a letter denying disability benefits failed to gave notice of the plan's appeal procedures, Conley (P) sued employer Pitney Bowes (D), who raised a defense of administrative exhaustion.

CONCISE RULE OF LAW: In a bilateral contract based on promises that must be exchanged in a certain order, performance of the first is a constructive condition precedent to the other's duty to perform.

FACTS: Conley (P) was denied continued disability benefits for injuries resulting from an accident. Pitney Bowes' (D) plan included language requiring exhaustion of administrative procedures, as well as language stating that any notice of denial of benefits be accompanied by explicit instructions informing the plan participant of the procedures for appeal. The letter denying Conley (P) benefits did not inform him of any appeal procedures. When Conley (P) sued Pitney Bowes (D) for the benefits, a defense was raised based on the clause in the plan requiring exhaustion of administrative remedies, and the district court granted Pitney Bowes' (D) motion for summary judgment. Conley (P) appealed.

ISSUE: In a bilateral contract based on promises that must be exchanged in a certain order, is performance by the first a constructive condition precedent to the other's duty to perform?

HOLDING AND DECISION: (Arnold, J.) Yes. In a bilateral contract based on promises that must be exchanged in a certain order, performance by the first is a constructive condition precedent to the other's duty to perform. When a party has no actual knowledge of the plan's procedures for administrative exhaustion, any breach of the plan's notice requirement is material. A defense under the exhaustion clause may not be asserted absent performance of the notice clause, since the clauses are presumed to be the subject of promises made in exchange for each other. Since Pitney Bowes (D) was obligated to inform Conley (P) of the appeal procedure at the time it denied him benefits, Pitney Bowes' (D) performance had necessarily to precede exhaustion by Conley (P). Reversed.

DISSENT: (Gibson, J.) The court today elevates form over substance. This is not a case about an employee who failed to file an application for review because he was not told about the procedures. Here, Conley (P) relied on his lawyer, who dropped the ball.

EDITOR'S ANALYSIS: Clear-cut rules based on specified order of performance are frequently imposed by courts seeking consistency and order. If a party has let the time for the first performance pass and is then not in a position to perform himself when he calls for performance on the other side, the other party may be excused. This follows from practical concerns rather than any principles of contract interpretation.

QUICKNOTES

CONSTRUCTIVE CONDITION - A condition that is not express in the terms of a contract, but implied by law as a part of the binding agreement based on the circumstances and conduct between the contracting parties.

CONDITION PRECEDENT - The happening of an uncertain occurrence, which is necessary before a particular right or interest may be obtained or an action performed.

BILATERAL CONTRACT - An agreement pursuant to which each party promises to undertake an obligation, or to forbear from acting, at some time in the future.

NOTES:

ZIEHEN v. SMITH
Seller of real estate (D) v. Purchaser
N.Y. Ct. App., 148 N.Y. 558, 42 N.E. 1080 (1896).

NATURE OF CASE: Damages for breach of contract to convey.

FACT SUMMARY: Smith (P) contracted to purchase real estate from Ziehen (D), but was not aware of an action to foreclose a previous mortgage having commenced and notice of such having been filed with the county clerk. Ziehen (D) was equally ignorant, a former owner having been the one to obtain the mortgage.

CONCISE RULE OF LAW: If the vendor of real estate is unable to perform his part of an executory contract when such performance is due, a formal tender or demand by the vendee is not required for maintenance of an action by him to recover the money paid on the contract or damages.

FACTS: By an August 10, 1892 contract, Smith (P) agreed to pay $3,500 for land owned by Ziehen (D). $500 down payment was due at that time and September 15, 1892 was when another $300 was to be paid, an existing $1,000 mortgage was to be assumed, and a bond and mortgage for the $1,700 balance was to be placed on the property. The delivery of the conveyance was also due at that date. Unbeknownst to Ziehen (D), a former owner had placed a mortgage on the property and an action to foreclose same commenced on July 21, 1892. It was noted in the files of the county clerk. When the judgment of foreclosure resulted in a December 28, 1892 sale to a third party by the referee, Smith (P) sued to recover money paid and title examination expenses. Ziehen (D) appealed from a judgment granting same.

ISSUE: Must a vendee tender performance before he can recover damages for the breach of an executory contract if the vendor has disabled himself from performance or is unable to perform?

HOLDING AND DECISION: (O'Brien, J.) No. As a general rule one seeking recovery for breach of an executory contract must show performance or tender of same on his part. Such is not required, however, when it appears the vendor has disabled himself or is otherwise unable to perform. Under such circumstances it would be an idle or useless ceremony. However, it is not conclusively shown that Ziehen (D) was unable to convey the title the contract required simply because of the existence of the encumbrance. The judgment is, therefore, reversed.

EDITOR'S ANALYSIS: When a contract for sale of an item, title to pass in the future, is entered into, the seller need not possess the property until his performance is due. This is why tender is required. The buyer must establish that the seller could not deliver at the time his performance was due. An inability to perform prior to that point is immaterial. A tender or demand is not required where performance is impossible. For example, if the sale was of a specific item which was destroyed prior to the time of performance, a tender would not be required.

_____

QUICKNOTES
EXECUTORY CONTRACT - A contract in which performance of an obligation has yet to be rendered.

IMPOSSIBILITY - A doctrine relieving the parties to a contract from liability for nonperformance of their duties thereunder, if the subject matter of the contract ceases to exist, a person essential to the performance of the contract is deceased, or the service or goods contracted for has become illegal.

NOTES:

COHEN v. KRANZ
Home buyer (P) v. Seller (D)
N.Y. Ct. App., 12 N.Y.2d 242, 238 N.Y.S.2d 928, 189 N.E.2d 473 (1963).

NATURE OF CASE: Action for return of deposit for realty purchase.

FACT SUMMARY: Having contracted to buy Kranz's (D) home, Cohen (P) obtained an adjournment of the original November 15, 1959 closing date until December 15, 1959.

CONCISE RULE OF LAW: While a vendor of real estate with incurable title defects is automatically in default, a vendor with curable title must be put in default by the vendee's tender of performance and demand for a good title deed.

FACTS: Cohen (P) agreed to purchase Kranz's (D) house. Cohen (P) gave Kranz (D) a $4,000 down payment and the escrow was to close on November 15. Cohen (P) requested and was granted a 30- day extension of the closing date (December 15). On November 30, Cohen (P) informed Kranz (D) that he did not want the house because of defects in it which rendered title allegedly unmarketable. A demand was made for a return of the down payment on November 30 and again on December 15. Kranz (D) refused and suit was brought. The court found that a protective covenant existed, a fence extended over the property line, and the swimming pool lacked a proper certificate of occupancy. Judgment was rendered for Cohen (P). Kranz (D) appealed alleging that no tender had been offered at closing and he had never been informed of the nature of the defects so that he could attempt to cure them prior to closing.

ISSUE: Can a real estate vendor be in default because of curable title defects absent vendee's tender of performance and demand for good title deed?

HOLDING AND DECISION: (Burke, J.) No. Unlike a real estate vendor whose title has incurable defects, a vendor with curable title defects is not automatically in default. Rather, he must be placed in default by the vendee's tender of performance and demand for a good title deed. The defects herein being curable and Cohen (P) having made no tender, the appellate court's decision was correct. Failure to specify the objections to title and an unjustified attempt to cancel the contract by Cohen (P) not only made attempts to cure the minor defects before closing unnecessary and wasteful, it rendered them impossible. Judgment is affirmed.

EDITOR'S ANALYSIS: The nature of curable defects must be disclosed by the vendee. If they can be cured, the vendor is given a reasonable time to do so even if it extends a short time past the specified closing date. A vendee may not take unfair advantage of minor defects to escape his contractual duties. Equity will prevent such unfair surprise. Specific performance with a reduction in price due to minor curable or even incurable defects may be awarded by some courts if deemed equitable to do so.

QUICKNOTES

CONDITION - Requirement; potential future occurrence upon which the existence of a legal obligation is dependent.

SPECIFIC PERFORMANCE - An equitable remedy whereby the court requires the parties to perform their obligations pursuant to a contract.

NOTES:

BEECHER v. CONRADT
Buyer of land (D) v. Covenantee (P)
N.Y. Ct. App., 13 N.Y. 108 (1855).

NATURE OF CASE: To recover the amount due under a contract.

FACT SUMMARY: Conradt (P), under a contract transferred to him, was to convey land to Beecher (D) under an agreement whereby $396 was to be paid in five equal annual payments.

CONCISE RULE OF LAW: Failure to insist upon strict performance of an independent covenant can preclude a party from suit based on that designation when the lapse of time thus engendered has altered the nature of the covenants.

FACTS: On January 3, 1839, Varick entered into a contract with Beecher (D). Varick agreed to convey land upon the express condition that Beecher (D) perform his covenants. Beecher (D) covenanted to pay $396 in five equal annual payments. Conradt (P), who obtained the contract by transfer from Varick in December of 1850, refrained from suit until the last payment became due. At that time, he sued Beecher (D) for the full amount of the contract. Beecher (D) moved for nonsuit, alleging, inter alia, Conradt (P) had to show his own tender of conveyance or offer of same before commencement of the action. This point was overruled, and recovery ordered for Conradt (P) of the full price. From a Supreme Court affirmation, Beecher (D) appealed.

ISSUE: Does failure to enforce an independent covenant which results in full performance of all contractual covenants being simultaneously due prevent a suit based on that independent nature?

HOLDING AND DECISION: (Gardiner, J.) Yes. When formerly independent covenants are due to be fully performed, enforcement of the steps required to perform one of them having been neglected, suit for performance thereof becomes one for total performance of concurrent conditions. Thus, each party's performance is due, and neither party can place the other in default unless he is able to perform or make a tender of the promised performance. Thus, because of his inaction, Conradt (P) must sue for the whole price, for which Beecher (D) is entitled to receive the deed. The parties are in the same situation as if the money was all payable at one time. So, Conradt (P) must show performance as would entitle him to all the unpaid consideration. A new trial is thus ordered.

EDITOR'S ANALYSIS: This case simply illustrates the fact that the courts look with disfavor on one who is lax in enforcing his rights. Had recovery been permitted and the deed not been forthcoming, Conradt (P) would have been allowed to use the courts to alter the results of his inaction. His conduct was akin to an inducement to rely on the non-enforcement of the independent nature of the covenants. The result reached is like estoppel engendered by such action—estoppel to deny the usual construction that bilateral contracts contain mutual and concurrent conditions.

QUICKNOTES

CONCURRENT CONDITIONS - Dependent conditions that are to be performed at the same time.

CONSIDERATION - Value given by one party in exchange for performance, or a promise to perform, by another party.

COVENANT - A written promise to do, or to refrain from doing, a particular activity.

NOTES:

OSBORNE v. BULLINS
University professor (D) v. Store owner (P)
Miss. Sup. Ct., 549 So.2d 1337 (1989).

NATURE OF CASE: Appeal of award of damages for breach of contract.

FACT SUMMARY: After Osborne (D) refused to close his contract for Bullins (P), Bullins (P) sued for specific performance and was awarded judgment in the amount of the purchase price, secured by a vendor's lien.

CONCISE RULE OF LAW: In the event of a buyer's breach, a court may award the seller the amount of the purchase price in lieu of specific performance.

FACTS: Osborne (D), a university professor, approached Bullins (P), who had only a seventh-grade education, and offered to purchase his store for $85,000. The sales contract, prepared by Osborne's (D) brother, an attorney, provided that the sale would close within 60 days from delivery of the deed. However, at the end of 60 days, Osborne (D) refused to close, citing financing problems, although he produced no evidence that he had tried to borrow $85,000 from anyone. Bullins (P) sued for specific performance, and the trial court found he was so entitled but directed Bullins (P) to execute a warranty deed conveying the premises to Osborne (D) that would be released to Osborne (D) when he paid the judgment of $85,000. Osborne (D) appealed.

ISSUE: In the event of a buyer's breach, may a court award the seller the amount of the purchase price in lieu of specific performance?

HOLDING AND DECISION: (Robertson, J.) Yes. In the event of a buyer's breach, a court may award the seller the amount of the purchase price in lieu of specific performance. The traditional legal remedy for a buyer's breach would require, in this case, that Bullins (P) sell the property to someone else and be limited to a judgment against Osborne (D) for the difference between the purchase price of $85,000 and the amount he could realize from the sale. However, where that remedy is inadequate or difficult to measure, then specific performance may be ordered by the court. In this case, it would be unfair to leave Bullins (P) with the burden of marketing his property to a third-party buyer since he contracted for liquidity in his assets, not just value. Therefore, the rather unorthodox remedy fashioned by the trial court—a money judgment against Osborne (D) that places the burden of marketing the property on Osborne (D)—fits the facts of this case and is within the authority of the court. Affirmed.

EDITOR'S ANALYSIS: This case illustrates the problems faced by modern courts in classifying a money judgment against a buyer in a sale-of-land contract that is labeled as specific performance but has the attributes of a remedy at law. Whether the remedy is equitable or legal makes a difference in some states because of the traditional notion that a decree in equity may contain conditions and qualifiers, whereas a money judgment entered at law must be unconditional. The judge who wants to ensure, as in this case, that the seller will tender the deed upon payment of the purchase price by the breaching buyer must issue a conditional decree that the buyer deposit the deed with the court; the court may then intervene if there is any dispute regarding the title. Even though the remedy is, in reality, a judgment at law for the unpaid purchase price, it may still be labeled as specific performance for practical purposes.

QUICKNOTES

SPECIFIC PERFORMANCE - An equitable remedy whereby the court requires the parties to perform their obligations pursuant to a contract.

MONEY DAMAGES - Monetary compensation sought by, or awarded to, a party who incurred loss as a result of a breach of contract or tortious conduct on behalf of another party.

EQUITABLE REMEDY - A remedy that is based upon principles of fairness as opposed to rules of law.

NOTES:

STEWART v. NEWBURY
Excavator (P) v. Employer (D)
N.Y. Ct. App., 220 N.Y. 379, 115 N.E. 984 (1917).

NATURE OF CASE: Action for damages for breach of a construction contract.

FACT SUMMARY: Stewart (P), who contracted to do excavating for Newbury (D), alleged that he was to be paid in the "usual manner," i.e. 85% every 30 days, 15% being retained until work was completed, even though this was not written into the contract. When Newbury (D) failed to pay, Stewart (P) stopped work.

CONCISE RULE OF LAW: Where a contract is made to perform work and no agreement is made as to payment, the work must be substantially performed before payment can be demanded.

FACTS: Stewart (P), who contracted to do excavating work for Newbury, claimed that over the telephone Newbury (D) promised to pay in the "usual manner." That is to say, 85% each 30 days or end of the month, 15% being retained until completion of the work. Newbury (D) denied so promising. Excavation began in July and continued until the end of September when Newbury (D) refused to pay the first bill. Stewart (P) claimed that Newbury (D) would not permit him to continue work because there were alleged variations from specifications. The trial judge charged the jury that (1) if no agreement for payment was made, the builder could expect payment at reasonable intervals, if it were not understood that payments were due monthly; and (2) if payments were not made, the builder could abandon the work.

ISSUE: Can a builder expect payment at reasonable times if no agreement was made as to payment, and, if not paid at reasonable times, abandon the work?

HOLDING AND DECISION: (Crane, J.) No, it is settled that where a contract is made to perform work and no agreement is made as to payment, the work must be substantially performed before payment can be demanded. As the case was submitted also upon the ground that variation from specifications may have constituted breach, and since it is impossible to tell under which theory the jury arrived at its conclusion, the judgment must be reversed and a new trial ordered.

EDITOR'S ANALYSIS: It is not unusual in a bilateral contract that the parties will neglect to state in what order their promises will be performed. First, a party must perform before he is entitled to payment. That is to say, performance is a constructive condition precedent to payment. Periodic payments, as herein illustrated, are not implied. If periodic payments are agreed to, performance is a constructive condition precedent to the first payment which is a constructive condition precedent to the next stage of performance,

etc. These rules are ordinary business practice and have been said to be the "practice of centuries."

QUICKNOTES
SUBSTANTIAL PERFORMANCE - Performance of all the essential obligations pursuant to an agreement.

NOTES:

TIPTON v. FEITNER

Hog seller (P) v. Buyer (D)

N.Y. Ct. App., 20 N.Y. 423 (1859).

NATURE OF CASE: Appeal from judgment in action on contract.

FACT SUMMARY: Tipton (P) and Feitner (D) made a contract for the sale of hogs. Both parties contended that the other breached the contract.

CONCISE RULE OF LAW: The occurrence of a condition precedent creates the duty of counter performance.

FACTS: On February 3, 1855, in New York City, the parties made the following oral agreement. Tipton (P) would sell Feitner (D) 88 dressed hogs at 7 cents a pound, and an unspecified number of live hogs at 5¼ cents a pound. The dressed hogs were in the city and were to be delivered immediately. They were delivered that day. The live hogs were to be delivered when they arrived in the city a few days later. Feitner (D) agreed to buy the hogs at these prices. He did not pay for the dressed hogs when they were delivered. The live hogs arrived five days later. They were not delivered, but were slaughtered by Tipton (P) and then sold to others. Tipton (P) sued for the price of the dressed hogs. Feitner (D) contended that Tipton (P) had not fulfilled the conditions of the contract, and could not recover. The trial court allowed Tipton (P) to recover the cost of the dressed hogs but allowed Feitner (D) to deduct his damages sustained by the breach of the second part of the contract. Feitner (D) appealed.

ISSUE: Does partial performance of a contract create the duty of counter performance?

HOLDING AND DECISION: (Denio, J.) Yes. The occurrence of a condition precedent creates the duty of counter performance. In contracts for the sale of property, real or personal, delivery and payment are each conditions of the other, unless the parties specify otherwise. Here, there is no mention of payment in the contract, nor is there a mention of the extension of credit. In view of this we must hold that the parties intended that delivery and payment were to be concurrent acts. But the question then arises whether the contract was entire or divisible. The answer lies in the contract itself. There is no express provision in the agreement other than the promise to pay. The agreement deals with two types of hogs, live and dressed. The price for each is different. The time of delivery is different. On these facts we hold that a separate payment was required with each delivery. The defendant is not injured by this ruling; he has an action on the second part of the contract, or he can set off his loss against the judgment. Judgment affirmed.

EDITOR'S ANALYSIS: Where a court is given a choice in deciding whether a contract is entire or divisible, it will generally rule that it is divisible. This allows a court greater leeway in protecting the commercial expectations of the parties, and protecting them from unfair loss. When a court rules a contract divisible, each separate transaction forms a different deal. Thus, the failure of one transaction does not cause the failure of the whole contract.

QUICKNOTES

PART PERFORMANCE - Partial performance of a contract, promise or obligation.

CONDITION PRECEDENT - The happening of an uncertain occurrence, which is necessary before a particular right or interest may be obtained or an action performed.

NOTES:

OSHINSKY v. LORRAINE MFG. CO.

Shirting seller (P) v. Buyer (D)

187 F. 120 (2d Cir. 1911).

NATURE OF CASE: Appeal by writ of error in action on contract.

FACT SUMMARY: Lorraine Mfg. Co. (D) refused to accept goods it ordered after the delivery date.

CONCISE RULE OF LAW: A party is not bound to honor a contract after the specified date of performance.

FACTS: Oshinsky (P) and Lorraine Mfg. Co. (D) entered into a contract, under which Oshinsky (P) was to deliver a quantity of "shirtings" by November 15 , 1908. Certain pieces were delivered before that date, but the bulk did not arrive until November 16. Lorraine Mfg. Co. (D) refused to accept delivery. Oshinsky (P) sued for breach. At trial the court ruled that time was of the essence, and that the time provision in the contract was ambiguous. Judgment for Oshinsky (P). Lorraine Mfg. Co. (D) appealed.

ISSUE: Where time is of the essence does failure to perform at a specified date release the other party from their obligation?

HOLDING AND DECISION: (Noyes, J.) Yes. Where time is of the essence, a party is not bound to contract after the date of performance has passed. Here the date was clearly specified as November 15. The specification of a date in a contract requires performance on that date and no other. As the goods were not delivered by that date we find that Oshinsky (P) had failed to perform as required by the contract. Judgment reversed.

EDITOR'S ANALYSIS: Failure to perform on time, where time is an express condition of the contract, discharges the obligation of the innocent party. Where the time of performance is not an express condition, a delay in performance will not cause discharge unless the breach is considered material. The materiality of the delay is determined by looking to the purposes of the contract, and the consequences of the delay. The courts have tended to enforce this rule more strictly in cases involving the sale of goods, but it is applicable to other contracts as well. Under the U.C.C., if no time of performance is specified, the parties are allowed a reasonable time to perform, and a party who desires strict performance must make a provision for same in the agreement.

QUICKNOTES

EXPRESS CONDITION - A condition that is expressly stated in the terms of a written instrument.

TIME IS OF THE ESSENCE - Contract provision specifying that the time period in which performance is rendered constitutes an essential term of the agreement.

NOTES:

BARTUS v. RICCARDI
Hearing aid seller (P) v. Buyer (D)
Utica City Ct., Oneida County, N.Y., 55 Misc.2d 3, 284 N.Y.S.2d 222 (1967).

NATURE OF CASE: Suit on contract for payment of the price.

FACT SUMMARY: Bartus (P) sued to recover the price of a hearing aid ordered by Riccardi (D) who returned it as nonconforming.

CONCISE RULE OF LAW: Under the U.C.C. a seller has the right to correct defective performance within a reasonable time provided notice of intent is given.

FACTS: Bartus (P) was a seller of hearing aids. On January 15, 1966, Riccardi (D) contracted to purchase a Acousticon Model A-660 hearing aid from him. He specified this model because he had been informed by a hearing clinic that this was the best one for his needs. Two weeks later the hearing aid was delivered and Riccardi went to pick it up. At that time he was informed by Bartus (P) that the hearing aid was a model A-665, a new and improved version of the A-660. Riccardi (D) denied he understood this. He accepted the hearing aid and used it for some 15 hours over the next few days. Then, not satisfied with its performance, he returned to the clinic where he was informed that the hearing aid was a different model from that which he had been advised to get. He returned the hearing aid to Bartus (P), on February 8, complaining that it gave him a headache and was not the model he ordered. Bartus (P) offered to get the correct model. Riccardi (D) neither consented nor refused the offer. The manufacturer was advised of the complaint, and they advised Riccardi (D) by mail that they would replace the unit or supply the model ordered. Riccardi (D) then decided that he did not want a hearing aid. Bartus (P) sued for the balance due on the contract. Riccardi (D) contended that he properly exercised his right of rejection.

ISSUE: Is a breaching party permitted to cure defective performance by a subsequent act?

HOLDING AND DECISION: (Hymes, J.) Yes. The U.C.C. gives a seller a reasonable time to cure defective performance, provided he has reason to believe the tender will be accepted, and he has given notice of his intention. Here, Bartus (P) offered to cure the defective performance as soon as he was aware of it. Riccardi (D) did nothing to give the impression that this was unacceptable. Thereafter and within a reasonable time Bartus (P) delivered the hearing aid. Thus, Bartus (P) had complied with the provisions of the U.C.C. Judgment for plaintiff.

EDITOR'S ANALYSIS: The U.C.C. has added new dimensions to the law of contracts. Under the U.C.C. strict performance is no longer the rule. The parties are given a reasonable time to act provided proper notice is given. The U.C.C. does not negate the common-law rules, but rather it liberalizes them. For instance, if a party desires strict performance of a contract he must make it a term of the contract. If a party chooses to reject nonconforming goods he must do so in a reasonable time and give proper notice. In this way some of the harsh results seen in the common-law cases can be mitigated.

QUICKNOTES

CURE - In a commercial transaction, the seller has a right to correct a delivery of defective goods within the time originally provided for performance as specified in the contract.

MATERIAL BREACH - Breach of a contract's terms by one party that is so substantial as to relieve the other party from its obligations pursuant thereto.

SUBSTANTIAL PERFORMANCE - Performance of all the essential obligations pursuant to an agreement.

NOTES:

PLATEQ CORP. OF NORTH HAVEN v. MACHLETT LABS., INC.

Seller (P) v. Buyer (D)

Conn. Sup. Ct., 189 Conn. 433, 456 A.2d 786 (1983).

NATURE OF CASE: Appeal of judgment in a breach of contract action.

FACT SUMMARY: Machlett (D) ordered from Plateq (P) some specially manufactured goods but cancelled the contract after it had indicated acceptance.

CONCISE RULE OF LAW: Acceptance of goods occurs when the buyer, after a reasonable opportunity to inspect the goods, signifies to the seller that he will take them in spite of their nonconformity or fails to make an effective rejection.

FACTS: Machlett (D) ordered from Plateq (P) two lead covered steel tanks and stands to be constructed by Plateq (P) according to specifications supplied by Machlett (D). Performance was late but mostly complete when one of Machlett's (D) engineers did an inspection and noted some deficiencies. Plateq (P) promised to remedy the deficiencies and have the product ready for delivery the following day. The engineer (D) led Plateq (P) to believe that Machlett (D) would be sending a truck to pick up the products within a day or two. A few days later, Machlett (D) sent a notice of cancellation that failed to particularize the grounds upon which cancellation was based. Plateq (P) sued Machlett (D) to recover damages arising out of Machlett's (D) cancellation of the contract. The trial court found for Plateq (P) and Machlett (D) appealed.

ISSUE: Did Machlett (D) accept the goods before it attempted to cancel the contract of sale?

HOLDING AND DECISION: (Peters, J.) Yes. Machlett (D) accepted the goods before it attempted to cancel the contract of sale. Acceptance of goods occurs when the buyer, after a reasonable opportunity to inspect the goods, signifies to the seller that he will take them in spite of their nonconformity or fails to make an effective rejection. At the time of the engineer's (D) inspection, performance was in substantial compliance with the terms of the contract. It was at that time that Machlett (D) was notified that the goods would be ready for tender the following day. Machlett (D) responded to this notification by promising to send its truck to pick up the tanks in accordance with the contract. Machlett (D) had therefore accepted the goods it had ordered from Plateq (P). Although the contract provides for inspection for radiation leaks after installation of the tanks at its premises, Machlett (D) did not postpone its inspection rights to that time. A buyer may be found to have accepted goods despite their known nonconformity and despite the absence of actual delivery to the buyer. Furthermore, the tanks had been accepted because Machlett (D) failed to make an effective rejection. A buyer cannot rely as a basis for rejection upon unparticularized defects in his notice of rejection, if the defects were such that with seasonable notice, the seller could have cured them by making a substituted conforming tender. Plateq (P) was ready to make a tender on the day following the last inspection by Machlett's (D) engineer and would have done so but for its receipt of Machlett's (D) telegram of cancellation. The unparticularized telegram of cancellation thus wrongfully interfered with Plateq's (P) contractual right to cure any remaining post-installation defects. In addition, Machlett (D) has not met its burden of proof to show that the goods were substantially nonconforming and therefore did not cancel the contract. Affirmed.

EDITOR'S ANALYSIS: Many courts invoke estoppel to preclude the use of unstated objections to the opposing party's performance, when a specific objection could have been made.

NOTES:

PLANTE v. JACOBS
Home builder (P) v. Buyers (D)
Wis. Sup. Ct., 10 Wis.2d 567, 103 N.W.2d 296 (1960).

NATURE OF CASE: Action to establish a lien upon property for breach of a constitution contract.

FACT SUMMARY: When the Jacobs (D) believed that Plante (P), whom they contracted to build a home upon their lot for $26,765, used faulty workmanship and incomplete construction, they stopped further payments to him after having paid $20,000. Plante (P) then refused to complete and sued to establish a lien on the property.

CONCISE RULE OF LAW: There can be no recovery on a contract as distinguished from quantum meruit unless there is substantial performance which is defined as where the performance meets the essential purpose of the contract.

FACTS: Plante (P) contracted with Frank and Carol Jacobs (D) to furnish materials and construct a house upon their lot in accordance with plans and specifications for $26,765.00. Plante (D) received $20,000 during the course of construction when a dispute arose between the parties as to faulty workmanship and incomplete construction. The Jacobs (D) refused to continue payments and Plante (P) refused to complete construction. Plante (P) then sued to establish a lien on the property so as to recover the unpaid balance plus extras. The Jacobs (D) alleged that faulty workmanship on at least 20 items plus decreasing the width of the living room by one foot did not amount to substantial performance.

ISSUE: Was there substantial performance of the contract?

HOLDING AND DECISION: (Hallows, J.) Yes. There can be no recovery at common law on a contract as distinguished from quantum meruit unless there is substantial performance which is determined by whether the performance meets the essential purpose of the contract. When applied to house construction, this does not mean that every detail must be in strict compliance with specifications and plans. Here the specifications were standard printed forms and the plan was a "stock floor plan." While the Jacobs (D) received a house with which they were dissatisfied, the contract was substantially performed. The misplacing of a wall by one foot so as to narrow the living room did not affect the value of the home. Gutters and rainspouts, kitchen cabinets, and clothes closet poles were omitted. As the measure of damages for substantial, but incomplete, performance, Plante (P) should receive the contract price less the damages caused the Jacobs (D) by incomplete performance. For faulty construction, the "diminished value" rule pertains which is the difference between the value of the house as it would stand complete and as it stands

faulty but substantially complete. The trial court applied the "lost of repair" rule which allows the cost to repair a number of small defects and omissions. If the separation of defects would lead to confusion, the diminished value rule can be applied to all defects. There was no confusion here in separating the defects. Whether a defect comes under the diminished value or cost of repair rule depends upon the magnitude of the defect. However, the trial court was not in error in applying the cost of repair rule (usually applied to small items) to repairing a patio floor, plaster cracks in ceiling, and repair of a non-structural patio wall. The misplaced wall in the living room was of a magnitude sufficient as to place it under the diminished value rule but as misplacing the wall was of no effect to the value of the house and as it would have been economical waste to move it, no legal damage was suffered.

EDITOR'S ANALYSIS: The doctrine of substantial performance is applied when the unperformed portion does not destroy the purpose or value of the contract. Of course, this is like saying that the breach must not be material. Here, when the Jacobs (D) occupied the house they showed that it served its purpose and thereby assumed the burden to show performance was not substantial to the terms of the contract. The primary application of the doctrine of substantial performance is with building contracts where fairly large defaults have been treated as immaterial, while a small default is often sufficient to breach a sales contract due to practical considerations. The unhappy buyer can return the goods or refuse delivery. The unhappy landowner keeps the incomplete structure, hence, greater are the possibilities for unjust enrichment.

QUICKNOTES

SUBSTANTIAL PERFORMANCE - Performance of all the essential obligations pursuant to an agreement.

QUANTUM MERUIT - Equitable doctrine allowing recovery for labor and materials provided by one party, even though no contract was entered into, in order to avoid unjust enrichment by the benefitted party.

UNJUST ENRICHMENT - The unlawful acquisition of money or property of another for which both law and equity require restitution to be made.

NOTES:

WORCESTER HERITAGE SOCIETY, INC. v. TRUSSELL

Preservation society (P) v. Historic house purchaser (D)

Mass. Ct. App., 31 Mass. App. Ct. 343, 577 N.E.2d 1009 (1991).

NATURE OF CASE: Appeal from denial of rescission in action for breach of contract.

FACT SUMMARY: When Trussell (D) purchased an historic house from the Worcester Heritage Society (P), he agreed to do a complete historic restoration on the exterior within one year, but two years later, with the work still uncompleted, the Society (P) sued for rescission of the contract.

CONCISE RULE OF LAW: A court may refuse to order rescission where only a breach of contract has occurred rather than an utter failure of consideration or a repudiation by the party in breach.

FACTS: In 1984, Trussell (D) purchased a vacant and uninhabitable historic house for $20,100 from the Society (P), agreeing to do a complete historic restoration on the exterior portion of the house within a year. If the exterior restoration was not completed within a year, the Society (P) retained the option to hire workers to complete the job at Trussell's (D) expense. A year and a half after the transfer, Trussell (D) lost his job, and his work on the house, although hampered by lack of funds, proceeded slowly but steadily. The Society (P) sued for rescission of the contract and reconveyance of the house. The trial court found that the exterior work was 65% to 75% complete and refused rescission. The Society (P) appealed.

ISSUE: May a court refuse to order rescission where only a breach of contract has occurred rather than an utter failure of consideration or a repudiation by the party in breach?

HOLDING AND DECISION: (Armstrong, J.) Yes. A court may refuse to order rescission where there has been only a breach of contract rather than an utter failure of consideration or a repudiation by the party in breach. In the absence of fraud, an injured party may not maintain an action to set aside a contract unless the breaching party's nonperformance is so material that it goes to the "essence" of the contract. In this case, Trussell's (D) actions do not amount to a repudiation of the contract. On the contrary, although he has exceeded the one-year deadline in the contract, he still intends to complete the restoration. Neither has there been a total failure of consideration, since Trussell (D) paid the purchase price and invested additional sums and his own labor in the restoration work. The Society's (P) primary concern was the exterior appearance of the houses that it rescued, and Trussell's (D) uncompleted work was mainly at the rear of the house and therefore unnoticeable to the public. Furthermore, Trussell's (D) "sweat equity" might be forfeited if a rescission were ordered. Finally, the contract expressly contemplated the possibility of delay by its option to engage outside workers, a self-help remedy which the Society (P) is now free to employ. Affirmed.

EDITOR'S ANALYSIS: Although there are no firm rules that govern the right of rescission, it is generally permitted for failure of consideration, fraud in the making, inability to perform, repudiation, or a breach that substantially defeats the purpose of the contract. This case illustrates the general trend that rescission is not permitted in the event of a slight, casual, or technical breach, but only for breaches that are both material and willful, or so substantial and fundamental as to defeat the object of the parties in making the contract. The only important issue is how defective the performance of the contract has been. However, if the party seeking rescission has an adequate remedy at law, he will not be entitled to rescission, except in cases where damages cannot be ascertained with reasonable certainty (which probably means that this exception is not an exception at all but, rather, an example of another inadequate remedy at law).

QUICKNOTES

RESCISSION - The canceling of an agreement and the return of the parties to their positions prior to the formation of the contract.

REPUDIATION - The actions or statements of a party to a contract that evidence his intent not to perform, or to continue performance, of his duties or obligations thereunder.

CONSIDERATION - Value given by one party in exchange for performance, or a promise to perform, by another party.

NOTES:

WHOLESALE SAND & GRAVEL, INC. v. DECKER
Earth work provider (P) v. Property owner (D)
Sup. Jud. Ct. of Me., 630 A.2d 710 (1993).

NATURE OF CASE: Appeal from judgment in a breach of contract claim.

FACT SUMMARY: Decker (D) hired another contractor to complete work begun by Wholesale (P) when Wholesale (P) refused to finish the job.

CONCISE RULE OF LAW: An anticipatory repudiation of a contract is a definite and unequivocal manifestation of an intention on the part of the repudiator that he will not render the promised performance when the time fixed for it in the contract arrives.

FACTS: On June 13, 1989, Decker (D) and Wholesale Sand & Gravel (P) entered into a contract whereby Wholesale (P) agreed to perform earth work, including the installation of a gravel driveway, on Decker's (D) property. The contract contained no provision specifying a completion date for the project, and the only reference to time was that payment was to be made within ninety days. Goodenow, the president of Wholesale (P), told Decker (D) that the driveway portion of the work would be completed within one week. Wholesale (P) began work the following weekend but experienced immediate difficulties when their bulldozers became stuck in the mud. Because the ground was too wet to allow Wholesale (P) to perform the work without substantially exceeding the contract price, Goodenow decided that they should wait for the ground to dry out. On July 12, 1989, Decker (D) contacted Goodenow concerning the lack of work on the driveway and Goodenow responded that he would "get right on it." Decker (D) called again to inquire on July 19, 1989, and informed Goodenow that they had one week to complete the driveway. Weeks later, wholesale (P) still had not started work again, so Decker (D) hired another contractor to complete the work. Wholesale (P) commenced an action for breach of contract; however, the trial court entered a judgment in favor of Decker (D) finding that Wholesale's (P) conduct constituted an anticipatory repudiation of the contract. Wholesale (P) appealed.

ISSUE: Is an anticipatory repudiation a definite and unequivocal manifestation of an intention on the part of the repudiator that he will not render the promised performance when the time fixed for it in the contract arrives?

HOLDING AND DECISION: (Roberts, J.) Yes. An anticipatory repudiation of a contract is a definite and unequivocal manifestation of an intention on the part of the repudiator that he will not render the promised performance when the time fixed for it in the contract arrives. Wholesale (P) removed its equipment from the work site and never returned, despite repeated promises. It was reasonable for Decker (D) to conclude that Wholesale (P) would never complete the work under the contract. The trial court properly found that Wholesale's (P) conduct reflected an unequivocal and definite unwillingness or inability to perform within a reasonable time. Affirmed.

DISSENT: (Wathen, J.) This court and the trial court misapplied the doctrine of anticipatory repudiation. The record does not contain any explicit words or conduct that show that Wholesale (P) did not intend to perform, but merely that they were waiting for circumstances to permit performance.

EDITOR'S ANALYSIS: The common law doctrine of anticipatory repudiation, or voluntary disablement, was devised to allow one party to be excused from performance because of the actions or inactions of the other party. Without this doctrine, the party with less leverage or bargaining power can be held at the mercy of the other party and without alternatives. However, the standard for enforcing application of the rule is stringent, and the actions of the repudiating party must show a definite, unequivocal, and unyielding renunciation of intent to perform.

QUICKNOTES

ANTICIPATORY REPUDIATION - Breach of a contract subsequent to formation but prior to the time performance is due.

NOTES:

K&G CONSTRUCTION CO. v. HARRIS
General contractor (P) v. Subcontractor (D)
Md. Ct. App., 223 Md. 305, 164 A.2d 451 (1960).

NATURE OF CASE: Appeal from a judgment for defendant for the value of work performed and lost profits.

FACT SUMMARY: When Harris (D), subcontractor for K&G (P), negligently damaged K&G's (P) property, K&G (P) refused to make further installment payments until Harris (D) admitted liability for the damage, and Harris (D) refused further performance until payments were resumed.

CONCISE RULE OF LAW: The failure of a contractor's (or subcontractor's) performance to constitute "substantial" performance may justify the owner in refusing to make a progress payment.

FACTS: K&G (P), owner and general contractor, entered into a contract with Harris (D), subcontractor, for the excavating and earth-moving work required on a housing project. The contract contained a provision that Harris (D) agreed to perform the work "in a workmanlike manner and in accordance with the best practices." Also, Harris (D) was to submit to K&G (P) by the 25th of each month a requisition for work performed during the preceding month, and K&G (P) agreed to pay 90% of each requisition by the 10th of the following month. Harris (D) performed work which, under the terms of the contract, would have entitled him to a progress payment on August 10th. On August 9th, Harris (D), while grading the yard, damaged K&G's property at a cost of $3,400. Both Harris (D) and his insurer denied liability for the damage. Because the damage was not repaired or paid for, K&G (P) refused to make the progress payment to Harris (D) on August 10th. Harris (D) continued work until September 12, when it discontinued work because of K&G's (P) refusal to pay the July and August installments. Harris (D) notified K&G (P) that it was willing to resume work, but only on payment. K&G (P) had the remaining work done by another subcontractor at a cost of $450 and sued for this cost and the prior damage from grading the yard. Harris (D) counterclaimed for the value of the work performed and for the lost profits on the remainder of the job. The jury found for K&G (P) for the grading damage, but the court awarded judgment to Harris (D) on both counterclaims. K&G (P) appealed.

ISSUE: Does the failure of a contractor's performance to constitute "substantial" performance justify the owner in refusing to make a progress payment?

HOLDING AND DECISION: (Prescott, J.) Yes. The failure of a contractor's (or subcontractor's) performance to constitute "substantial" performance may justify the owner in refusing to make a progress payment. Here, when the subcontractor's employee negligently damaged the contractor's property, this constituted a breach of Harris' (D) promise to perform his work in a

"workmanlike manner and in accordance with the best practices." In permitting the subcontractor Harris (D) to proceed with work on the project after August 9th, the contractor K&G (P) treated the breach by Harris (D) as a partial one. As the promises were mutually dependent and the subcontractor Harris (D) had made a material breach in his performance, K&G (P) justifiably refused to make the August 10 payment and was not in default on that date. On September 12, Harris (D) again breached the contract by discontinuing work, rendering him liable to K&G (P) for the stipulated amount of $450, the increased cost of having the excavating done. Reversed.

EDITOR'S ANALYSIS: Simpson, Contracts (1965) at p. 373: "A breach by one party may suspend or, if material, may altogether discharge the other party's performance. In either case, it affords a complete excuse for such other party's nonperformance." However, the right to "suspend" performance must be clearly distinguished from the right to refuse absolutely. The difference between the two is the difference between saying: "I refuse to perform until you perform," and "I will not perform because your performance was not timely."

QUICKNOTES

SUBSTANTIAL PERFORMANCE - Performance of all the essential obligations pursuant to an agreement.

ADEQUATE ASSURANCES - Refers to a situation in which one party is excused from performance of his obligations under a contract if the other party to the contract indicates that he does not intend to perform when the time for performance thereunder arrives; the nonbreaching party in that case is excused from further performance, unless he receives adequate assurances that performance will be rendered.

ANTICIPATORY REPUDIATION - Breach of a contract subsequent to formation but prior to the time performance is due.

NOTES:

HATHAWAY v. SABIN
Event manager (P) v. Concert promoter (D)
Vt. Sup. Ct., 63 Vt. 527, 22 A. 633 (1891).

NATURE OF CASE: Action for breach of contract.

FACT SUMMARY: Sabin (D) contracted to furnish the hall for a concert and to pay Hathaway $75 for the entertainment. Sabin (D) later canceled the concert because of a snowstorm.

CONCISE RULE OF LAW: The reasonable belief that the other party to a contract will be unable to perform does not relieve one of his own duty to perform his contractual obligations.

FACTS: Sabin (D) agreed to furnish a hall for a concert and to pay Hathaway (P) $75 for entertainment. During the 36 hours prior to the evening for which the concert had been scheduled, the area was engulfed by a violent snowstorm. Local streets were rendered virtually impassable, and regular train service to the nearby town of Barre had been suspended. Since the musicians who were scheduled to perform at the concert were lodged in Barre, Sabin (D) telephoned the manager of the hall and canceled the concert, although it would not have been necessary to begin preparing the hall until late in the afternoon. Eventually, a special train was sent to Barre, and the musicians arrived in time for the scheduled concert which was, of course, not held. Hathaway (P) sued Sabin (D) for breach of contract and was awarded $75 plus interest.

ISSUE: Does a belief that the other party to a contract will not be able to perform relieve a party to a contract of his obligations thereunder?

HOLDING AND DECISION: (Munson, J.) No. A reasonable belief that the other party to a contract will be unable to perform does not relieve a person of his own duty to perform his contractual obligations. In the present case, Sabin (D) was mistaken in the belief that Hathaway (P) would be unable to perform. Considering that Sabin (D) canceled the concert early in the day instead of waiting as long as possible for the musicians to arrive, it is probable that he (D) was looking for an excuse to cancel the concert because he anticipated it would be poorly attended.

EDITOR'S ANALYSIS: As a general rule, performance under a contract will only be excused (as opposed to being discharged, see below), where the other party to the contract has in fact (1) breached (either presently or prospectively—by anticipatory breach or voluntary disablement), (2) prevented counter-performance, (3) waived counter-performance, or (4) can be estopped from demanding counter-performance on account of representations to the promisor that such performance will not be required. In addition, performance may be discharged by (1) modification of the contract based on valuable consideration, accord and satisfaction, (2) novation, (3) account stated, (4) rescission, (5) written release (regardless of consideration), (6) impossibility (including the U.C.C. concepts of commercial impracticality and frustration of purpose), and (7) the occurrence of a condition subsequent. Note above that, had Hathaway (P) actually been unable to perform, and had he communicated this to Sabin (D), the doctrine of anticipatory breach would have excused performance.

QUICKNOTES

ANTICIPATORY REPUDIATION - Breach of a contract subsequent to formation but prior to the time performance is due.

BREACH OF CONTRACT - Unlawful failure by a party to perform its obligations pursuant to contract.

NOVATION - The substitution of one party for another in a contract with the approval of the remaining party and discharging the obligations of the released party.

ACCORD - An agreement between two parties, one of which has a valid claim against the other, to settle the controversy.

CONDITION SUBSEQUENT - Potential future occurrence that extinguishes a party's obligation to perform pursuant to the contract.

NOTES:

154

CHERWELL-RALLI, INC. v. RYTMAN GRAIN CO.
Grain seller (P) v. Buyer (D)
Conn. Sup. Ct., 180 Conn. 714, 433 A.2d 984 (1980).

NATURE OF CASE: Appeal from award for breach of contract.

FACT SUMMARY: Rytman (D) claimed that Cherwell-Ralli, Inc. (P) had failed to give adequate assurances of continued performance due to grain shortages.

CONCISE RULE OF LAW: The right of a party to a contract to demand adequate assurances of performance by the other party is predicated on reasonable grounds for insecurity regarding such performance.

FACTS: Cherwell-Ralli (P) agreed to deliver certain products to Rytman (D) on a weekly basis. Rytman (D) was to specify the amount of product to be delivered in each installment. Soon after performance began, Rytman (D) fell behind in its payments to Cherwell-Ralli (P). Despite calling the arrearages to Rytman's (D) attention on several occasions, Cherwell-Ralli (P) continued to make deliveries. On April 15, 1973, Rytman (D) became concerned that Cherwell-Ralli (P) was going to discontinue its shipments due to grain shortages. Its president contacted the president of Cherwell-Ralli (P) who assured him that the deliveries would continue so long as Rytman (D) paid for its past debts. Rytman (D) sent a check in the amount of the arrearages but stopped payment on it several days later when it heard from a truck driver, who was not an employee of Cherwell-Ralli (P), that the deliveries were stopping. Cherwell-Ralli (P), upon learning of the stop payment, did discontinue shipments and brought suit for breach of contract in the amount past due. Rytman (D) admitted the amount past due but claimed counter damages owing from Cherwell-Ralli's (P) breach in failing to assure it adequately of continued service after the check was stopped. The trial court ruled for Cherwell-Ralli (P). Rytman (D) appealed.

ISSUE: May a party to a contract who does not have reasonable grounds to doubt performance by the other party demand adequate assurance of such performance?

HOLDING AND DECISION: (Peters, J.) No. Rytman's (D) stopping payment on its check and subsequent failure to pay on its past due account clearly constituted a breach of the delivery contract entitling Cherwell-Ralli (P) to cease performance. The only question remaining was whether Cherwell-Ralli (P) failed to provide adequate assurance of its performance to Rytman (D), and, even if it did, whether such a failure would have constituted a breach of contract. The answer to both questions is "no." In the first instance, if adequate assurances were required, the statement by Cherwell-Ralli's (P) president that performance would continue, and the continuation of such performance until Rytman (D) stopped payment on the check, clearly sufficed. However, the right of a party to a contract to demand adequate assurances of performance by the other is predicated on reasonable grounds for insecurity regarding such performance. Rytman (D) clearly lacked any reasonable grounds to doubt Cherwell-Ralli's (P) performance. Affirmed.

EDITOR'S ANALYSIS: U.C.C. § 2-713 provides that a buyer's damages for non-delivery or repudiation of a sales contract shall be "the difference between the market price at the time when the buyer learned of the breach and the contract price, together with any incidental and consequential damages provided [for elsewhere in the U.C.C.], but less expenses saved in consequences of the seller's breach."

QUICKNOTES

ADEQUATE ASSURANCES - Refers to a situation in which one party is excused from performance of his obligations under a contract if the other party to the contract indicates that he does not intend to perform when the time for performance thereunder arrives; the nonbreaching party in that case is excused from further performance, unless he receives adequate assurances that performance will be rendered.

ANTICIPATORY REPUDIATION - Breach of a contract subsequent to formation but prior to the time performance is due.

NOTES:

GREGUHN v. MUTUAL OF OMAHA INS. CO.

Stonesman (P) v. Insurance Company (D)

Utah Sup. Ct., 23 Utah 2d 214, 461 P.2d 285 (1969).

NATURE OF CASE: Appeal from a judgment for plaintiff for future benefits under a life insurance policy.

FACT SUMMARY: After the jury found that Greguhn (P) was permanently disabled as a result of an accident, the court awarded Greguhn (P) a lump sum judgment for future benefits, based on his life expectancy.

CONCISE RULE OF LAW: In a unilateral contract for the payment in installments after default of one or more, no repudiation can amount to an anticipatory breach of the rest of the installments not yet due.

FACTS: Greguhn (P), a stonemason, was severely injured in an accident which was covered under his life insurance contract with Mutual (D). Mutual (D) notified Greguhn (P) that his ailment would be considered an "illness without confinement" and Greguhn (P) sued Mutual (D) claiming total and permanent disability within the terms of the policy. The jury returned a general verdict for the plaintiff. The trial court calculated the amount due under the insurance policy, but also found that Mutual (D) had repudiated its policy, thereby entitling Greguhn (P) to a lump sum judgment for future benefits to accrue under the policy. The lump sum was based on Greguhn's (P) life expectancy, and was in lieu of the installment payments provided for in the insurance contract. Mutual (D) appealed.

ISSUE: Is the doctrine of anticipatory breach applicable to unilateral contracts?

HOLDING AND DECISION: (Tuckett, J.) No. The doctrine of anticipatory breach has not ordinarily been extended to unilateral contracts. In a unilateral contract for the payment in installments after default of one or more, no repudiation can amount to an anticipatory breach of the rest of the installments not yet due. The great majority of decisions permits recovery under a disability policy only of installments accrued and unpaid. Should Mutual (D) fail in the future to make payment in accordance with the terms of the policy without just cause or excuse and Greguhn (P) is compelled to file another action of delinquent installments, the court at that time should be able to fashion such relief as will compel performance. Remanded.

DISSENT: (Ellett, J.) In those actions which have been brought to interpret, apply, or enforce the terms of a policy and where no repudiation of further liability is involved, the recovery is properly limited to accrued and past-due installments. However, where there is a repudiation of all contractual obligations, I think it is the better policy to allow full recovery in one action, as was done in the case at bar. I would affirm.

EDITOR'S ANALYSIS: Massachusetts is the only state that refuses to allow a damage remedy on the basis of a purely anticipatory breach. However, a clear repudiation in Massachusetts has important remedial consequences. Repudiation of contract duties to mature in the future may so alter the character of a partial breach of present duty as to produce a total breach of contract. *Parker v. Russell*, 133 Mass. 74 (1882); Corbin, Contracts, Sec. 987. Also, restitution is apparently available after a sufficiently emphatic repudiation, even without breach of a present duty. See *Johnson v. Starr*, 321 Mass 566, 74 N.E. 2d 137 (1947), which involved not a contract for insurance, but an agreement to render household services in return for a promise to devise land. The Mass. court, when the promisor repudiated, allowed recovery for the claimant in quantum meruit for the value of the services.

QUICKNOTES

ANTICIPATORY REPUDIATION - Breach of a contract subsequent to formation but prior to the time performance is due.

UNILATERAL CONTRACT - An agreement pursuant to which a party agrees to act, or to forbear from acting, in exchange for performance on the part of the other party.

NOTES:

REIGART v. FISHER
Buyer (D) v. Home seller (P)
Md. Ct. App., 149 Md. 336, 131 A. 568 (1925).

NATURE OF CASE: Appeal from a judgment ordering specific performance of a land sale contract.

FACT SUMMARY: When Reigart (D), vendee, learned that the land described in the sales contract was significantly less than contract specifications, he refused further performance and Fisher (P), vendor, sued.

CONCISE RULE OF LAW: Where there is a substantial defect with respect to the nature, character, or situation, and in regard of which he is not put on inquiry, specific performance will not be decreed as against him.

FACTS: Reigart (D) contracted with Fisher (P) to buy a country home described in the contract as "containing about seven acres more or less." In fact, the quantity was 4.764 acres. When this was disclosed, Reigart (D) demanded return of his down payment and refused further performance. Fisher (P) sued for specific performance. From a judgment for Fisher (P), Riegart (D) appealed.

ISSUE: Where there is a substantial defect with respect to the nature, character, situation, extent, or quality of the estate, which is unknown to the vendee and in regard of which he is not put on inquiry, will specific performance be decreed as against him?

HOLDING AND DECISION: (Adkins, J.) No. Where there is a substantial defect with respect to the nature, character, situation, extent, or quality of the estate, which is unknown to the vendee and in regard of which he is not put on inquiry (notice), specific performance will not be decreed against him. Any misrepresentation or misdescription of the estate or interest or extent or value of the property in a material and substantial point, so far affecting the subject matter of the contract, that it may reasonably be supposed that but for such misdescription or misrepresentation the contract would never have been made, at once releases the purchaser from the bargain. Here, however, it certainly cannot be said that the misrepresentation as to acreage so far affected the attractiveness of the place that it could reasonably be supposed that but for such misrepresentation the contract would not have been made. Nor that by reason of the shortage in acreage, which in value was less than six percent of the purchase price, defendant Reigart failed to get substantially what he intended to buy and what constituted the object and inducement of the purchase. Affirmed.

EDITOR'S ANALYSIS: Compare Reigart with *Keating v. Price*, 58 Md. 532 (1882), where Price (D) contracted to buy 20 acres and found the land short by one-fourth acre. Price (D), vendee, had informed that vendor, Keating (P), earlier that he intended to use the land for a phosphate and canning factory, and had a specific

and clear need for the missing one-fourth acre. The court refused to order specific performance, holding that the variance here was not "so immaterial that (Price) is considered as getting substantially what he intended to buy and what constituted the object and inducement of his purchase."

QUICKNOTES

MATERIAL BREACH - Breach of a contract's terms by one party that is so substantial as to relieve the other party from its obligations pursuant thereto.

SPECIFIC PERFORMANCE - An equitable remedy whereby the court requires the parties to perform their obligations pursuant to a contract.

NOTES:

CHAPTER 6
THE RIGHTS AND DUTIES OF NONPARTIES

QUICK REFERENCE RULES OF LAW

1. **Third Party Beneficiaries.** A third party for whose benefit a contract is made may bring an action for its breach. (Lawrence v. Fox)

2. **Third Party Beneficiaries.** A niece for whose benefit a promise was made to her aunt may successfully bring an action for breach of that promise. (Seaver v. Ransom)

3. **Third Party Beneficiaries.** In order to recover as a third party beneficiary, the plaintiff must show that the defendant and the lessor intended to give her the benefit of the promised performance. (Anderson v. Fox Hill Village Homeowners Corp.)

4. **Third Party Beneficiaries.** Unless a contract between two parties is intended to directly (as opposed to incidentally) benefit a third party, no action for its breach can be maintained by that party. (H.R. Moch Co. v. Rensselaer Water Co.)

5. **Third Party Beneficiaries.** An attorney-client relationship may give rise to a valid third-party beneficiary contract on which the third party may maintain a malpractice action. (Heyer v. Flaig)

6. **Third Party Beneficiaries.** In the absence of detrimental reliance, parties may modify a contract to strip a donee beneficiary of unvested benefits. (Robson v. Robson)

7. **Third Party Beneficiaries.** A third-party beneficiary's rights against the promisor rise no higher than those of the promisee; however, its rights may rise higher against the promisor than they could against the promisee. (Rouse v. United States)

8. **Assignment and Delegation.** A promise of the assignee to assume the assignor's duties is not to be inferred from the assignee's acceptance of an assignment of a bilateral contract, in the absence of circumstances surrounding the assignment which indicate a contrary intention. (Langel v. Betz)

9. **Assignment and Delegation.** An assignment is binding upon the obligor where there is an intent to relinquish the right to the assignee and the obligor is notified. (Herzog v. Irace)

10. **Assignment and Delegation.** An option under seal is specifically enforceable by an assign regardless of whether the nominal consideration was ever actually paid. (Cochran v. Taylor)

11. **Assignment and Delegation.** Rights and duties under a vending contract may be assigned. (Macke Co. v. Pizza of Gaithersburg, Inc.)

12. **Assignment and Delegation.** A contractual provision clearly prohibiting assignment will be given effect by the courts (unless it violates public policy or a principle of law). (Allhusen v. Caristo Constr. Corp.)

13. **Assignment and Delegation.** The notice provision required by law in all consumer credit contracts that subjects holders to all claims and defenses which the debtor could assert against the seller does not entitle a consumer to an affirmative recovery from a creditor/assignee. (Ford Motor Credit Co. v. Morgan)

14. **Assignment and Delegation.** While parties to a contract cannot modify the terms of a contract assigned without the consent of the assignee, they may rescind the original contract, and enter into a new one, if performance by the assignor had become impossible. (Homer v. Shaw)

LAWRENCE v. FOX
Lender (P) v. Lendee of debtor (D)
N.Y. Ct. App., 20 N.Y. 268 (1859).

NATURE OF CASE: Action by a third party to recover damages for breach of contract.

FACT SUMMARY: Fox (D) promised Holly for consideration that he would pay Holly's debt to Lawrence (P).

CONCISE RULE OF LAW: A third party for whose benefit a contract is made may bring an action for its breach.

FACTS: One Holly owed Lawrence (P) $300. Holly loaned $300 to Fox (D) in consideration of Fox's (D) promise to pay the same amount to Lawrence (P), thereby erasing Holly's debts to Lawrence (P). Fox (D) did not pay Lawrence (P) and Lawrence (P) brought this action for breach of Fox's (D) promise to Holly.

ISSUE: Is a third party precluded for want of privity of contract from maintaining an action on a contract made for his benefit?

HOLDING AND DECISION: (Gray, J.) No. "[In the case of] a promise made to one for the benefit of another, he for whose benefit it is made may bring an action for its breach." This principle, which has been long applied in trust cases, is in fact a general principle of law.

CONCURRENCE: (Johnson, J.) The promise should be regarded as made to Lawrence (P) through his agent, which Lawrence could ratify once it came to his knowledge, although he was not privy to it.

DISSENT: (Comstock, J.) In general, there must be privity of contract. Here Lawrence (P) had nothing to do with the promise on which he brought the action. "It was not made to him, nor did the consideration proceed from him. If [Lawrence (P)] can maintain the suit, it is because an anomaly has found its way into the law on this subject."

EDITOR'S ANALYSIS: This is the leading case which started the general doctrine of "third-party beneficiaries." In the parlance of the original Restatement of Contracts, Lawrence (P) was a "creditor" beneficiary. Restatement 2nd, § 133 has eliminated the creditor/donee distinction which the original Restatement fostered and has lumped both under the label of "intended" beneficiary. Although the court in the present case went to some effort to discuss trusts and agency, ultimately the court allowed Lawrence (P) to recover because it was manifestly "just" that he should recover. Such has been the creation of many a new legal doctrine. The dissenting justices were primarily worried about freedom of contract and the continuing ability of promisor and promisee to rescind or modify their contract. As the doctrine has developed, various rules have arisen to handle these situations.

QUICKNOTES

PRIVITY OF CONTRACT - A relationship between the parties to a contract that is required in order to bring an action for breach.

THIRD-PARTY BENEFICIARY - A party who benefits from a promise made pursuant to a contract although he is not a party to the agreement.

INTENDED BENEFICIARY - A third party who is the recipient of the benefit of a transaction undertaken by another.

NOTES:

SEAVER v. RANSOM
Niece (P) v. Executor of estate (D)
N.Y. Ct. App., 224 N.Y. 233, 120 N.E. 639 (1918).

NATURE OF CASE: Action by a third party to recover damages for breach of a contract.

FACT SUMMARY: Berman made a promise to his wife for the benefit of their niece, Seaver (P), who sued Berman's executor (D) for breach of that promise.

CONCISE RULE OF LAW: A niece for whose benefit a promise was made to her aunt may successfully bring an action for breach of that promise.

FACTS: One Mrs. Berman, on her deathbed, wished to leave some property to her niece, Seaver (P). Her husband induced his dying wife to sign a will leaving all property to him by promising that he would leave a certain amount in his own will to Seaver (P). Mr. Berman died without making such a provision for Seaver (P). Seaver (P) brought suit against Ransom (D), as executor of Berman's estate, for Berman's breach of his promise to his dying wife.

ISSUE: Does a niece for whose benefit a promise was made to her aunt have an action for breach of that promise?

HOLDING AND DECISION: (Pound, J.) Yes. Although a general rule requires privity between a plaintiff and a defendant as necessary to the maintenance of an action on the contract, one of several exceptions to the rule is the case where a contract is made for the benefit of another member of the family. Here Mrs. Berman was childless and Seaver (P) was a beloved niece. However, "the constraining power of conscience is not regulated by the degree of relationship alone. The dependent or faithful niece may have a stronger claim than the affluent or unworthy son. No sensible theory of moral obligation denies arbitrarily to the former what would be conceded to the latter." The reason for this "family" exception (and other exceptions) to the rule is that it is just and practical to permit the person for whose benefit a contract is made to enforce it against one whose duty it is to pay. "The doctrine of *Lawrence v. Fox* is progressive, not retrograde." Finally, in this particular case, the "equities" are with Seaver (P).

EDITOR'S ANALYSIS: In this case, the court (as does the original Restatement of Contracts) uses the term "donee beneficiary" to describe Seaver (P). The Restatement 2nd erases the creditor/donee distinction and labels both types of beneficiaries as "intended." Although the court here is very insistent on the close family relationship, subsequent New York cases have erased that requirement for donee beneficiaries as the doctrine governing third-party beneficiaries has expanded. These subsequent cases represent the now-prevailing view in the country.

QUICKNOTES

INTENDED BENEFICIARY - A third party who is the recipient of the benefit of a transaction undertaken by another.

THIRD-PARTY BENEFICIARY - A party who benefits from a promise made pursuant to a contract although he is not a party to the agreement.

DONEE BENEFICIARY - A third party, not a party to a contract, but for whose benefit the contract is entered with the intention that the benefits derived therefrom be bestowed upon the person as a gift.

NOTES:

ANDERSON v. FOX HILL VILLAGE HOMEOWNERS CORP.

Injured pedestrian (P) v. Owner of parking lot (D)
Mass. Sup. Jud. Ct., 424 Mass. 365, 676 N.E.2d 821 (1997).

NATURE OF CASE: Appeal from summary judgment for the defense on suit for damages resulting from a slip and fall accident.

FACT SUMMARY: Icy conditions caused Anderson (P) to slip and fall in a parking lot on property leased by Fox Hill (D).

CONCISE RULE OF LAW: In order to recover as a third party beneficiary, the plaintiff must show that the defendant and the lessor intended to give her the benefit of the promised performance.

FACTS: When Anderson (P) got out of her car at work, she slipped and fell on the icy parking lot. Under the lease between Fox Hill (D) and the lessor, Fox Hill (D) had assumed sole responsibility for operation and maintenance of the retirement complex on the property. Anderson (P) worked at a nursing facility, also located on the premises. Fox Hill (D) had also agreed to promptly remove snow and ice from all driveways and walkways. Anderson (P) sued for damages arising from the slip and fall caused by the icy condition on the property. The district court granted Fox Hill's (D) motion for summary judgment, and Anderson (P) appealed.

ISSUE: In order to recover as a third party beneficiary, must the plaintiff show that the defendent intended to give her the benefit of the promised performance?

HOLDING AND DECISION: (Lynch, J.) Yes. In order to recover as a third party beneficiary, the plaintiff must show that the defendant and the lessor intended to give her the benefit of the promised performance. The intent must be clear and definite. In this lease there was no indication, express or implied, that any obligations had been imposed for the benefit of employees of the nursing facility. Anderson (P) was only an incidental beneficiary and cannot recover under the lease. Nor can she recover under a tort theory since landowners are liable only for injuries caused by defects existing on their property, and the law does not regard the natural accumulation of snow and ice as an actionable property defect. Affirmed.

EDITOR'S ANALYSIS: The intent to confer a third party beneficiary benefit is to be determined from the language of the contract. Under the Restatement (Second) of Contracts, either a promise to pay a debt to a beneficiary or a gift promise would involve a manifestation of intention sufficient to make reliance by the beneficiary reasonable. The significant intention is that of the promisee in cases involving a protected beneficiary.

NOTES:

H.R. MOCH CO. v. RENSSELAER WATER CO.
Building owner (P) v. Utility company (D)
N.Y. Ct. App., 247 N.Y. 160, 159 N.E. 896 (1928).

NATURE OF CASE: Action for breach of third party beneficiary contract.

FACT SUMMARY: H.R. Moch Co. (P) sued Rensselaer Water Co. (D) as a third party beneficiary to its contract with the city to supply water to fire hydrants.

CONCISE RULE OF LAW: Unless a contract between two parties is intended to directly (as opposed to incidentally) benefit a third party, no action for its breach can be maintained by that party.

FACTS: A building owned by H.R. Moch Co. (P) was destroyed by a fire because there was insufficient water pressure in the fire hydrant to extinguish it. The city paid Rensselaer Water Co. (D) $42.50 per year per hydrant to provide adequate water. H.R. Moch (P) brought suit for breach of that contract alleging that it was a third-party beneficiary contract because it was for the general protection of the public. H.R. Moch (P) also alleged a breach of implied warranty and the breach of a statutory duty.

ISSUE: May a member of the public bring suit on a contract between the city and a private company which is for the general welfare?

HOLDING AND DECISION: (Cardozo, J.) No. There must be some intention shown to make the private party liable to the public before members of the public may bring suit on the contract. It must be established that a direct and immediate benefit/duty was created to the public before a third-party beneficiary contract may be found. An incidental benefit flowing from obligations/duties solely between the parties to the contract will not give rise to standing in the incidental beneficiary. No such duty/benefit is present herein. The city has no legal duty to supply its inhabitants with fire protection and nothing in the contract indicates that residents were intended to be granted a private cause of action or that the city was contracting on behalf of its citizens. The Rensselaer Water Co. (D) has not accepted a common-law duty to protect all citizens through its contract. H.R. Moch (P) is not within the loss protected under the contract duties and protection cannot be extended since inaction alone does not constitute a direct threat of injury. There must be some assumption of a relationship between the parties which is not present herein. The assumption of duties between two parties will not give rise to duties to an indefinite number of nonparties to the contract. This is a case involving negligence, not willful/malicious acts. No warranty ran to the public and no legal duties were present. Judgment for Rensselaer Water Co. (D).

EDITOR'S ANALYSIS: In *Anderson v. Rexroad*, 175 Kan. 676 (1954), the court stated that waterworks cases such as *H.R. Moch* are cases unto themselves and their precedential value is minimal. The court, however, distinguished this case involving street construction under a clause holding the contractor liable for any damage to private property. In *Doyle v. South Pittsburgh Water Co.*, 414 Pa. 199 (1964), the court held that a claim against a water company could be held liable by a private party. It was the lack of water as much as the fire which caused a destruction of plaintiff's house.

QUICKNOTES

INTENDED BENEFICIARY - A third party who is the recipient of the benefit of a transaction undertaken by another.

THIRD-PARTY BENEFICIARY - A party who benefits from a promise made pursuant to a contract although he is not a party to the agreement.

INCIDENTAL BENEFICIARY - A third party beneficiary who receives benefits from the performance of a contract without the intentions of the contracting parties to do so.

NOTES:

HEYER v. FLAIG
Daughters of client (P) v. Attorney (D)
Cal. Sup. Ct., 70 Cal. 2d 223, 449 P.2d 161 (1969).

NATURE OF CASE: Action in malpractice.

FACT SUMMARY: Flaig (D), an attorney, negligently drafted a will, but the injured beneficiaries did not bring suit until more than two years after it had been drafted.

CONCISE RULE OF LAW: An attorney-client relationship may give rise to a valid third-party beneficiary contract on which the third party may maintain a malpractice action.

FACTS: Kilburn wished to leave all of her property to her two daughters (P). Kilburn had Flaig (D), an attorney, prepare her will, informing him at that time that she shortly planned to remarry. The husband-to-be was not excluded from the will as drawn up by Flaig (D) even though he knew of her plans to remarry. As a result, the new husband received a statutory share after Kilburn's death. Heyer (P) and the other daughter (P) brought a malpractice action against Flaig (D) more than 2 years after the will had been drafted, but less than 2 years after Kilburn's death. Heyer (P) alleged that she and her sister were third-party beneficiaries under the will and could maintain an action against Flaig (D) for malpractice. A demurrer on the ground that the action was barred under the 2-year statute of limitations was sustained over Heyer's (P) objection that her cause of action did not begin to run until Kilburn's death.

ISSUE: Can an attorney-client relationship create a third-party beneficiary contract under which a malpractice action may be brought?

HOLDING AND DECISION: (Tobriner, J.) Yes. There is an implied contractual promise to use reasonable skills (based on the circumstances) in performing the work requested by the client. For breach of that duty/promise, the client may sue in malpractice for damages. Where, as in the case of a will, the work is for the direct benefit of third parties (beneficiaries), we have a classic third-party beneficiary contract and the third parties may maintain a malpractice action against the attorney. Failure to provide for the known contingency of a new husband is negligence for which a cause of action arises. The injury is the statutory share awarded the husband reducing the bequest to the daughters. The cause of action does not accrue to the third-party beneficiaries until the date of death of testatrix when they have enforceable rights under the contract and the harm can no longer be remedied. Until date of death a will is ambulatory and may freely be revoked/modified. Therefore, the statute of limitations did not begin to run until Kilburn's death, less than 2 years before the action was brought. Reversed.

EDITOR'S ANALYSIS: Creditors or assigns of the beneficiaries may not bring suit for malpractice. They are only incidental beneficiaries under the contract/will. In *Exercycle of Michigan, Inc. v. Wayson*, 341 F.2d 335 (C.A.A., 7th, 1965), Exercycle sold national franchises giving the franchisee exclusive territorial rights and non-exclusive rights to sell in unassigned territories. Franchises were forbidden to sell in territories assigned to others. It was held that this created a primary duty/benefit in franchisees to sue other franchisees selling in their exclusive territory.

QUICKNOTES
CREDITOR BENEFICIARY - A creditor who receives the benefits of a contract between a debtor and another party, pursuant to which the other party is obligated to tender payment to the creditor.

THIRD-PARTY BENEFICIARY - A party who benefits from a promise made pursuant to a contract although he is not a party to the agreement.

NOTES:

ROBSON v. ROBSON
Corporation owner (D) v. Wife (P)
514 F.Supp. 99 (N.D. Ill. 1981).

NATURE OF CASE: Action to enforce a third-party beneficiary contract provision.

FACT SUMMARY: A contract was modified to negotiate payments that were to be made to the ex-wife of one of the parties under a third-party beneficiary clause.

CONCISE RULE OF LAW: In the absence of detrimental reliance, parties may modify a contract to strip a donee beneficiary of unvested benefits.

FACTS: Raymond Robson (D) and R.F. Robson contracted regarding the disposition of ownership interests in a small corporation. Part of the contract provided that in the event of R.F's death, $500 per month would be paid to his wife, Lise Robson (P), for a specified term. R.F. and Lise (P) subsequently divorced, and shortly before R.F's death the provision benefitting Lise (P) was deleted. Lise (P) brought an action to enforce the third-party beneficiary provision. Both sides moved for summary judgment.

ISSUE: In the absence of detrimental reliance, may parties modify a contract to strip a donee beneficiary of unvested benefits?

HOLDING AND DECISION: (Aspen, J.) Yes. In the absence of detrimental reliance, parties may modify a contract to strip a donee beneficiary of unvested benefits. Unlike a creditor beneficiary, who obtains vested rights at the moment of a contract's execution, a donee beneficiary is akin to one who has been promised a gift. Unless the prospective donee can demonstrate reasonable detrimental reliance, he cannot enforce a promise for a gift. Where a donee beneficiary's interest is contingent upon the occurrence of certain events, until those events occur the benefits may be withdrawn. Summary judgment for Raymond (D).

EDITOR'S ANALYSIS: As the court stated, it is the general rule that a creditor beneficiary may enforce a third-party beneficiary clause any time after execution, and the clause may not be rescinded. This is because the rights of the creditor beneficiary vest immediately. Further, detrimental reliance may be presumed, since the creditor beneficiary will waive his right to seek to recover from the promisee, assuming that he will be paid by the promisor.

QUICKNOTES

DONEE BENEFICIARY - A third party, not a party to a contract, but for whose benefit the contract is entered with the intention that the benefits derived therefrom be bestowed upon the person as a gift.

CREDITOR BENEFICIARY - A creditor who receives the benefits of a contract between a debtor and another party, pursuant to which the other party is obligated to tender payment to the creditor.

DETRIMENTAL RELIANCE - A change in position by one party to a contract, prompted by the acts or representations of the other contracting party and having detrimental results for the party effecting the change.

NOTES:

ROUSE v. UNITED STATES
Purchaser of house (D) v. Federal government (P)
215 F.2d 872 (D.C. Cir. 1954).

NATURE OF CASE: Action by a third party to recover damages for breach of contract.

FACT SUMMARY: Rouse (D) promised to pay Bessie Winston's creditor but refused to do so after discovering flaws in his own contract with Bessie and in Bessie's contract with her creditor.

CONCISE RULE OF LAW: A third-party beneficiary's rights against the promisor rise no higher than those of the promisee; however, its rights may rise higher against the promisor than they could against the promisee.

FACTS: The Government's (P) assignor sold a heating plant to Bessie, who gave her promissory note for $1,008.37 payable in monthly installments of $28.01. Bessie later sold her house to Rouse (D), who agreed in the contract of sale "to assume payment of $850 for the heating plant payable $28 per Mo." Bessie defaulted on her note and the Government (P) sued Rouse (D) as a third party beneficiary of Rouse's (D) contract with Bessie. Rouse (D) defended, arguing (1) that Bessie fraudulently misrepresented the condition of the heating plant and (2) that the Government's (P) assignor didn't install the heater properly in the first place. The trial court struck Rouse's (D) defense and granted the Government (P) summary judgment. Rouse (D) appealed.

ISSUE: May a promisor assert against a third party beneficiary a defense which he would have against the promisee?

HOLDING AND DECISION: (Edgerton, J.) Yes. The rights of the third party beneficiary rise no higher than those of the promisee; or, in other words, one who promises to make a payment to the promisee's creditor can assert against the creditor any defense that the promisor could assert against the promisee. Thus, Rouse's (D) defense of fraud, which he would certainly have been entitled to show against Bessie, is equally effective against the beneficiary (or any valid assignee of the original beneficiary). Accordingly, the trial court erred in striking the first defense. On the other hand, the second defense was properly struck. Here, Rouse's (D) promise was to pay a specified sum of money to the beneficiary (P) and it is irrelevant whether or not the promisee (Bessie) was actually indebted in that amount. "Where the promise is to pay a specific debt . . . this interpretation will generally be the true one." [2 Williston, § 399] Reversed and remanded.

EDITOR'S ANALYSIS: This well-known case is a law student's dream insofar as it clearly lays out what defenses are, and are not, available to a promisor in an action by a third-party beneficiary. While the promisor usually may assert against the beneficiary any defense which he could assert against the promisee, he usually may not assert defenses which the promisee might have raised against the beneficiary. In support of its denial of Rouse's (D) second defense, the court rests on Williston's presumption as to the nature of the promisor's promise. Unless it is clearly indicated that a promisor is only undertaking to pay "the debt" of the promisee (whatever it may turn out to be), it will be presumed that the promise is to pay the specific amount, regardless of whether it is actually owed. Whether this "presumption" necessarily effects a "just" result in all (or even most) ambiguous cases is open to some question.

QUICKNOTES

THIRD-PARTY BENEFICIARY - A party who benefits from a promise made pursuant to a contract although he is not a party to the agreement.

FRAUD - A false representation of facts with the intent that another will rely on the misrepresentation to his detriment.

NOTES:

LANGEL v. BETZ

Seller of land (P) v. Assignor of buyer (D)

N.Y. Ct. App., 250 N.Y. 159, 164 N.E. 890 (1928).

NATURE OF CASE: Action for specific performance.

FACT SUMMARY: Langel (P) made a contract with Betz's (D) assignor for the sale of certain land. The assignment contract contained no delegation to Betz (D) as assignee of the performance of the assignor's duties. Betz (D) refused to perform on the contract with Langel (P).

CONCISE RULE OF LAW: A promise of the assignee to assume the assignor's duties is not to be inferred from the assignee's acceptance of an assignment of a bilateral contract, in the absence of circumstances surrounding the assignment which indicate a contrary intention.

FACTS: Langel (P) made a contract with Hurwitz for the sale of certain real property. Hurwitz, the vendee, assigned the contract to Benedict, who in turn assigned it to Betz (D). The assignment contract contained no delegation to Betz (D) as assignee of the performance of the assignor's duties. Betz (D) requested and obtained an extension of the time in which to close title. Betz (D) then refused to perform.

ISSUE: Can a promise of the assignee to assume the assignor's duties be inferred from the assignee's acceptance of an assignment of a bilateral contract in the absence of circumstances surrounding the assignment which indicate a contrary intention?

HOLDING AND DECISION: (Pound, J.) No. The mere assignment of a bilateral executory contract may not be interpreted as a promise by the assignee to the assignor to assume the performance of the assignor's duties, so as to have the effect of creating a new liability on the part of the assignee to the other party to the contract assigned. The assignee may, however, expressly or impliedly, bind himself to perform the assignor's duties. But a promise to do so will not be inferred in the absence of circumstances surrounding the assignment which indicate an intention on the part of the assignee to so bind himself. Here there were no such circumstances. Betz's (D) request for and obtaining an extension of the performance date was not such an assertion of a right under the contract as to make it enforceable against him here.

EDITOR'S ANALYSIS: It is a general principle that an assignment of a contract does not operate to cast upon the assignee the duties and obligations or the liabilities imposed by the contract on the assignor in the absence of the assignee's express assumption of such liabilities. The U.C.C. provides, in Section 2-210(4), that "assignment of `the contract' or an assignment in similar terms is an assignment of rights and unless the language or the circumstances indicate the contrary, it is a delegation of performance of the duties of the assignor and acceptance by the assignee constitutes a promise by him to perform those duties. This promise is enforceable by either the assignor or the other party to the original contract."

NOTES:

HERZOG v. IRACE
Assignee (P) v. Attorneys (D)
Me. Sup. Ct., 594 A.2d 1106 (1991).

NATURE OF CASE: Appeal of an award of damages for breach of assignment.

FACT SUMMARY: Although notified of Jones' assignment of a personal injury claim to Herzog (P), Jones' attorneys, Irace and Lowry (D) failed to pay the settlement to Herzog (P).

CONCISE RULE OF LAW: An assignment is binding upon the obligor where there is an intent to relinquish the right to the assignee and the obligor is notified.

FACTS: Jones, who had been injured in a motorcycle accident, hired attorneys Irace and Lowry (D) to represent him in a personal injury action. Jones required surgery for his injuries which was performed by Herzog (P), a physician. Since Jones was unable to pay for this treatment, he signed a letter stating that he "request that payment be made directly . . . to John Herzog" of money received in settlement for his claim. Herzog (P) notified Irace and Lowry (D) of the assignment in 1988. The following year Jones received a $20,000 settlement for his claim. Jones instructed Irace and Lowry (D) to pay the money to him rather than to Herzog (P). Irace and Lowry (D) followed this instruction; Jones failed to pay Herzog (P) for the medical treatment. Herzog (P) brought a breach of assignment action against Irace and Lowry (D), and the trial court ruled in favor of Herzog (P). The superior court affirmed, and Irace and Lowry (D) appealed.

ISSUE: Is an assignment binding upon the obligor where the assignor has intended to relinquish the right and the obligor has been notified?

HOLDING AND DECISION: (Brody, J.) Yes. An assignment is binding upon an obligor when the assignor has intended to relinquish his rights and the obligor has been notified. The letter directing payment to be made directly to Herzog (P) clearly and unequivocally demonstrated Jones' intent to relinquish his control over any money received for his personal injury claim. Irace and Lowry (D) were duly notified of this assignment and therefore the settlement money should have been paid to Herzog (P). Although the assignment did interfere with the ethical obligations that Irace and Lowry (D) owed to Jones, the professional conduct rules do not prohibit the client's right to assign the proceeds of a lawsuit to a third party. Affirmed. The client's right prevails over any limitations on his lawyers.

EDITOR'S ANALYSIS: Although assignment of contract rights are generally valid, some limitations on the right exist. Nearly every jurisdiction has a statute which restricts the assignment of wages. Furthermore, public policy considerations may protect assignors who attempt to assign future rights. Restatement (Second) § 317 (2) does not allow assignment where the duty to the obligor would be materially changed.

QUICKNOTES

ASSIGNMENT - A transaction in which a party conveys his or her entire interest in property to another.

OBLIGOR - Promisor; a party who has promised or is obligated to perform.

NOTES:

COCHRAN v. TAYLOR
Grantor (D) v. Grantee of option to purchase (P)
N.Y. Ct. App., 273 N.Y. 172, 7 N.E.2d 89 (1937).

NATURE OF CASE: Action for specific performance.

FACT SUMMARY: Taylor (D) granted an option to purchase real property under seal and for a consideration of $1.

CONCISE RULE OF LAW: An option under seal is specifically enforceable by an assign regardless of whether the nominal consideration was ever actually paid.

FACTS: Taylor (D) granted an option to purchase real and personal property to Chenault. The option was under seal and recited that a consideration of $1 had been paid for it. Taylor (D) attempted to repudiate the option prior to its expiration. Chenault assigned the option to Cochran (P) who brought suit to specifically enforce it. Taylor (D) alleged that the $1 consideration was never actually paid and that it was not assignable. The court denied specific performance finding that the option was revocable not being supported by consideration. No decision was reached on Taylor's (D) claim of fraud.

ISSUE: May an assignee specifically enforce an option under seal supported by nominal consideration regardless of whether it was actually paid?

HOLDING AND DECISION: (Rippey, J.) Yes. Options are fully assigned unless restricted under the option. An option under seal is presumed to be supported by adequate consideration but open to rebuttal. However, where the party has stated that he has received the consideration he is estopped from denying it has been paid. Since the option was supported by consideration it was irrevocable during the time it was to be held open. Cochran (P) properly notified Taylor (D) that he intended to exercise the option and would render the performance called for under the option at the time it was due. Since the option had not yet expired and was irrevocable, Taylor (D) was bound to perform per the terms of the option. Reversed and remanded for a new trial on the issue of fraud.

EDITOR'S ANALYSIS: Traditionally, courts have accepted the seal as a substitute for consideration. At common law it was customary, if not obligatory, for a party to affix his seal to any document which was intended to be legally operative. Today the popularity of the seal has diminished substantially, and most states have enacted statutes which provide that the seal is mere presumptive evidence that consideration has been given.

QUICKNOTES

ASSIGNMENT - A transaction in which a party conveys his or her entire interest in property to another.

NOMINAL CONSIDERATION - Consideration that is so insignificant that it does not represent the actual value received from the agreement.

SEAL - An impression made upon wax, wafer, or other substance that signifies the execution of a document.

SPECIFIC PERFORMANCE - An equitable remedy whereby the court requires the parties to perform their obligations pursuant to a contract.

NOTES:

MACKE CO. v. PIZZA OF GAITHERSBURG, INC.
Vending machine operator (P) v. Pizza company (D)
Md. Ct. App., 259 Md. 479, 270 A.2d 645 (1970).

NATURE OF CASE: Appeal from judgment denying assignment of vending contract.

FACT SUMMARY: Pizza of Gaithersburg (D) refused to accept an assignment of a vending license.

CONCISE RULE OF LAW: Rights and duties under a vending contract may be assigned.

FACTS: Pizza of Gaithersburg (D) contracted with Virginia Coffee Service, Inc. to operate drink vending machines in its locations. Virginia Coffee assigned the contract to Macke (P). Pizza of Gaithersburg (D) refused to accept the assignment and refused to permit Macke (P) to operate the machines. Macke (P) brought suit for breach. The trial court held that the contract could not be assigned, and held for Pizza of Gaithersburg (D). Macke (P) appealed.

ISSUE: May rights and duties under a vending contract be assigned?

HOLDING AND DECISION: (Singley, J.) Yes. Rights and duties under a vending contract may be assigned. Generally speaking, rights and duties under an executory bilateral contract may be freely assigned. The exception to this is when the contract in question provides for personal services or otherwise is dependent on some unique characteristic of one or both of the parties. The execution of a vending contract, while having an element of service, is not so personal as to render the contract one for personal services. For that reason the assignment was valid. Reversed.

EDITOR'S ANALYSIS: The general rule as stated is fairly universally accepted, and has been for some time. It was reflected in the first Restatement of Contracts, at § 160(3). The lower court here did not disagree with the general rule, but considered the contract in question to be one for personal services.

QUICKNOTES

BILATERAL CONTRACT - An agreement pursuant to which each party promises to undertake an obligation, or to forbear from acting, at some time in the future.

PERSONAL SERVICES CONTRACT - A contract whose bargained-for performance includes specific conduct or activity that must be performed by one party.

DELEGATION - The authorization of one person to act on another's behalf.

ASSIGNMENT - A transaction in which a party conveys his or her entire interest in property to another.

NOTES:

ALLHUSEN v. CARISTO CONSTR. CORP.
Assignee (P) v. General contractor (D)
N.Y. Ct. App., 303 N.Y. 446, 103 N.E. 2d 891 (1952).

NATURE OF CASE: Action by an assignee to recover damages for breach of contract.

FACT SUMMARY: One Kroo assigned to Allhusen (P) rights under his contract in spite of an anti-assignment clause.

CONCISE RULE OF LAW: A contractual provision clearly prohibiting assignment will be given effect by the courts (unless it violates public policy or a principle of law).

FACTS: Caristo (D), a general contractor, subcontracted with Kroo to do painting. The subcontract contained the following provision: "The assignment by the second party (Kroo) of this contract or any interests therein, or of any money due or to become due by reason of the terms here without the written consent of the first party [Caristo (D)] shall be void." Kroo subsequently and without written consent from Caristo (D) assigned rights (including "moneys due and to become due") to a third company which in turn assigned them to Allhusen (P). The contracts were not "assigned" and no question of improper delegation was involved. Allhusen (P) sought to recover on the assignment but Caristo (D) contended that the contract prohibition against assignments must be given effect.

ISSUE: Will a contractual provision clearly prohibiting assignment be held effective?

HOLDING AND DECISION: (Froessel, J.) Yes. A term of a contract with language clearly prohibiting assignment will be upheld, although in the absence of such clear language a prohibitory clause will normally be interpreted as merely a covenant not to assign (for which the obliger may have an action for breach). In the present case it is clearly and unequivocally provided that an "assignment . . . shall be void." In such a situation courts, while striving to uphold freedom of assignability, have recognized the greater interest in freedom of contract. "No sound reason appears why an assignee should remain unaffected by a provision in the very contract which gave life to the claim he asserts." Such a holding is not violative of public policy, and the question of free alienation of property does not seem to be involved.

EDITOR'S ANALYSIS: Although some cases have held an anti-assignment clause to be an unlawful restraint on alienation (the present court to the contrary notwithstanding), most courts have refused to interfere with "freedom of contract" so explicitly. Instead, a court, while allowing an anti-assignment clause in theory, will tend to find that the particular provision before it is not drafted with sufficient clarity to accomplish its purpose of prohibiting assignment. As such, the provision is held merely a promise not to assign for breach of which the obligor has a theoretical action. ("Theoretical" because damages for such a breach will ordinarily be nominal.) In the present case, the court could not shut its eyes to the clear language and even admitted that "violence" would be done to that language by construing it as a mere promise. [See also U.C.C. § 2-210(2) and Restatement 2nd §§ 149(2)c and 154(2); and cf. U.C.C. § 9-318(4), comments to which expressly reject the present decision.]

QUICKNOTES
ASSIGNMENT - A transaction in which a party conveys his or her entire interest in property to another.

DELEGATION - The authorization of one person to act on another's behalf.

FREEDOM OF CONTRACT - The constitutional right to enter into contractual relationships and freely determine the parameters of party obligations without undue legal interference.

NOTES:

FORD MOTOR CREDIT CO. v. MORGAN
Creditor (P) v. Car loan defaulter (D)
Mass. Sup. Ct., 404 Mass. 537, 536 N.E.2d 587 (1989).

NATURE OF CASE: Appeal from denial of damages on counterclaim for breach of contract.

FACT SUMMARY: When the Morgans (D) defaulted on their monthly automobile payments, and Ford Credit (P) repossessed the car and sought recovery of the outstanding balance, the Morgans (D) counterclaimed on the theory that any wrongful acts of the dealer were fully attributable to Ford Credit (P), as assignee of the contract.

CONCISE RULE OF LAW: The notice provision required by law in all consumer credit contracts that subjects holders to all claims and defenses which the debtor could assert against the seller does not entitle a consumer to an affirmative recovery from a creditor/assignee.

FACTS: When financing their new car, the Morgans (P) signed a standard retail installment contract containing the following notice required by the Federal Trade Commission: "Any holder of this consumer credit contract is subject to all claims and defenses which the debtor could assert against the seller of goods or services obtained pursuant hereto." The Morgans (P) experienced several problems with their car, as well as with their financial situation, until eventually they stopped making monthly installment payments altogether. Ford Credit (P) sued to recover possession of the car and to recover the $2,628 due on the installment contract. The Morgans (D) interposed a defense against Ford Credit's (P) collection claim, based on the dealer's false representations regarding the car, and also counterclaimed for damages of $7,061, arguing that any wrongful acts of the dealer were fully attributable to, and may provide a basis for, affirmative recovery from Ford Credit (P), the assignee of the contract. The trial court determined that the Morgans (D) had a valid defense against Ford Credit's (P) collection claim, but they were not entitled to any damages on their counterclaims. The Morgans (D) appealed.

ISSUE: Does the notice provision required by law in all consumer credit contracts that subjects holders to all claims and defenses which the debtor could assert against the seller entitle a consumer to an affirmative recovery from a creditor?

HOLDING AND DECISION: (O'Connor, J.) No. The notice provision required by law in all consumer credit contracts that subjects holders to all claims and defenses which the debtor could assert against the seller does not entitle a consumer to an affirmative recovery from a creditor. The only exceptions are breaches so substantial that rescission and restitution would be justified, such as in a case of nondelivery or total failure of performance. The FTC did not intend that the rule would entitle a consumer to a full refund of funds paid on account. Instead, the purpose of the rule is to cut off the creditor's rights as a holder in due course and to prevent the creditor from asserting his right to be paid by the consumer despite misrepresentation, breach of warranty, or even fraud on the part of the seller. Eliminating holder in due course status prevents the assignee from demanding further payment when there has been assignor wrongdoing and gives the consumer the "weapon" of nonpayment. In this case, the Morgans (D) were unable to show that they qualified for affirmative recovery under one of the exceptions listed above. Furthermore, their contention that U.C.C. § 9-318 enables a consumer to recover affirmatively against an assignee-creditor like Ford Credit (P) is without merit. Section 9-318 has been interpreted to incorporate the common law principle that the assignee stands in the assignor's shoes, meaning that the debtor can raise the same defenses against the assignee as he could against the assignor. It does not mean the assignee is liable for the assignor's wrongs. Neither the contract provision required by the FTC nor U.C.C. § 9-318 puts the assignee in the shoes of the assignor for purposes of being affirmatively liable for claims which could be brought against the assignor. The Morgans (D) were entitled to no more than a judgment in their favor on Ford Credit's (P) original claim. Affirmed.

EDITOR'S ANALYSIS: Ford Credit reflects the general principle that an assignment of a contract does not operate to cast upon the assignee the duties and obligations or the liabilities imposed by the contract on the assignor, unless the assignee expressly assumes such liabilities. Note that once a right under a contract is assigned, the assignor ordinarily no longer has any interest in the claim. He loses some of his incentive to perform because the consideration that was to come to him from the obligor is now passed on to the assignee. Eliminating incentive should not seriously impair the obligor's chance of obtaining performance, however, because the assignee and the obligor may both bring suit against the assignor if he fails to perform. For example, the court in Ford Motor Credit noted that the Morgans (D) might still have had a valid claim against Neponset Lincoln Mercury, the dealer.

QUICKNOTES

ASSIGNMENT - A transaction in which a party conveys his or her entire interest in property to another.

RESCISSION - The canceling of an agreement and the return of the parties to their positions prior to the formation of the contract.

RESTITUTION - The return or restoration of what the defendant has gained in a transaction to prevent the unjust enrichment of the defendant.

HOMER v. SHAW

Steelwork company (P) v. Obligee (D)

Mass. Sup. Jud. Ct., 212 Mass. 113, 98 N.E. 697 (1912).

NATURE OF CASE: Action by assignee to recover under a contract.

FACT SUMMARY: Homer's (P) assignor entered into a contract with Shaw (D) to do certain work, but shortly after starting, the assignor informed Shaw (D) that he would be unable to finish. The assignor, however, remained in charge of the work and Homer (P) contended that the money received thereafter was earned under the original contract and thus belonged to him as assignee.

CONCISE RULE OF LAW: While parties to a contract cannot modify the terms of a contract assigned without the consent of the assignee, they may rescind the original contract, and enter into a new one, if performance by the assignor had become impossible.

FACTS: Homer's (P) assignor entered into a contract to transport, erect, and paint certain steelwork for $6 per ton, to be paid monthly for all work completed. Shortly after starting the work, the assignor informed Shaw (D) that he could not finish the work because Homer (P) had not advanced the money to him as agreed and his workers could not be paid and would quit. After this notice, without any change, the assignor remained in charge of the work until its completion. The trial court found that the parties, facing changed circumstances, had mutually agreed to a cancellation of the original contract, and thereafter entered into an independent contract by the terms of which Shaw (D) paid the workmen the wages due, while the assignor received a weekly salary for his personal services of supervision. Thus, the court concluded that Homer (P) had no claim against Shaw (D) under the assignment of the original contract. Homer (P) contended that the money received by the assignor should be considered as earned under the original contract, and thus rightfully his under the assignment.

ISSUE: May the parties to a contract assigned to a third party rescind the contract where performance by the assignor had become impossible due to unforeseen circumstances, and enter into a new independent contract eliminating the assignee's claims?

HOLDING AND DECISION: (Braley, J.) Yes. While parties to a contract cannot modify the terms of a contract assigned without the consent of the assignee, they may rescind the original contract, and enter into a new independent one, if performance by the assignor had become impossible due to unforeseen circumstances. Here, the trial court was correct in concluding that Shaw (D) and the assignor had canceled the original contract and entered into a new independent one under which Homer (P) had no claims against Shaw (D). Had Shaw (D) merely advanced the necessary money to the assignor under the terms of the original contract,

Homer's (P) assignment would have been given priority over Shaw's (D) loan. This, however, was not the case and the lower court decision is affirmed.

EDITOR'S ANALYSIS: The traditional view expressed in this case that parties cannot modify the terms of a contract without the consent of the assignee has not been adopted by the U.C.C. Under U.C.C. § 9-318, it is provided that any modification or substitution of an executory provision by the original parties made in good faith and in accord with reasonable commercial standards will be effective against an assignee, despite notice of the assignment, unless the assignment specifically provides that such modification or substitution is a breach by the assignor.

QUICKNOTES

ASSIGNMENT - A transaction in which a party conveys his or her entire interest in property to another.

RESCISSION - The canceling of an agreement and the return of the parties to their positions prior to the formation of the contract.

IMPOSSIBILITY - A doctrine relieving the parties to a contract from liability for nonperformance of their duties thereunder, if the subject matter of the contract ceases to exist, a person essential to the performance of the contract is deceased, or the service or goods contracted for has become illegal.

NOTES:

GLOSSARY

COMMON LATIN WORDS AND PHRASES ENCOUNTERED IN THE LAW

A FORTIORI: Because one fact exists or has been proven, therefore a second fact that is related to the first fact must also exist.

A PRIORI: From the cause to the effect. A term of logic used to denote that when one generally accepted truth is shown to be a cause, another particular effect must necessarily follow.

AB INITIO: From the beginning; a condition which has existed throughout, as in a marriage which was void ab initio.

ACTUS REUS: The wrongful act; in criminal law, such action sufficient to trigger criminal liability.

AD VALOREM: According to value; an ad valorem tax is imposed upon an item located within the taxing jurisdiction calculated by the value of such item.

AMICUS CURIAE: Friend of the court. Its most common usage takes the form of an amicus curiae brief, filed by a person who is not a party to an action but is nonetheless allowed to offer an argument supporting his legal interests.

ARGUENDO: In arguing. A statement, possibly hypothetical, made for the purpose of argument, is one made arguendo.

BILL QUIA TIMET: A bill to quiet title (establish ownership) to real property.

BONA FIDE: True, honest, or genuine. May refer to a person's legal position based on good faith or lacking notice of fraud (such as a bona fide purchaser for value) or to the authenticity of a particular document (such as a bona fide last will and testament).

CAUSA MORTIS: With approaching death in mind. A gift causa mortis is a gift given by a party who feels certain that death is imminent.

CAVEAT EMPTOR: Let the buyer beware. This maxim is reflected in the rule of law that a buyer purchases at his own risk because it is his responsibility to examine, judge, test, and otherwise inspect what he is buying.

CERTIORARI: A writ of review. Petitions for review of a case by the United States Supreme Court are most often done by means of a writ of certiorari.

CONTRA: On the other hand. Opposite. Contrary to.

CORAM NOBIS: Before us; writs of error directed to the court that originally rendered the judgment.

CORAM VOBIS: Before you; writs of error directed by an appellate court to a lower court to correct a factual error.

CORPUS DELICTI: The body of the crime; the requisite elements of a crime amounting to objective proof that a crime has been committed.

CUM TESTAMENTO ANNEXO, ADMINISTRATOR (ADMINISTRATOR C.T.A.): With will annexed; an administrator c.t.a. settles an estate pursuant to a will in which he is not appointed.

DE BONIS NON, ADMINISTRATOR (ADMINISTRATOR D.B.N.): Of goods not administered; an administrator d.b.n. settles a partially settled estate.

DE FACTO: In fact; in reality; actually. Existing in fact but not officially approved or engendered.

DE JURE: By right; lawful. Describes a condition that is legitimate "as a matter of law," in contrast to the term "de facto," which connotes something existing in fact but not legally sanctioned or authorized. For example, de facto segregation refers to segregation brought about by housing patterns, etc., whereas de jure segregation refers to segregation created by law.

DE MINIMUS: Of minimal importance; insignificant; a trifle; not worth bothering about.

DE NOVO: Anew; a second time; afresh. A trial de novo is a new trial held at the appellate level as if the case originated there and the trial at a lower level had not taken place.

DICTA: Generally used as an abbreviated form of obiter dicta, a term describing those portions of a judicial opinion incidental or not necessary to resolution of the specific question before the court. Such nonessential statements and remarks are not considered to be binding precedent.

DUCES TECUM: Refers to a particular type of writ or subpoena requesting a party or organization to produce certain documents in their possession.

EN BANC: Full bench. Where a court sits with all justices present rather than the usual quorum.

EX PARTE: For one side or one party only. An ex parte proceeding is one undertaken for the benefit of only one party, without notice to, or an appearance by, an adverse party.

EX POST FACTO: After the fact. An ex post facto law is a law that retroactively changes the consequences of a prior act.

EX REL.: Abbreviated form of the term ex relatione, meaning, upon relation or information. When the state brings an action in which it has no interest against an individual at the instigation of one who has a private interest in the matter.

FORUM NON CONVENIENS: Inconvenient forum. Although a court may have jurisdiction over the case, the action should be tried in a more conveniently located court, one to which parties and witnesses may more easily travel, for example.

GUARDIAN AD LITEM: A guardian of an infant as to litigation, appointed to represent the infant and pursue his/her rights.

HABEAS CORPUS: You have the body. The modern writ of habeas corpus is a writ directing that a person (body) being detained (such as a prisoner) be brought before the court so that the legality of his detention can be judicially ascertained.

IN CAMERA: In private, in chambers. When a hearing is held before a judge in his chambers or when all spectators are excluded from the courtroom.

IN FORMA PAUPERIS: In the manner of a pauper. A party who proceeds in forma pauperis because of his poverty is one who is allowed to bring suit without liability for costs.

INFRA: Below, under. A word referring the reader to a later part of a book. (The opposite of supra.)

IN LOCO PARENTIS: In the place of a parent.

IN PARI DELICTO: Equally wrong; a court of equity will not grant requested relief to an applicant who is in pari delicto, or as much at fault in the transactions giving rise to the controversy as is the opponent of the applicant.

IN PARI MATERIA: On like subject matter or upon the same matter. Statutes relating to the same person or things are said to be in pari materia. It is a general rule of statutory construction that such statutes should be construed together, i.e., looked at as if they together constituted one law.

IN PERSONAM: Against the person. Jurisdiction over the person of an individual.

IN RE: In the matter of. Used to designate a proceeding involving an estate or other property.

IN REM: A term that signifies an action against the res, or thing. An action in rem is basically one that is taken directly against property, as distinguished from an action in personam, i.e., against the person.

INTER ALIA: Among other things. Used to show that the whole of a statement, pleading, list, statute, etc., has not been set forth in its entirety.

INTER PARTES: Between the parties. May refer to contracts, conveyances or other transactions having legal significance.

INTER VIVOS: Between the living. An inter vivos gift is a gift made by a living grantor, as distinguished from bequests contained in a will, which pass upon the death of the testator.

IPSO FACTO: By the mere fact itself.

JUS: Law or the entire body of law.

LEX LOCI: The law of the place; the notion that the rights of parties to a legal proceeding are governed by the law of the place where those rights arose.

MALUM IN SE: Evil or wrong in and of itself; inherently wrong. This term describes an act that is wrong by its very nature, as opposed to one which would not be wrong but for the fact that there is a specific legal prohibition against it (malum prohibitum).

MALUM PROHIBITUM: Wrong because prohibited, but not inherently evil. Used to describe something that is wrong because it is expressly forbidden by law but that is not in and of itself evil, e.g., speeding.

MANDAMUS: We command. A writ directing an official to take a certain action.

MENS REA: A guilty mind; a criminal intent. A term used to signify the mental state that accompanies a crime or other prohibited act. Some crimes require only a general mens rea (general intent to do the prohibited act), but others, like assault with intent to murder, require the existence of a specific mens rea.

MODUS OPERANDI: Method of operating; generally refers to the manner or style of a criminal in committing crimes, admissible in appropriate cases as evidence of the identity of a defendant.

NEXUS: A connection to.

NISI PRIUS: A court of first impression. A nisi prius court is one where issues of fact are tried before a judge or jury.

N.O.V. (NON OBSTANTE VEREDICTO): Notwithstanding the verdict. A judgment n.o.v. is a judgment given in favor of one party despite the fact that a verdict was returned in favor of the other party, the justification being that the verdict either had no reasonable support in fact or was contrary to law.

NUNC PRO TUNC: Now for then. This phrase refers to actions that may be taken and will then have full retroactive effect.

PENDENTE LITE: Pending the suit; pending litigation underway.

PER CAPITA: By head; beneficiaries of an estate, if they take in equal shares, take per capita.

PER CURIAM: By the court; signifies an opinion ostensibly written "by the whole court" and with no identified author.

PER SE: By itself, in itself; inherently.

PER STIRPES: By representation. Used primarily in the law of wills to describe the method of distribution where a person, generally because of death, is unable to take that which is left to him by the will of another, and therefore his heirs divide such property between them rather than take under the will individually.

PRIMA FACIE: On its face, at first sight. A prima facie case is one that is sufficient on its face, meaning that the evidence supporting it is adequate to establish the case until contradicted or overcome by other evidence.

PRO TANTO: For so much; as far as it goes. Often used in eminent domain cases when a property owner receives partial payment for his land without prejudice to his right to bring suit for the full amount he claims his land to be worth.

QUANTUM MERUIT: As much as he deserves. Refers to recovery based on the doctrine of unjust enrichment in those cases in which a party has rendered valuable services or furnished materials that were accepted and enjoyed by another under circumstances that would reasonably notify the recipient that the rendering party expected to be paid. In essence, the law implies a contract to pay the reasonable value of the services or materials furnished.

QUASI: Almost like; as if; nearly. This term is essentially used to signify that one subject or thing is almost analogous to another but that material differences between them do exist. For example, a quasi-criminal proceeding is one that is not strictly criminal but shares enough of the same characteristics to require some of the same safeguards (e.g., procedural due process must be followed in a parol hearing).

QUID PRO QUO: Something for something. In contract law, the consideration, something of value, passed between the parties to render the contract binding.

RES GESTAE: Things done; in evidence law, this principle justifies the admission of a statement that would otherwise be hearsay when it is made so closely to the event in question as to be said to be a part of it, or with such spontaneity as not to have the possibility of falsehood.

RES IPSA LOQUITUR: The thing speaks for itself. This doctrine gives rise to a rebuttable presumption of negligence when the instrumentality causing the injury was within the exclusive control of the defendant, and the injury was one that does not normally occur unless a person has been negligent.

RES JUDICATA: A matter adjudged. Doctrine which provides that once a court of competent jurisdiction has rendered a final judgment or decree on the merits, that judgment or decree is conclusive upon the parties to the case and prevents them from engaging in any other litigation on the points and issues determined therein.

RESPONDEAT SUPERIOR: Let the master reply. This doctrine holds the master liable for the wrongful acts of his servant (or the principal for his agent) in those cases in which the servant (or agent) was acting within the scope of his authority at the time of the injury.

STARE DECISIS: To stand by or adhere to that which has been decided. The common law doctrine of stare decisis attempts to give security and certainty to the law by following the policy that once a principle of law as applicable to a certain set of facts has been set forth in a decision, it forms a precedent which will subsequently be followed, even though a different decision might be made were it the first time the question had arisen. Of course, stare decisis is not an inviolable principle and is departed from in instances where there is good cause (e.g., considerations of public policy led the Supreme Court to disregard prior decisions sanctioning segregation).

SUPRA: Above. A word referring a reader to an earlier part of a book.

ULTRA VIRES: Beyond the power. This phrase is most commonly used to refer to actions taken by a corporation that are beyond the power or legal authority of the corporation.

ADDENDUM OF FRENCH DERIVATIVES

IN PAIS: Not pursuant to legal proceedings.

CHATTEL: Tangible personal property.

CY PRES: Doctrine permitting courts to apply trust funds to purposes not expressed in the trust but necessary to carry out the settlor's intent.

PER AUTRE VIE: For another's life; in property law, an estate may be granted that will terminate upon the death of someone other than the grantee.

PROFIT A PRENDRE: A license to remove minerals or other produce from land.

VOIR DIRE: Process of questioning jurors as to their predispositions about the case or parties to a proceeding in order to identify those jurors displaying bias or prejudice.

REV 1-95

CASENOTE LEGAL BRIEFS